The Maple Sugar Book

The Maple Sugar Book

TOGETHER WITH

REMARKS ON PIONEERING AS A WAY OF

LIVING IN THE TWENTIETH CENTURY

BY HELEN AND SCOTT NEARING

GALAHAD BOOKS · NEW YORK CITY

CONTENTS

v

Chapter Seven

MAKING MAPLE SYRUP

Chapter Eight

MAKING MAPLE SUGAR

Chapter Nine

MARKETING MAPLE PRODUCTS

PART III. A LIVING FROM MAPLE

Chapter Ten

PIONEERS, O PIONEERS!

MAPLE SUGARING

"In contemplating the present opening prospects in human affairs, I am led to expect that a material part of the general happiness which heaven seems to have prepared for mankind, will be derived from the manufacture and general use of Maple Sugar."

Letter to Thomas Jefferson by Benjamin Rush, August 19, 1791.

"The acquisition of the Sugar Maple must necessarily enrich the Country, and give comfort to the people where it exists. . . . Every land owner must be desirous of having on his estate so generous a product of nature. . . . We therefore recommend it, and most seriously recommend it, for no one can tell how soon we shall want to partake of its bounty."

E. Jones, The Acer Saccharinum, 1832.

"The land-holder who appropriates a few rods of land to the preservation or cultivation of the sugar tree not only increases the value of his estate, but confers a benefit upon future generations."

Superintendent of United States Census, 1860.

FOREWORD

WE HAD three things in mind when we set ourselves to write this book. The first was to describe in detail the process of maple sugaring. The second was to present some interesting aspects of maple history. The third was to relate our experiment in homesteading and making a living from maple to the larger problem faced by so many people nowadays: how should one live?

In the first part of this book, particularly in the chapters on the Indians and the early settlers, we have used a great deal of source material. We have not been satisfied with secondary sources but, whenever they were available, have gone back to the originals. And whenever possible we have quoted verbatim the words of those who watched or helped or performed during sugaring. Articles, letters, books, documents have all been examined and checked with the greatest possible care and presented in the original form and wording. This method of utilizing material, instead of weaving it all into a legend of our own, has necessitated numerous quotations. We do not apologize for them because we feel they give genuine color and present the early history of maple sap, syrup, and sugar with the greatest possible authenticity.

Where we could tap original editions we did so, though some of the European volumes were not easily available in this country. Perhaps it might be in place here to express appreciation for the courtesies extended to the authors in their researches in the history and rare-book rooms of the main public libraries in New York, Boston, and Chicago, the Library of Congress in Washington, and the Vermont and Chicago Historical Societies. If their crypts hold more information on maple sugar and syrup than we have given here, it is not for lack of industry in seeking.

This is a book whose foresection may interest the student of history. The maple farmer can go straight to the chapters on sugaring, and try to poke holes in our theory or practice. The city subway swayer can turn to the end of the book and learn how to live in the country, with a bit of work.

Josiah Quincy, one-time mayor of Boston and president of Harvard, wrote in a letter of January 15, 1817: "Would it not be a desideratum to have the mode of managing this manufacture, the expense of raising the trees, the effect of the tapping upon their longevity, and all the particulars having a bearing on the question of the expediency of turning agricultural attention to this branch, stated from experiment and observation?" We have done what we could in this book to take on Quincy's challenge. We do not claim to be experts in the art of sugaring. We learn as we go along, and we have been learning for only fifteen years. In this book on sugaring we hope to learn more through any comment and criticism it may occasion.

We have also tried to find answers for some of the nagging, disrupting, distressing social experiences that are distorting the lives of friends and acquaintances. We believe that we have made some headway in our daily lives and we take this opportunity to share our hard-won experience with those of our fellows who are facing like problems and who are ready to pay the price of thoroughgoing solutions.

What we have been developing here in the Green Mountains is a source of livelihood that leaves us time and room to live life simply and surely and worthily. Henry Thoreau wrote in his journal on February 18, 1850: "There is little or nothing to be remembered written on the subject of getting an honest living. Neither the New Testament nor Poor Richard speaks to our condition. I cannot think of a single page which entertains, much less answers, the questions which I put to myself on this subject. How to make the getting our living poetic! for if it is not poetic, it is not life but death that we get." Sugaring can bring one an honest living. And anyone who has ever sugared remembers the poesy of it to the end of his days. When the time of year comes round with sap rising and snow melting, there is an insistent urge to take one's part in the process—to tap the trees, to gather the sap, to boil out the sweet syrup of the maple.

Sugar makers sugar because they like to. We are of their company and share their joy in the sap season. We have had an equal satisfaction in writing this story of maple. May it persuade many a reader to hang out his buckets during the first upsurge of the coming spring.

HELEN AND SCOTT NEARING

Forest Farm
Jamaica, Vermont

PART I

Sugaring in the Past

CHAPTER ONE

Sugar from Trees

"Honey is found in the trees and is gathered amongst briar and bramble bushes."
   Peter Martyr, The Decades of the Newe Worlde of West India, *1521.*

"There is in some parts of New England a kind of tree . . . whose juice that weeps out of its incisions, if it be permitted slowly to exhale away the excess moisture, doth congeal into a sweet and saccharine substance, and the like was confirmed to me by the agent of the great and populous colony of Massachusetts."
   Robert Boyle, Philosophical Works, *1663.*

"There is a kind of tree called maple, which grows very large and high. . . . When gashes are made in these trees in the spring, there runs out from them a quantity of water which is sweeter than sugar and water, or at least more pleasant to drink."
   Pierre Boucher, Histoire véritable et naturelle des mœurs et productions du pays de la Nouvelle France, vulgairement dite Canada, *1664.*

3

"*The mapple-tree yields a Sap, which has a much pleasanter taste than the best Limonade or Cherry-water, and makes the wholesomest drink in the World. . . . Of this Sap they make Sugar and Syrrup, which is so valuable, that there cannot be a better remedy for fortifying the Stomach. 'Tis but few of the Inhabitants that have the patience to make Mapple-water, for as common and used things are always slighted, so there is scarce anybody but Children that give themselves the trouble of gashing these Trees.*"

Louis, Baron de La Hontan,
Nouveaux voyages dans l'Amérique Septentrionale, *1703.*

"*The name that this maple bears (Acer saccharinum) announces the interesting property it possesses of furnishing through incisions a sweet liquid. . . . Who would not marvel to see realized to a certain extent among the savages of America, in the frozen forest of Canada, those enchanted pictures that the ancient poets have left us of the golden age, when they painted for us the trees distilling honey through their bark?*"
Henri Louis Duhamel du Monceau, Traité des Arbres et Arbustes, *1755.*

"*When made in small quantities—that is, quickly from the first run of sap and properly treated—it has a wild delicacy of flavor that no other sweet can match. What you smell in freshly cut maple-wood, or taste in the blossom of the tree, is in it. It is then, indeed, the distilled essence of the tree.*"

John Burroughs, Signs and Seasons, *1886.*

WERE earth devoid of trees, life on this planet would be scarcely livable. This highest form of vegetation is a contributor to the soil we cultivate, to the food we eat, to the houses we live in, to the fuel we burn, to the shade in summer, to the air we breathe, to the rains that water earth, and lastly, to the beauty of the landscape.

Man has used and enjoyed this tremendous source of delight and livelihood since the beginning of time. We are more deeply indebted to the whole gigantic earth-swaddling network of roots, branches, and mobile foliage than to any other part of the vegetable kingdom. The roots seek and find excess moisture in the soil; by growing and pushing downward and outward they keep the soil aerated; they prevent soil erosion; and even when dead and decayed the roots add their measure to the soil's fertility.

The upreaching bodies or trunks of trees are windbreakers and borders. They give leaven to plains and rolling valleys, and clothe the hills and peaks with raiment. When massacred in midlife or when old and dead they give their bodies to be burned. Their fuel value is high, yet as lumber for building they are even more valuable. Doors, frames, posts, rafters, timbers of all sorts, flooring, shingles—all are of the bodies of trees. Their branches and twigs are largely used by humans for fuel, unless left in the woods to rot and form richer soil.

The leaves are the fluttering flags that attract the sunlight, and through the action of sun and air transform those qualities into nourishment for the parent tree. They breathe in sunlight and breathe out moisture. They also, when dead, play a part in forest culture and human economy by adding yearly to the carpet of the forest's ferny floor and thus maintaining a necessary precondition of life—a rich and healthy soil.

The tree lives in and absorbs the earth qualities. It uses air, water, and sun. "Trees enjoy the totality of the sources of energy in nature," points out Edmond Bordeaux Szekely. "The work of a single tree during a single day is very considerable. . . . First of all the roots work unceasingly to absorb the various chemical materials from the earth, and also absorb a large amount of water. Experiments and observations made by botanists prove that in the course of a day trees exhale as much as two hundred gallons of water into the atmosphere, and there are trees which even exceed this amount, particularly after a rainy period when the earth is a great well of water. Thousands and thousands of leaves of every tree constantly evaporate and breathe out water into the atmosphere, while the immense surfaces of these hundreds and thousands of leaves on a tree are constantly absorbing the maximum quantity of solar energy, nitrogen of the atmosphere, and various other elements and materials and many different radiations which they accumulate and elaborate, by means of millions and millions of chlorophyll cells. . . . The output of the greatest factories of the world is as nothing beside the work of the forests, not only from the point of view of quantity, but also from that of quality; for the products of nature from a biological, chemical point of view are incomparably superior in precision to all the products of our factories." [2]

Trees, however, are more than keen competitors of up-to-date factories, more than mere tissue-building machines or engines of living matter. From time immemorial, as Sir John Frazer notes in numerous instances in his *Golden Bough,* trees have been worshiped, held as sacred, and even depicted as living, important entities. Some few today still hold to this reverence of the tree's individuality. Algernon Blackwood, in his story "The Man Whom the Trees Loved," writes of "their huge, unutterable selves," and W. H. Hudson, in "An Old Thorn," speaks of "the sense of a strange intelligence and possibility of power" in trees. R. H. Francé, in his book *Germs of Mind in Plants,*[3] writes of their possessing "psychic activity." "The sense-life of animals," he says, "is only a higher developed stage of that of plants. The lowest animal, in this sense, is wholly comparable with the highest plants. The difference, which at the first glance causes the animals to appear as living and the plants as lifeless, is due only to the tempo of events. All reaction movements are quicker in animals. The movements of flowers have been photographed and transferred to a cinematograph, and then reproduced in the tempo of animal movements. They gave the fantastic picture of some fabulous being in tremendous agitation. But in spite of the slowing up, the life functioning is the same, just as the nerves of animals are essentially identical with the simple temporary instruments of the vegetable nervous systems."

Others are enthusiastic about the pattern, design, and construction of the tree. John Evelyn, in an ancient book, *Sylva,*[4] marvels: "Consider how it assimilates, separates, and distributes these several supplies; how it concocts, transmutes, augments, produces and nourishes . . . By what exquisite percolations and fermentations it proceeds." "Tree growth," says F. Schuyler Mathews, "is a constant source of wonder to one who contemplates Nature. The rigid bole, the bracing and far-searching roots, the out-spreading top with its myriad members and its infinite variety of form and expression, all combine to make an organism in which strength, durability, gracefulness, and tenderness are all at once the dominant characteristics. In all the range of Nature there is no object which so commonly inspires the tenderer and finer emotions, and which would leave the earth so bare of loveliness if it were to be removed." [5] Thoreau, in his journal for January 18, 1859, takes the tree out of the commonplaceness of everyday acceptance. "Many times I thought that if the particular tree . . . under which I was walking or riding was the only one like it in the country, it would be worth a journey across the continent to see it. Indeed, I have no doubt that such journeys would be undertaken on hearing a true account of it. But instead of being confined to a single tree, this wonder was as cheap and common as the air itself." [6] In his book *Maine Woods*,[7] Thoreau wrote of a tree: "It is as immortal as I am, and will perchance go to as high a heaven, there to tower above me still." Walt Whitman characteristically rants at man, in his *Specimen Days in America*, for his puniness in comparison to a tree. "How it rebukes, by its tough and equable serenity in all weathers, this gusty-tempered little whiffet, man, that runs indoors at a mite of rain or snow." [8]

Tree life, obviously, has many aspects. It is more than mere vegetation, more than mere firewood. It has a life of its own and is an end in itself. That mankind finds it useful is of secondary importance. A staid textbook of botany puts it thus: "The plant covering of the earth's surface is a living one, and plants must be thought of as living and at work. They are as much alive as are animals, and so far as mere living is concerned, they live in much the same way. . . . The more we know of living things the more is it evident that life processes are alike in them all, whether plants or animals." [9] Francé says "plants resemble, in their general features, animals and men, so that we can draw no fundamental distinction between them." [10] The tree is a living organism even as man, with organs of growth, nourishment, movement, respiration, reproduction. It is the highest form of vegetable life and the oldest living thing in the world today.

That a sweet syrup would emerge from forest trees was part of Virgil's dream of the Golden Age.[11] At that time (around 40 B.C.) honey of wild bees was the chief means of sweetening and was probably the first sugar food used by men. The care and cultivation of bees for their honey has been known at least for three thousand years. With the ancients it was almost their sole source of sugar. Besides being a condiment, it was used as a medicine, and helped to produce a kind of mead.

The first historic mention of sugar is found in China in the eighth century B.C., where it is spoken of as a product of India. The sugar cane was native in Bengal and cultivated there. After the fifth century B.C. it was introduced to the Euphrates valley and to China. Fellow travelers of Alexander the Great who invaded India in the fourth century B.C., in search of glory and loot, brought back tales of a reed that produced honey without the aid of bees. "Honey cane" it was called originally, and Herodotus spoke of sugar as "manufactured honey." Pliny, in his *Natural History,* describes it as resembling salt and speaks of its medicinal properties. It was used as an antiseptic and germicide, and sprinkled on wounds to keep them from mortifying. Dioscorides in the same era (about 50 A.D.), in his *Materia Medica,* states that "there is a sort of concreted honey which is called sugar, found upon canes in India and Arabia; it is in consistence like salt, and is brittle between the teeth." The Greeks and Romans called it "sweet salt," "Indian salt," "sweet gravel." In the Bible (Jeremiah 6:20) is mentioned a "sweet cane from a far country."

Crystallized sugar was in evidence about 1300 years after

the first historical mention of sugar. The Arabs and Egyptians were the pioneers in crystallizing. In India at the end of the thirteenth century we first hear of evaporating the cane juice, dissolving the residue in water, and clarifying this solution with milk. They then solidified their sugar into cakes or crystallized it into candy. W. W. Skeats, in tracing the history of sugar, says: "It long continued to be regarded as a rare and costly spice, and it remained so up to the time of the discovery of America at the end of the fifteenth century.[12]

It was not until the close of the seventeenth century, when tea and coffee drinking were becoming habits, that sugar came to be more generally used. By the 1800's, sugar was established as a regular part of the diet. "The articles of sugar and salt," wrote G. Imlay in 1792, "though not absolutely necessary to life, have become from habit so essential, that I doubt if any civilized people would be content to live without them." [13] "It is not to be supposed that such a delicious and innocent article could longer be subject to the controul of physician, and confined to the apothecary's shop . . . For such is the influence of sugar, that once touching the nerves of taste, no person was ever known to have the power of relinquishing the desire for it." [14] Joseph B. Felt, in a book printed in 1853 on *The Customs of New England,* said that "so strongly has it [sugar] become entrenched in the public appetite, not only for the morning and evening drinks but for many others, to which it imparts a pleasant taste, there is little prospect that it will be put aside and pass out of mind." [15]

What is this sugar and what are its qualities? The word is broadly applied to all substances having a sweet flavor. Chemically, it is classified as a carbohydrate, and a carbohydrate is a substance made up of carbon, hydrogen, and oxygen. Sugar to the chemist is termed "sucrose," and is merely one of over a hundred saccharides, which in turn belong to the still larger group of carbohydrates. Dextrose, fructose, lactose, maltose, levulose, glucose, and saccharose are some of the more commonly known terms.

In an analysis of *The World's Commercial Products*,[16] the authors state that sugar is one of the most important products of the plant world and that almost all plants contain sugar at some point in their growth. Sugar, which is necessary to plant life and growth, is produced under appropriate conditions of warmth and sunlight. A part of the sugar is used immediately and the remainder is stored in the plant cells and used as required, literally "for a rainy day." H. V. Knaggs, in a book on *The Romance of Sugar*,[17] writes: "With the exception of the gaseous element nitrogen present in the atmosphere, and certain mineral salts, which are used to stabilize and strengthen the structure, practically the whole fabric of the plant or the tree is composed of sugar in one form or another."

Sugar is manufactured in the plant and tree for its own use and is in the proportions best suited to its growth. "It is now common knowledge among botanists," says E. N. Transeau in his *Textbook of Botany*,[18] "that sugar is the first kind of food made by green plants, and that all other kinds of food are made by chemical alterations of this sugar. . . . The material make-up of all living organisms is dependent upon chemical derivatives of the sugar made by plants. . . . The potential energy in sugar is the primary source of the chemically bound energy supply of all organisims. . . . Most of the energy that man transforms by various means into heat, light, electricity, and mechanical energy may be traced back through various transformations to the potential energy of sugar." Sugar, then, is the first product of the plant's activities and the primary source of its continuing energy.

Sugar, or sucrose, is found in the cells of plants, in many fruits, in the nectar of flowers, and in various forest trees. In ripe fruits, natural sugar predominates. Vegetables such as carrots, beets, turnips, pumpkin, and corn contain much of it. The chief source of our modern crystallized sugar is the sugar cane that grows abundantly in India, Egypt, the Philippines, Cuba, Japan, Hawaii. The sugar next in importance is derived from the beet root and is grown in many parts of the world, notably Europe and the northern part of the United States. Sugar lies in watery solution in the sap of palms, birch trees, walnuts, hickories, sycamore, ash, basswood, butternut, and maple. All the above-mentioned trees yield a sweetish sap, but only the sap of the maple and the palm are crystallized into commercially profitable sugar.

Of the two thousand known palm trees, nine are used for the production of sugar. The date palm (*Arenga saccharifera*) in the tropics yields the strongest sugar solution of any known tree—from 15 to 20 per cent. The sap can be collected for almost five months a year. There is on record a palm which gave forty-two quarts in twenty-four hours. A Dutch acquaintance of ours knows of a hundred-year-old tree in Java that gave twenty-five thousand pounds of sugar during its lifetime. The collecting of juice from the palm is a tedious business. Tapping or cutting produces not a drop of sap. The very inactive tissue requires a strong stimulus or succession of stimuli to induce exudation. Therefore the date palm must be repeatedly beaten or sliced at. "The Malaya people strike the spike of the flower with a wooden mallet repeatedly for nearly a fortnight, after which the sugary juice is yielded from an incision. In India, the method employed is perhaps more humane. The long spadix is held tightly between the fingers and kneaded from above downwards, the process being similar to the milking of a cow. This milking process is repeated day after day for a week. Cutting of the tip is then followed by a copious yield of sap. The preliminary hammering may be compared to the 'butting' of the calf, the 'kneading' to the usual process of milking. . . . As a result of this treatment the inactive tissue becomes as active as a glandular tissue, and is thus able to maintain the exudation even though there be no internal sap-pressure to urge it." [19] This same Dutch friend of ours, when in Java, in his own compound, tried tapping a date palm, without success. "Of course you'll never get sap," said the natives. "You have to marry the tree." (Shades of Sir James Frazer!)

The maple is a hardy tree adapted to a rigorous climate and a wide variety of soils. Their family (the botanical genus

*Acer**) is composed of over a hundred species, scattered over the Northern Hemisphere. China and Japan are said to be their original home and the center of population, Japan having about forty native maples. (It has been estimated that fully 30 per cent of the deciduous forests of Japan are composed of different species of maple.) Twelve species are said to be found in the Himalayas, and thirteen in Europe and the Orient. Thirteen are native to North America, nine being found in the eastern half of the continent, two in the Rocky Mountain region, and two on the Pacific coast. The maple flourishes best "in mountainous places, where the soil though fertile is cold and humid. . . . It is nowhere more abundant than between the 43rd and 46th degrees of latitude, which comprise Canada, New Brunswick, Nova Scotia, the States of Vermont and New Hampshire, and the District of Maine; in these regions it enters largely into the composition of the forests with which they are still covered. Further south, it is common . . . in the State of New York, and in the upper parts of Pennsylvania. . . . It is rapidly disappearing from the forests about New York and Philadelphia, where it is no longer drained for sugar, but is felled for fuel and other purposes." [20]

The best of the North American sugar-yielding maples are the hard or rock maple *(Acer saccharum)*, the soft or white or silver maple *(Acer saccharinum)*, the red maple *(Acer rubrum)*, and the black maple *(Acer nigrum)*. All the maples yield a sweet sap, but it is most abundant in the hard maple, which furnishes 75 per cent of the commercial syrup and sugar made of maple. From the same amount of sap, the white and red maple yield from half to two thirds the proportion of sugar obtained from the hard, and it is of inferior quality. "No sirup made from the sap of the soft maple is

* Linnaeus, the early codifier of all species of plants and the father of modern systematic botany, in his *Species Plantarum* in 1753 classed all maples as the tribe or genus *Acer*. As the only maple of Europe that had a sweet sap was the soft maple, he called it the *Acer saccharinum*. Then the hard maple, with an even sweeter sap, was reported in North America, and for a time was also called *Acer saccharinum*. Careful botanists today differentiate the one from the other by calling the hard, or rock, maple *Acer saccharum*.

of light color or has a delicate taste, the tendency of this variety being to give a reddish-brown sirup with a strong flavor, but in a great many instances the soft maple is tapped early in the season, because its sap flows much more freely at that time than that of the hard maple, and by mixing the two the first sirup of the year can be produced earlier than if only the hard maple were tapped." [21]

In the oldest books on arboreal lore, maples were mentioned as rarities in Europe, and there was no reference to their sugar-yielding sap. The "mapel-trēow" was so spelled by Chaucer in the fourteenth century, and it is variously referred to from then on in Middle English literature as the mayple, the mapell and the mapple. In 1588 Jean Liebault, the French naturalist, wrote of "balmes and oyles" distilled from trees, but never a word on maple. John Gerade, author of *The Herball or Generall Historie of Plantes*,[22] writes: "The great Maple is a stranger in England, only it groweth in the walkes and places of pleasure of noble men, where it especially is planted for the shadowe sake." In *The Whole Art and Trade of Husbandry*,[23] Barnabe Googe speaks of the "juyce" and the "sappe" of many trees, but not of the maple. Closer to our own day, Charles Sprague Sargent writes of the maple in Europe: "The sugar Maple, like the Hickories, the White Oaks, and other upland trees of eastern America, does not flourish in the Old World, and really fine specimens, if they exist at all in Europe, are extremely rare, although 150 years have passed since it was introduced, and at different times considerable attention has been given to its cultivation." [24]

Maple sugar and syrup are apparently, then, a specialized North American product. The bulk of these commodities is made in six states: Vermont, New York, Ohio, Michigan, Pennsylvania, and New Hampshire (in order of output). These states furnish 95 per cent of the country's maple sugar and 80 per cent of its syrup. Little or no syrup is made south of 35° latitude or west of 95° longitude. North Carolina, Tennessee, Iowa, and Missouri mark the south and west limits of the growth of the sugar maple. The provinces of

New Brunswick and Southern Quebec in Canada mark the
northern boundaries. The rock maple grows naturally in
the middle Eastern district of the United States, finds the
conditions it likes best and thrives there, with little the inhabitants can say, or need do about it. It is self-seeding and
self-perpetuating. It is a crop that needs neither sowing nor
hoeing. Maple trees are self-supporting, need not be fed,
watered, curried down, or housed. They need no cultivating,
fertilizing, or spraying. They go on growing and leafing out
and storing up sugar while the farmer goes about his other
business. In the spring the trees are standing in their old
familiar places and replete with sap for the tapping.

This idyllic picture should not give the impression that
sugar making is easy, or that the syrup pours from the tree
full flavored and full bodied.* Maple sap is thin, barely
sweet, and as colorless as spring water. In fact, the earliest
settlers called it sugar water, and maple water. City dwellers
often imagine the sap to be the same shade and flavor as
maple syrup, an amber-colored fluid. Seen "in the raw,"
dripping from the trees to the buckets, it is a disappointment
and a disillusionment to them. Arthur Guiterman, the poet,
is not the only one who has poesied unrealistically, "The
sweet sap welled like molasses from the bung," "The brown
sap oozed," and raved over "barrels filled with golden flow."
Then it would truly be manna: "a sweetish substance obtained
from incisions in the stems of various trees or shrubs" and the
maple might well be renamed the manna tree. But sugar
making is no dream of Elysian delight, with the trees "distilling honey." It involves arduous work, as anyone who has
tried it will have found out. "My readers must not suppose
that sugarmaking is a light and pleasurable employment. On
the contrary, it is one of the most laborious occupations,
while it lasts, that falls to the lot of the settler to perform." [25]

*C. M. Fisher, on page 108 of the 1878 *Vermont Agricultural Report,*
speaks of a lady who "supposed that the trees were hollow, and that the sap
ran up the hollow in the tree, and in order to obain it we must bore a hole
into it, and the sap would run out the same as water from a pump stock.
I think any sugar maker would like one such tree in close proximity to the
front end of his evaporator, if it would run a good stream of sap."

A Mr. Richard Parkinson, English gentleman of the old school, wiped his hands of the whole business after a short trial in the early 1800's. "Some experiments," said he, "have lately been made on the maple or sugar-tree, so much spoken of by the writers on America. I had two of them growing on my farm: but it appeared to me that if a man had no sugar but what he made from the maple-tree, and he knew no more of making that sort of sugar than I do, if his wife were not a very patient woman her calmness would be tried; or she must learn to drink her tea without sugar." [26] He recommended "an agreeable substitute—honey, . . . more easily obtained," with "industrious little insects" supplying the sweetening for his wife's tea and "apple-pye."

A defender of the art of sugar making steps forward in the person of Mr. E. Jones, lauding the process and production in an enthusiastic volume called *The Acer Saccharinum*.[27] He chides, "Not withstanding what Mr. Parkinson says, we recommend to the new settlers to reserve on their farms a sufficient number of the Sugar Maple to give them abundance of sugar annually for their families: it is an article of importance in domestic economy, and may thus be had with little labour and no expense." Joseph Bouchette, in the same year, concurs and says, "the process of obtaining it is extremely simple, and is so far, generally speaking, from being considered laborious, that the sugar season . . . is rather deemed one of festivity than toil." [28] Another writer also belittles the difficulties and labor involved. According to this gentleman it is easily done and can be delegated to mere women. "The force required," says Alexander Reed, "is one man, one boy with a horse and small sled, to collect the water; with occasionally a little extra help. In many instances the females of the family do all the work, except cutting and hauling the wood for fuel." [29]* The Irish *Emigrant's Guide* has this to say

*"In the backwoods the women do the chief of the sugarmaking; it is rough work, and fitter for men; but Canadians think little of that. I have seen women employed in stronger work than making sugar. I have seen women under-brushing, and even helping to lay up and burn a fallow, and it grieved me, for it was unfit for them." C. P. Traill, *The Canadian Settler's Guide*, London: Stanford, 1860. P. 62.

to prospective settlers: "The process of boiling the sap into sugar is simple, and easily acquired. By a little examination and experience, the settler may in a few days obtain a perfect knowledge of the process; and if for a short time the labour be found severe, the reward will be sweet." [30] S. F. Perley in the 1862 *Report of the Maine Board of Agriculture* speaks of sugaring as "a little pleasant labor, at a leisure season of the year." [31]

Later in this book we will go into detail on the various steps involved in the process of gathering the sap and boiling it down into syrup and sugar. The reader may then judge for himself whether it is work. Virgil said, "The Sire of gods and man, with hard decrees, forbids our plenty to be born with ease." The world about us is replete with food, clothing, and shelter, but most of it is unprocessed and cannot be utilized for our comfort or need without a vast amount of bestirring on the part of man and beast. Said Xenophon, the Greek historian and philosopher, "Nature supplies good things in abundance, yet she suffers them not to be won without toil."

We want food? Fruits are there to be plucked from the trees, vegetables in the ground. But only because someone labored to develop or help them grow. We want a house? Stone, sand, and timber cover the earth. We have only to dig, lift, pull, or hew. The wind roars or the sun burns, and we want covering? The materials lie at hand whereof to knit, to sew, to fabricate. With the materials at hand, however, labor and ingenuity must make something of them.

There is an old Indian legend that once upon a time the maple trees gave forth a sap that was almost pure syrup, but when the god Ne-naw-Bo-zhoo tasted it he found it too good and too easy to obtain. He felt it would be prized too cheaply. "The great Ne-naw-Bo-zhoo, the most remarkable, wonderful and supernatural being that ever trod upon the earth . . . has done much mischief and also much benefits to the inhabitants of the earth whom he called his 'nephews.' " He diluted the sap of the maple until the sweetness was barely discernible. " 'Now,' said he, 'my nephews will have to labor hard to make sugar from this sap, and it will be much more valuable to them in the future time.' " [32]

The story has truth in it, for the sap of the maple is certainly diluted, and the "nephews of Ne-naw-Bo-zhoo," sugar makers in any part of the country, work hard to get it, and prize it accordingly.

Maple sugar was valued in the early colonial days because it proved, with carriage dear and distances between trading towns far, the most available and unfailing source of sweetening. Rochefoucauld wrote, in the late eighteenth century, "As the maple-tree, where-ever it grows, multiplies with astonishing rapidity, we found, almost every where on our journey, no want of excellent sugar." [33]

Many looked on this handy fount of saccharinity, in a wilderness being newly developed, as a direct act of God. Benjamin Rush, the best-known physician of his time on the American continent and a signer of the Declaration of Independence, wrote in a letter to Thomas Jefferson, "The gift of the sugar maple trees is from a benevolent Providence." [34] Robert B. Thomas's *Farmer's Almanack* for March, 1808, says, "Heaven has been extremely propitious to our country, in causing the growth of this valuable tree, the maple." William Chapin calls the maple "a standing miracle of goodness." [35] Another author ascribes the good fortune of the colonists to Nature's divine beneficence. "Neither the sugar-cane nor the beet will grow in very cold climates; and under many circumstances the inhabitants of these countries would be unable to procure this grateful condiment, if Nature, always watchful for the wants of her creation, had not scattered over the surface of many northern countries, several species of hardy trees, whose juices contain large quantities of saccharine matter." [36] "Such," exclaims Brissot in 1791, "is the beneficent tree which has, for a long time, recompenced the happy colonists, whose position deprived them of the delicate sugar of our islands." [37]

The sanctification of the maple, its sap, and its sugar, was not shared by a French missionary, Henri Nouvel, who in the pursuit of his duties in the wilds of Canada found "maple-water" not holy enough for his purposes. He reports back to France in 1672: "I made various excursions on the ice in quest of stray sheep—finding five children to Baptize, and a sick young man, for whose salvation Providence was more watchful than I. For, having inadvertently baptized him, not with natural water, but with a certain liquor that runs from the trees toward the end of Winter, and which is known as 'Maple-water,' which I took for natural water, I discovered my mistake when, wishing to give this patient a dose of Theriac, I asked for some maple-water,—which, being naturally sweet, is more suitable for such a purpose. I was given some of the same liquor that I had used in baptizing him, and was thus obliged to repair that error,—happily a little before his death." [38]

Thomas Fessenden, in a poem inspired by syrup of the maple, brought the subject down to earth earthy when he amorously rhapsodized, "The lips of my charmer are sweet as a hogshead of maple molasses." [39]

Beyond furnishing the settlers with a needful commodity, there was another reason why this sugar from a native tree was hailed as a godsend by most of the population. A movement was on foot from the beginning of the eighteenth century (with its initial impulse in England) to abolish the slave trade and all it implied in the hunting of humans, their exploitation by forced labor, and the profit made from the sale of their living bodies. The slave trade, it was said at that time, was contrary to the laws of God and the rights of man. In no occupations were the slaves more widely used than on the sugar plantations. John Lincklaen and Gerrit Boon were sent from Europe as agents of the Holland Land Company in 1791 "to gain information at first hand upon the maple sugar industry. . . . Mr. Boon was a sugar refiner by occupation sent out . . . to try if the making of sugar from the cane by slave labour could not be superseded by its manufacture from the hard maple by free labour." [40] Coxe Tench writes in 1794 of the Pennsylvanians' "great and increasing dislike to negro slavery, and to the African trade among the people of the state," and about "this new prospect of obtaining a sugar not

made by the unhappy blacks." [41] Early almanacs exhort their
readers in March: "Prepare for making maple sugar, which
is more pleasant and patriotic than that ground by the hand
of slavery, and boiled down by the heat of misery." [42] "Make
your own sugar, and send not to the Indies for it. Feast not
on the toil, pain and misery of the wretched." [43] "Sugar made
at home must possess a sweeter flavor to an independent
American of the north, than that which is mingled with the
groans and tears of slavery." [44] William Drown's *Compendium of Agriculture* affirms: "The cane sugar is the result
of the forced labor of the most wretched slaves, toiling under
the cruel lash of a cutting whip. While the maple sugar is
made by those who are happy and free." [45] Zadock Thompson
of Vermont, in extolling the merits of the maple sugar, emphasizes "two important recommendations. It is the product
of our own state, and it is never tinctured with the sweat, and
the groans, and the tears, and the blood of the poor slave." [46]

In his letter of August 19, 1791, to Thomas Jefferson, Benjamin Rush cites an early record of conscientious objection
to the use of slaves on the sugar plantations. "Cases may occur
in which sugar may be required in medicine, or in diet, by
persons who refuse to be benefited even indirectly from the
labour of slaves. In such cases the innocent Maple Sugar will
always be preferred. . . . Dr. Knowles, a physician of worthy
character in London, had occasion to recommend a diet to
a patient, of which sugar composed a material part. His
patient refused to submit to his prescription, and gave as a
reason for it that he had witnessed so much of the oppression
and cruelty which were exercised upon the slaves, who made
the sugar, that he had made a vow never to taste the product
of their misery as long as he lived." Dr. Rush ends his letter
in moving words: "I cannot help contemplating a Sugar
Maple Tree with a species of affection, and even veneration;
for I have persuaded myself to behold in it the happy means
of rendering the commerce and slavery of our African
brethren in the sugar islands, as unnecessary as it has always
been inhuman and unjust. I shall conclude this letter by
wishing that the patronage which you have afforded to the

Maple Sugar, as well as the Maple Tree, by your example (Mr. Jefferson is purported to have used no other sugar in his family than maple and to have planted an orchard of maples on his farm in Virginia) may produce an influence in our country as extensive as your reputation for useful science and genuine patriotism." [47]

M. Bonnet, a French author of the eighteenth century, goes further than any in vaunting the virtues of the unsullied sap and of the native country that it enhances. "When we consider the intrinsic and beneficent qualities of sugar, the place it holds amongst the catalogue of our wants, the sacrifices it costs to reason and to humanity, and on the other hand that we see a new people placed in a country where nature every year opens her reservoirs to let flow, during six weeks, that salutary sap from millions of sources, we are forced to admit that Providence, which supplies them so well with a matter whose absolute want would make them partakers of the immorality, we might say of the crimes, of ancient people, has a view upon them, which requires that nothing might stain the purity of their principles and their morality." [48] The same author in a later book says, "This tree is the best argument that can be given in favor of the freedom of the negroes. . . . What answer can be given to the slaves by the congress assembled to pronounce definitely concerning their fate, when, holding in their hands a branch of sugar maple, they will come and say to it: read on this leaf the decree of our liberty pronounced by nature." [49]

The author of *Acer Saccharinum,* Mr. Jones, a Britisher, mixing maple and politics, pointed out in prophetic words further benefits accruing from using the fruits of the maple tree rather than that of the cane. "It is not subject to political revolutions, but the cane is," he says.[50] "The source here presented seems so promising, that if, from revolutions or other causes, all Europe were deprived of foreign sugars, this tree alone, planted in sufficient numbers, and properly attended to, would supply all its wants; and it may not perhaps be too much to say, that the time may come when that shall take place, whether from turbulent causes, or from experience of its convenience and utility." [51] "As to our being supplied with sugar from the East Indies, we do not like to augur misfortunes, but it is always prudent to be prepared against them. . . . Who can tell what may be the state of Indostan in a century or two; and that is no great length of time in the age of a nation. What man in England thought, a hundred years ago, that our North American Colony would shake off its allegiance, and become a dangerous Republic?" [52]

"However, putting all public calamities out of the question, and judging of the Sugar Maple Tree from its own intrinsic merits, its properties, and their different uses" [53] we, in this twentieth century, find that it is a patient and lavish giver of its sap, that it is an important contributor to the comfort and livelihood of individuals and to the welfare of the state, that its sugar is healthful and harmless, and it is good to the taste. The trees of the world give of their greenness for shade and health, of their trunks and limbs for fuel and lumber, and of their fruit for nourishment. The maple adds its sugary sap for drink and delectation. It has been said that sweetness is to the taste what beauty is to the eye. The sugar maple, "that admirable tree," [54] rates on both scores.

CHAPTER TWO

Indians, the First Maple-Sugar Makers

"If they [the Indians] are pressed by thirst, they get juice from trees and distil a sweet and very agreeable liquid, which I have tasted several times."

Marc Lescarbot, Histoire de la nouvelle France, *1609.*

"When in a state of famine, they [the Indians] eat the shavings or bark of a certain tree, which they call Michtan, which they split in the Spring to get from it a juice, sweet as honey or as sugar."

Paul Le Jeune, Nouvelle France en l'année *1634.*

"The Maple is also a good wood. . . . That tree has sap different from that of all others. There is made from it a beverage very pleasing to drink, of the colour of Spanish wine but not so good. It has a sweetness which renders it of very good taste; it does not inconvenience the stomach. . . . This is the drink of the Indians, and even of the French, who are fond of it."

Nicolas Denys, Histoire naturelle des Peuples, des Animaux, des Arbres et Plantes de l'Amérique Septentrionale, *1672.*

22

"The Sugar-Tree . . . which, I am told, is of a tedious Growth, is found very plentifully towards the Heads of some of our Rivers. The Indians tap it, and make Gourds to receive the Liquor, which Operation is done at distinct and proper times, when it best yields its Juice, of which, when the Indians have gotten enough, they carry it home, and boil it to a just Consistence of Sugar, which grains of itself, and serves for the same Uses, as other Sugar does."

John Lawson, The History of Carolina, *1718.*

"There is no lack of sugar in these forests. In the spring the maple-trees contain a fluid resembling that which the canes of the island contain. The women busy themselves in receiving it into vessels of bark, when it trickles from these trees; they boil it, and obtain from it a fairly good sugar."

Sebastien Rasles, Lettres édifiantes et curieuses, *1724.*

"This is truly an American industry; in fact, we are indebted to the Indian for the first knowledge of it. He tapped the tree, collected the sap, and boiled it in rude receptacles. We practise today the same old method, although it has been much improved."

John Gifford, Practical Forestry, *1907.*

THE Indians had a name for it—*Sinzibuckwud* (drawn from wood)—the Algonquin word for maple sugar. The Ojibways called the maple *Ninautik* (our own tree), with a preference for the rock maple, *Sheesheegummawis* (sap flows fast). The Cree tribe called the maple tree *Sisibaskwatattik,* and the sugar *Sisibaskwat.*

Although the earliest settlers called it "Indian melasses" and "Indian sugar," there have been proponents of the notion that the natives of North America did not tap the trees or make maple syrup until the Europeans came and taught them how. An early traveler who raised that point in the presence of a Kickapoo chief drew a scornful reply. " 'Can it be that thou art so simple as to ask me such a question, seeing that the Master of Life has imparted to us an instinct which enabled us to substitute stone hatchets and knives for those made of steel by the whites; wherefore should we not have known as well as they how to manufacture sugar? He has made us all, that we should enjoy life; he has placed before us all the requisites for the support of existence, food, water, fire, trees, etc.; wherefore then should he have withheld from us the art of excavating the trees in order to make troughs of them, of placing the sap in these, of heating the stones and throwing them into the sap so as to cause it to boil, and by this means reducing it to sugar?'"[1] The very method described, so primitive and unlike European processes, offers excellent evidence that sugar making was an established Indian custom before the first settlers appeared on the scene.

The Indian words for *maple* and *sugar* would indicate that the Indians had their own terminology and names for the sugar and the tree before the French, English, or Dutch ever knew America existed. No Indian name for maple sugar resembles or relates to any European word for same. Their names were their own and part of their immemorial language. If the invaders had taught them the uses and processes of maple syrup and sugar, European terms would have been used or at least imitated. And so it proves to be in the case of *white sugar*, which Paul Le Jeune, in 1637, said the Indians called "French snow." Lacombe, in his phonetical *Dictionnaire de la Langue des Cris,* gives *Sokaw* as the Indian's word for *white sugar,* obviously an atempt to pronounce *sucre* or *sugar.*

Furthermore, early French and English explorers and narrators would have recorded teaching the Indians the making of this novel sugar. Whereas, as it happens, the texts prove just the opposite. Among the earliest references to the making of maple sugar, we find in the memoirs of Sebastien Rasles, a missionary to the Abnakis in the 1690's, these words: "It is curious to know that the method of extracting the bayberry wax and making maple sugar, articles of considerable importance to us, has been learned of the aborigines."[2] Robert Beverley's *History and Present State of Virginia,* printed in 1705, devoted a whole chapter to the discovery of "the Honey or Sugar Trees." His statement seems conclusive enough. "The Sugar-Tree yields a kind of

Sap or Juice, which by boiling is made into Sugar. This Juice is drawn out, by wounding the Trunk of the Tree, and placing a Receiver under the Wound. The Indians make One Pound of Sugar, out of Eight Pounds of the Liquor. Some of this Sugar I examined very carefully. It was bright and moist, with a large full Grain; the Sweetness of it being like that of good Muscovada. Though this Discovery has not been made by the English above Twelve or Fourteen Years; yet it has been known among the Indians, longer than any now living can remember." [3]

In 1724 Père Joseph François Lafitau, in writing a book on the customs of the Americans, gives a complete account of the Indian method of sugar making, has a full-page illustration of the action, and concludes: "The French make it better than the Indian women, from whom they have learned how to do it." [4]

One more eighteenth-century witness we will call in defense of the Indians' previous knowledge and practice of sugaring. Nicolas Bossu, in 1786, tells of smoking the peace pipe with a group of Indians: "After the first ceremonies were over, they brought me a calebash of the vegetable juice of the maple tree. . . . The French who are settled at the Illinois have learnt from the Indians how to make this syrup, which is an exceeding good remedy for colds and rheumatisms." [5]

P.F.X. de Charlevoix makes a point in a March 11, 1721, letter to the Duchesse des Diguières that is debatable and disproved by other and earlier accounts. "It is very probable that the Indians, who are perfectly well-acquainted with all the virtues of their plants, have at all times, as well as at this day, made constant use of this liquor. But it is certain they were ignorant of the art of making a sugar from it, which we have since learnt them. They were satisfied with giving it two or three boilings, in order to thicken it a little, and to make a kind of syrup from it, which is pleasant enough." [6] That they carried the process through to its final stage is more likely than not, especially when one considers that they had no vessels to store syrup in and could handily carry blocks of sugar with them anywhere.*

In an article contributed to the *American Anthropologist,*[7] H. W. Henshaw states that "considering the great familiarity of the Indians with the natural edible products of America, and the general ignorance of the European on this subject, it is fairly to be inferred that the *a priori* likelihood of the discovery of the properties of the maple sap is all in favor of the Indian." He further confirms that the evidence "appears to offer at least presumptive proof that the Indians were in no wise indebted to the European for their knowledge of maple sugar. Like the cultivation of the maize, the tobacco, the pumpkin, bean and cotton, the art of maple-sugar-making, simple as it was, was aboriginal, resulting from their own observation and inventive powers." The haughty Kickapoo chief stands fairly vindicated before his conquerors and successors.

There is an Iroquois legend about the sap of the maple and how Woksis, the Indian chief, first tasted it as a sweet syrup because he had an ingenious wife. Woksis was going hunting one day early in March. He yanked his tomahawk from the tree where he had hurled it the night before, and went off for the day. The weather turned warm and the gash in the tree, a maple, dripped sap into a vessel that happened to stand close to the trunk. Woksis's squaw, toward evening, needed water in which to boil their dinner. She saw the trough full of sap and thought that would save her a trip to get water. Anyway, she was a careful woman and didn't like to waste anything. She tasted it and found it good—a little sweet, but not bad. So she used it for cooking water. Woksis, when he came home from hunting, scented the inimitable maple aroma, and from far off knew that something especially good was stewing. The water had boiled down to syrup,

---

*"Maple sirup also is made to some extent, but the Indians prefer to dissolve the sugar in water when sirup is desired, instead of retaining it in vessels, which, among them, are always scarce, or else perhaps not to be had at all." Walter James Hoffman, "The Menomini Indians," *14th Annual Report of The Bureau of Ethnology.* Washington, 1896. Part I, P. 288.

which sweetened their meal with maple. So, says the legend, was the happy practise inaugurated.

The Indians welcomed the return of spring by festivities and celebrations. They called the period "sugar month" or "maple moon." [8] One of the ancient religious festivals of the Iroquois Indians is dedicated to the maple and includes a "Maple dance." Erminnie A. Smith, in the *Second Annual Report of the Bureau of Ethnology*,[9] describes a special dance done at the tapping of the trees, "the performance of which will, it is hoped, bring on warmer weather and cause the sap to flow." This intimate fusion of their work and religious custom is further evidence of the antiquity, the veneration, and the knowledge of maple among them.

"Sugar making," says Henry P. Schoolcraft, a specialist on Indian history and customs, "forms a sort of Indian carnival. The article is profusely eaten by all of every age, and a quantity is put up for sale in a species of box made from the white birch bark, which are called mokuks. . . . The heydey scenes of the Seensibaukwut, or sugar-making, crown the labors of the spring. The pelt of animals is now out of season, winter has ended with all its rigors, and the introduction of warm weather prepares the Indian mind for a season of hilarity and feasting, for which the sale of his 'golden mokuks' gives him some means." [10] The same author, in his *Indian Tribes of the United States*[11] speaks again of the bark boxes called mokuks. "These sugar-boxes are in the shape of the lower section of a quadrangular pyramid. They are of a light-brown color, or, if new, of a nankeen-yellow. While the careful and industrious wife prepares and fills these boxes for sale, the children and youth carry sap from the trees, and have a grand frolic among themselves, boiling candy and pouring it out on the snow to cool, and gambolling about on the frozen surface with the wildest delight. Their mothers supply them, too, with miniature mokuks, filled with sugar from the first runnings of the sap, which make the choicest sugar."

Birch baskets, boxes, or mokuks for sugar are reported by other observers as an Indian stock in trade. In 1849, R. L.

Allen describes them: "They are made perfectly tight, of strips of white birch bark, sewed with thongs of elm. Many of the sap buckets are made of the same material, but different in form." [12] C. P. Traill speaks of "the Indian sugar (which looks dry and yellow and is not sold in cakes but in birch boxes or mowkowks as they call them) I have been told owes its peculiar taste to the birch-bark vessels that the sap is gathered in, and its grain to being kept constantly stirred while cooling." [13] The same containers were mentioned by an early settler in Canada who remembered seeing the Indians bringing their sugar to market. "A picturesque scene occurred in the spring of the year when the Indians came down from Manitoulin to sell their maple sugar. The journey was made in mackinaws,—open boats with a schooner rig; and the sugar was carried in mococks,—containers made of birch bark, each holding from twenty to thirty pounds." [14]

"This is a season of enjoyment with the Indians," reiterates Schoolcraft, "and they usually remain at their sugar-camps until the sap assumes too much acidity to be longer capable of being made into syrup, and the trees begin to put forth leaves." [15] "The season for sugar-making came when the first crow appeared. This happened about the beginning or middle of March, while there was yet snow on the ground. This period of the season was looked forward to with great interest, and, as among the Minnesota Ojibwa today, became a holiday for everybody. Each female head of a household had her own sugar hut, built in a locality abounding in maple trees which might or might not have been convenient to her camp, but which was the place always resorted to by her, and claimed by right of descent through her mother's family and totem." [16]

It is usually beneath the dignity of an Indian chief or brave to turn his hand to anything but war and hunting. However, chroniclers report that at the time of sugaring the Indian unbends and, "at this frolicsome season, assist the squaws in collecting sap." [17] If the braves bestirred themselves to menial labor at this time it must have been a very popular and singularly attractive occupation.

How did the Indians gather and boil the sap? Before the white man came they had no metallic vessels and none that would stand hot fires. Their pots were either of birch bark, of hollowed-out wood, or of clay that cracked under excessive heat. "In manufacturing their pottery for cooking and domestic purposes, they collect tough clay, beat it into powder, temper it with water, and then spread it over blocks of wood, which have been formed into shapes to suit their convenience or fancy. When sufficiently dried, they are removed from the moulds, placed in proper situations, and burned to a hardness suitable to their intended uses. . . . When these vessels are large, as is the case for the manufacture of sugar, they are suspended by grape vines, which, wherever exposed to the fire, are constantly kept covered with moist clay." [18] "The Nations of the South had only Vessels of baked Earth to dress their Meat. In the North they used Vessels of Wood, and they made Water boil by throwing in stones made red hot. They found our Iron and Tin Kettles much more convenient, and this is the Merchandise which we are sure to find a Vent for when we trade with them." [19]

To give an eyewitness account of the Indians cooking with hot stones, we quote from a book published in 1555.[20] "Their method of cooking is so new, that for its strangeness I desire to speak of it; thus it may be seen and remarked how curious and diversified are the contrivances and ingenuity of the human family. Not having discovered the use of pipkins [pots] to boil what they would eat, they fill the half of a large calabash with water, and throw on the fire many stones of such as are most convenient and readily take the heat. When hot, they are taken up with tongs of sticks and dropped into the calabash, until the water in it boils from the fervor of the stones. Then whatever is to be cooked is put in, and until it is done they continue taking out cooled stones and throwing in hot ones." "This custom is a very awkward and tedious one, and used only as an ingenious means of boiling their meat by a tribe who was too rude and ignorant to construct a kettle or pot." [21]

Another resourceful way in which they converted sap into

syrup without metal containers was by allowing sap to freeze overnight, throwing off the ice and collecting the thick syrup that was left. In fact, the sweetest, clearest syrup can be made by thus concentrating the sugar in the sap. "If sap could be evaporated without heat the sugar would be white as snow. . . . Freezing sap leaves the finest syrup ever tasted," says a *Vermont Agricultural Report*.[22] Here is a verbatim account of the freezing method written by an Englishman, who at eighteen, in the year 1755, was captured by the Indians and kept captive by them for five years. "Some time in February, we scaffolded up our furs and skins, and moved about ten miles in quest of a sugar camp, or a suitable place to make sugar, and encamped in a large bottom on the head waters of Big Beaver Creek. . . . Shortly after we came to this place the squaws began to make sugar. We had no large kettles with us this year and they made the frost, in some measure, supply the place of fire in making sugar. Their large bark vessels, for holding the stock water, they made broad and shallow, and as the weather is very cold here, it frequently freezes at night in sugartime, and the ice they break and cast out of the vessels. I asked them if they were not throwing away the sugar? They said no, it was water they were casting away, sugar did not freeze, and there was scarcely any in that ice. They said, I might try the experiment, and boil some of it, and see what I could get. I never did try it; but I observed, that after several times freezing, the water that remained in the vessel changed its colour, and became brown and very sweet." [23]

Reeds, shingles, or concave pieces of bark were used to run the sap from the tree. The vessels used to gather the sap were of bark. "During the early spring, when the birchbark is in prime condition for peeling, pieces were cut and folded into sap dishes or pans, each measuring from 7 to 10 inches in width, about 20 inches in length and 8 inches in depth. The ends were carefully folded and stitched along the edge with thin fibres of basswood bark or spruce root, in order that it might retain the shape. A woman in good circumstances would possess as many as from 1,200 to 1,500 birchbark vessels, all of which would be in constant use during the season of sugarmaking.

"The next articles to be made were sap buckets, which also were fashioned from birchbark, cut and folded at the corners so as to avoid breaking and consequent leakage. The folds were also seamed with pine resin. The buckets were of various sizes, though usually they held from 1 to 2 gallons.

"The folds at the top of the rim were held in place by means of a thin strip of wood neatly stitched with strands of basswood bark, and an additional cord was made to extend across the top to serve as a handle. Two buckets were attached to the wooden hooks suspended from a shoulder-yoke." [24]

The troughs or evaporators in which the sap was boiled down were of logs hollowed out like dugout canoes. Occasionally, tanned hides were used for storage purposes. A 1770 account gives such an example. "Bark vessels were placed under the ducts; and as they filled, the liquor was taken out in buckets and conveyed into reservoirs or vats of moose skin, each vat containing a hundred gallons." [25]

The Indians used the sap of walnuts and hickories, box elder, butternut, birch, sycamore, and basswood as well as maple. The roughest and crudest way by which they were known to have tapped the trees was to break off the ends of limbs and let the sap from the wounded part drip into a trough or vessel. They would also slash deep gashes in the trees with their tomahawks and set some rude container underneath for the sap. As trees were plentiful and seemingly endless in extent, little trouble was taken to spare them.

Here is a circumstantial account, written in 1724 by a Frenchman, as to how the Indians boiled their sap and made sugar. "In the month of March, when the sun has gathered a little strength and as the trees begin to be in sap, the Indians make with their hatchets transverse incisions in the trunks of the trees, from which trickles in abundance a water which they receive in large receptacles of bark. They afterwards cause this water to boil over the fire, which consumes all the watery matter, and which thickens the rest into the consistency of syrup, or even into cakes of sugar, according to the degree of heat to which they subject it. There is no further mystery to this." [26]

"About the middle of February is the time when the Indians of Housatunnuk leave their habitation and go with their families into the woods to make their year's stock of sugar. The season for this business lasts till the end of March and sometimes to the middle of April," writes Samuel Hopkins in his *Historical Memoirs Relating to the Housatonic Indians*.[27] He tells of a "settled minister to the Indians," John Sergeant, who "was loth they should be so long without instruction, and therefore concluded that he would go with one of the companies . . . and live with them during that season." Mr. Sergeant wrote a letter at the time to a friend, announcing his departure: "March 1, 1736. We have no remarkable news. Our Indians are this week gone out to make Sugar. Mr. Woodbridge and I design to go out to them next day after tomorrow and live with them till they return, if we can hold it out." He stayed the whole six weeks with them, "spending his time very agreeably among the Indians, being employ'd in the day time in teaching the children to read; and in the evening he taught the Indians to sing, in which they took great delight. . . . The snow now was about a foot and a half deep in those woods, and the weather cold. A deerskin with the hair on, spread upon some spruce boughs, and a blanket spread upon that, was his bed; and three blankets spread over him was his covering; where he slept very well. And tho' their Diet was low, yet it was cleanly and well dress'd. . . . Their drink was water. He had a good appetite, eat heartily and was in very good health all the time he was in the wilderness with them. 'I was,' says Mr. Sergeant 'treated very well while I was with them, and learned more of their manners and language than ever I had before.' " Following are Mr. Hopkins's notations on the manner of the Indians' sugar making. "They extract the sap by cutting the tree on one side, in such a form as that the sap will naturally gather into a small channel at the bottom of the hole cut, where they fix into the tree a small chip, of six or eight inches long, which carries the sap off from the tree into a vessel set to receive it. They tap a number of trees: and when the vessels are full they gather the sap and boil it to such a degree of consistence as to make sugar. After it is boil'd they take off the first, and stir it till it is cold, which is their way of graining it." [28]

James Smith, who lived for five years as captive of the Indians, and whose story of the freezing of sap we gave on page 30, left a long and factual description of the Indian way of working at sugaring.[29] "In this month [February, 1756] we began to make sugar. As some of the elm bark will strip at this season, the squaws, after finding a tree that would do, cut it down, and with a crooked stick, broad and sharp at the end, took the bark off the tree and of this bark made vessels in a curious manner, that would hold about two gallons each: they made above one hundred of these kind of vessels. In the sugar-tree they cut a notch, sloping down, and at the end of the notch stuck in a tomahawk; in the place where they stuck the tomahawk they drove a long chip, in order to carry the water out from the tree, and under this they set their vessels to receive it. As sugar trees were plenty and large here, they seldom or never notched a tree that was not two or three feet or over. They also made bark vessels for carrying the water that would hold about four gallons each. They had two brass kettles* that held about fifteen gallons each and other smaller kettles in which they boiled the water. But as they could not at times boil away the water as fast as it was collected they made vessels of bark that would hold about one hundred gallons each for retaining the water, and, though the sugar trees did not run every day, they had always a sufficient quantity of water to keep them boiling during the whole sugar season."

There are many allusions to the use of maple sap and syrup

---

* Solon Robinson, in a letter dated February 25, 1835, describing northwestern Indiana: "Adjoining the Door Prairie on the north is a very large body of Sugar tree timber. The Indians have many excellent Sugar Camps there. They are well furnished with large copper and brass kettles, which at the end of the season they bury until wanted again." *Indiana Historical Collection*, Vol. XXI, p. 63.

by the Indians as a drink. They attributed a tonic power to the sap, and in hot weather dissolved the sugar in cold water as a refresher.[30] Baron de la Hontan, in a letter to the Duke of Devonshire on May 28, 1689, describes a banquet given him by three Indian tribes. "For drink they gave me a very pleasant liquor, which was a syrup of maple beat up with water." It was also used in cooking and as an important part of their meals. A French explorer, Henri Joutel, in his diary for the year 1688 mentions maple "manna" being used in this way by his party. "The bad Weather oblig'd us to stay in that Place, till April. That Time of Rest was advantageous for the Healing of my Foot; and there being but very little Game in that Place, we had Nothing but our Meal or Indian Wheat to feed on. Yet we discover'd a Kind of Manna, which was a great help to us. It was a Sort of Trees, resembling our Maple, in which we made Incisions, whence flow'd a sweet liquor, and in it we boiled our Indian wheat which made it delicious, sweet and of a very agreeable Relish. There being no Sugar-Canes in that Country, those Trees supply'd that Liquor, which being boil'd up and evaporated, turn'd into a kind of Sugar somewhat brownish, but very good." [31] Lafitau says, "The Indians cooked their Indian wheat in their maple syrup like pralines, and they mixed their crushed sugar with ground flour which they took as provisions on all their trips. This flour keeps well and is very good." [32]

Father Sebastien Rasles, the missionary stationed among the Abnaki Indians in Lower Canada, wrote in 1722 to his nephew about his life with the natives. "As to my occupations, I assure you I neither see, nor hear, nor speak, anything but savage. My food is simple and light. I have never been able to acquire the taste for the meat and the smoked fish of the savages; my nourishment is nothing but Indian corn, which is pounded and of which I make every day a kind of porridge that I cook with water. The only relish that I add to it is in mingling a little sugar to correct the insipidity of it. There is no lack of sugar in these forests." [33]

A detailed account of the Indians' food, and the way in which maple helped ease its monotony, is given by James

Smith in his tale of life with the Indians in 1755. "The way we commonly used our sugar while encamped was by putting it in bear's fat until the fat was almost as sweet as the sugar itself, and in this we dipped our roasted venison." [34] "The Indians on their return from their winter hunt, bring in with them large quantities of bear's oil, sugar, dried venison, etc. At this time they have plenty, and do not spare eating or giving. . . . At this time homony, plentifully mixed with bear's oil and sugar, or dried venison, bear's oil and sugar, is what they offer to every one who comes in at any time of the day; and so they go on until their sugar, bear's oil and venison is all gone, and then they have to eat homony by itself, without bread, salt, or anything else; yet, still they invite every one that comes in, to eat, while they have anything; but, if they can in truth only say we have got nothing to eat, this is accepted as an honourable apology." [35]

As a little aside, on the nature of the Indian's sense of hospitality, we would like to share a story of Smith's about his Indian friend, Tontileango. "While the squaws were employed in making sugar, the boys and men were engaged in hunting and trapping. Tontileango would not go to town, but up the river and take a hunt. He asked me if I chose to go with them. I told him I did. We then got some sugar, bear's oil bottled up in a bear's gut, and some dry venison, which we packed up, and went up Canesadooharie, about 30 miles, and encamped. Tontileango went out to hunt, and when he was gone, a Wyandot came to our camp. I gave him a shoulder of venison which I had by the fire well roasted, and he received it gladly, told me he was hungry, and thanked me for my kindness. When Tontileango came home, I told him that a Wyandot had been at camp, and that I gave him a shoulder of roasted venison. He said 'That was very well, and I suppose you gave him also sugar and bear's oil, to eat with his venison.' I told him I did not; as the sugar and bear's oil was down in the canoe, I did not go for it. He replied, 'You have behaved just like a Dutchman. Do you not know that when strangers come to our camp, we ought always to give them the best that we have.' I acknowledged that I was wrong. He said that he could excuse this, as I was but young; but I must learn to behave like a warrior, and do great things, and never be found in any such little actions." [36]

Pehr Kalm, who wrote a lengthy dissertation for the Royal Swedish Academy of Science in 1751 on how sugar is made from various types of trees in North America, says, "When we reached the villages of the savages we received more than anything else gifts of large pieces of sugar which stood us well in hand on our trip into the wilderness. When the savages cooked gruel or mush for us from corn meal they added large lumps of sugar to make up for the lack of milk, for the savages have no livestock, if you except dogs and fleas." [37] In speaking of the strengthening properties of maple sugar, he adds, "I often heard the French in Canada say that if King Carl XII had eaten that food he could have conquered the whole world." [38]

The Indians seemed to be able to consume a lot of sugar and not be irked by its insipidity. Alexander Henry mentions their living solely on maple sugar at times. "Though, as I have said, we hunted and fished, yet sugar was our principal food during the whole month of April. I have known Indians to live wholly upon the same and become fat." [39] "On the mountain, we eat nothing but our sugar, during the whole period. Each man consumed a pound a day, desired no other food, and was visibly nourished by it." [40] Jonathan Carver confirms this: "And when they consume the sugar which they have extracted from the maple tree, they use it not only to render some other food palatable, but generally eat it by itself." [41]

"It is preferred by the Indians in their excursions from home," says Benjamin Rush. "They mix a certain quantity of maple sugar, with an equal quantity of Indian corn, dried and powdered, in its milky state. This mixture is packed in little baskets, which are frequently wetted in travelling, without injuring the sugar. A few spoonfulls of it mixed with half a pint of spring water, afford them a pleasant and strengthening meal." [42]

John Heckewelder, in his *History, Manners and Customs*

of Indian Nations,[43] speaks of the numbers of ways Indians use maple sugar or syrup in their food. Samuel Goodrich specifies cakes of "ground corn mixed with chestnuts, beans and berries" and sweetened with "sugar from the maple tree."[44] Berries, corn, and sugar are mentioned in another book as a favorite dish of Northeastern tribes of Indians. "From the sap of the maple tree they made a coarse-grained sugar, which, when mixed with freshly pounded 'sup-paun' and seasoned with dried whortle-berries, was baked into a dainty dish for high festivals."[45]

One circumstance that differs much from our modern dietary habits is the distaste among the primitive Indians for salt, and the preference of sugar as a flavoring medium. "The Ojibwa . . . who number less than 1,500, had during the preceding spring made almost ninety tons of sugar. When it is taken into consideration that nearly all of this sugar was consumed by the Indians themselves, it shows an almost abnormal fondness for sweets. It virtually forms a substitute for salt."[46] Other Indians ate the same way. "Salt is not used by the Menomini during meals, neither does it appear to have a place in the kitchen for cooking or baking. Maple sirup is used instead, and it is singular how soon one may acquire the taste for this substitute for salt, even on meats."[47] Whether the art of preserving fruit with sugar is an old invention of the Indians I am unable to say," says Johann Georg Kohl, "but I believe so, for it has been ascertained that the manufacture of sugar was pre-European among the Indians. Besides, the use of sugar as the universal and almost only condiment in Indian cookery is most extended. Sugar serves them, too, instead of salt, which even those who live among Europeans use very little or not at all. They are fond of mixing their meat with sweets, and even sprinkle sugar or maple syrup over fish boiled in water. . . . That great cookery symbol, the salt-box, which is regarded among salt-consuming nations with a species of superstitious reverence, is hence hardly ever found in an Indian lodge. But the large sugar makak may be always seen there, and when the children are impatient, the mother gives them some of the contents, and they will sit at the door and eat sugar by handfuls." [48] George Catlin, in his authoritative book on the American Indians, says, "I have, in travelling with the Indians, encamped by such places where they have cooked and eaten their meat, when I have been unable to prevail on them to use salt in any quantity whatever." [49]

A detailed description of the types of sugar made by the Indians is given in Kohl's volume.[50] "They prepare several sorts of sugar in their camps at the commencement of spring, when the snow begins to melt. The chief sort is 'grain sugar,' which is produced by boiling the sap of the maple-tree, and stirring it round and round till it crystallizes. Their principle stock of sugar is found in this granulated state.

"The second sort is what is termed 'cake sugar.' To produce it, they boil the juice, without stirring it till it becomes thick, and pour it, just prior to crystallization, into wooden moulds, in which it becomes nearly hard as stone. They make it into all sorts of shapes, bear's paws, flowers, stars, small animals, and other figures, just like our gingerbread-bakers at fairs. This sort is principally employed in making presents.

"A third variety is the 'gum' or 'wax sugar.' This is produced by throwing the thick-boiled sugar into the snow and cooling it rapidly. The sugar in that case does not crystallise, but becomes a soft coagulated mass, which remains tough for a lengthened period, and which can be twisted about between the fingers, or chewed as an amusement.

"Generally they prefer their maple sugar to the West Indian cane sugar, and say that it tastes more fragrant—more of the forest."

Frances Densmore, in writing of *The Uses of Plants by the Chippewa Indians,* gives much space to the use of maple sap for syrup and sugar. She also speaks of the dry sugar "stirred with a paddle, and at the proper time 'rubbed or worked' with the back of the granulating ladle, or in some instances pulverized by hand. This had to be done very rapidly before the sugar cooled too much. The stirring of the thick sirup and the granulating was a heavy task, and it was not unusual for men to assist in the work. From the granulating trough the warm sugar was poured into makuks." [51] She says that the fancy shapes Kohl mentions were made from molds "cut from soft wood and greased before the sirup was put into them so that it could easily be taken out. These molds were in shapes of various animals, also of men, and of the moon and stars, originality of design being sought." [52]

Sugar making by the North Temperate Zone Indians seems, then, to have been an aboriginal custom and culture trait. A history of the Northeastern American Indians must needs mention maple. It would be included in annals of their religion, their artifacts, customs, and language. "As the evidence of history and of language thus combine to support the same proposition, it seems only reasonable to accept their decision, that it is, after all, to the Indian that we are indebted for the important and natural product of maple sugar." [53]

CHAPTER THREE

The Early Settlers Make
Syrup and Sugar

*"Maple Sugar is made of the Juice of Upland Maple, or Maple Trees
that grow upon the Highlands. You box the Tree, as we call it, i.e. make
a hole with an Axe, or Chizel, into the side of the Tree, within a foot
of the Ground; the Box you make may hold about a Pint, and therefore
it must shelve inwards, or towards the bottom of the Tree; you must
also bark the Tree above the Box, to steer or direct the Juice to the
Box. You must also Tap the Tree with a small Gimblet below your
Box, so as to draw the Liquor off. When you have pierced or tapp'd
your Tree, or Box, you put in a Reed, or Pipe, or a bit of Cedar scored
with a Channel, and put a Bowl, Tray, or small Cask at the Foot of the
Tree, to receive your Liquor, and so tend the Vessels as they are full."*

Paul Dudley, An Account of the Method of Making Sugar
from the Juice of the Maple Tree in New England, *1723.*

"No more knowledge is necessary for making this sugar than is required to make soap, cyder, beer, sour crout, etc., and yet one or all of these are made in most of the farm houses of the United States. The kettles and other utensils of a farmer's kitchen, will serve most of the purposes of making sugar, and the time required for the labor, (if it deserve that name) is at a season when it is impossible for the farmer to employ himself in any species of agriculture."

Benjamin Rush, An Account of the Sugar Maple-Tree
of the United States, *1792.*

"Into these forests, in spring, the sugar-makers plunge, carrying with them a huge pot, a few buckets and other utensils, their axes, and a supply of food. They erect a shanty in the neighbourhood of the most numerous maple-trees, make incisions into as many as they can visit twice a-day to collect the sap, boil it down to the crystallizing point, and pour it into oblong brick-shaped moulds."

James Johnston, Notes on North America, *1851.*

THE backwoodsman of colonial days had perforce to be his own woodsman, sawyer, mason, builder, blacksmith, butcher, weaver, tailor, and farmer. There was yet another craft to be learned—that of sugar maker. Necessity in each case taught the emigré from Europe's shores to fend for himself and make the most of what he found in the new country. Some early settlers went in for trade or other civilized occupations, and stayed within the bounds of city or town. Others adventured forth into the wildwood and tried their hands at novel chores that gradually evolved into new-found skills. Hector St. John de Crèvecoeur, writing back to France in 1784, said, "Thus without the assistance of the West Indies, by the help of my trees and of my bees, we yearly procure the sweetening we want; and it is not a small quantity, you know, that satisfies the wants of a tolerable American family." [1]

In the same year Captain Charles Sias, with his wife and ten children, pushed his way into the forests and made the first actual settlement in Danville, Vermont. "The snow was very deep, and the way was trackless. . . . The lone family

began their hard labors upon the wilderness. They commenced by tapping the maples, which stood thick around
them in the most beautiful groves, affording them sugar in
abundance, and supplied, in a great degree, the lack of other
food." [2] Robert B. Thomas in his *Farmer's Almanack* for
March, 1804, wrote, "He that has money may eat honey. And
so, my home-made maple sweetening must answer my purpose."

Supplies were scanty and difficult of access. Things were
"made do" that were often primitive and far removed from
the products available in that day and age. An added spur to
the ingenuity of the early colonials, aside from the far distance from all sources of supply, was the firm intention and
desire to be self-sufficient and independent of the mother
country. They were like some young friends of ours who
today are pioneering in the backwoods of Vermont. An appeal to an indulgent grandparent would bring quick bounte-
ousness in reply, but, proud and Spartan, they prefer their
self-imposed penury to outside help. In the same way, many
early pioneers scorned help and outside products even when
help could be had.

The political break with England served further to inten-
sify this quality in the Americans of the 1700's, and led to a
development of extreme independence and self-sufficiency.
"The interruption suffered by foreign commerce [during the
American Revolution] gave a lively stimulus to domestic
ingenuity. To the revolution, the United States are indebted
for the cultivation of sugar from the maple tree. Determined
to use, so far as possible, no productions except of their own
growth or manufacture, the inhabitants tried every means
of supplying their conveniences from their native stores." [3]
"Those who have trees will not neglect the making of maple sugar, which is not only the most wholesome and pleasant
sweetening, but being the product of our own country, will
ever have the preference by every true American." [4] "There
ought not to be a pound of foreign sugar brought into the
State." [5]

Information on the benefits and practice of maple-sugar

making was included in tracts for immigrants to Canada and the United States. It was pointed out as one of the attractions of the New World that, whether settling in South or in North, one could grow one's own sugar in one's own back yard. "A branch of rural economy and comfort, peculiar to North America, is necessary to be noticed for the information of the emigrant, which is the manufacture of *maple sugar*. The settler should examine his farm, and where he can get from 200 to 500 or more maple trees together, and most convenient, that should be reserved for a *sugary*," says a Dublin-published volume in 1833, adding the following mild admonition: "If from among the trees intended for this use the brushwood be cut down and removed, the business can be carried on more conveniently." [6]

"Carry with you, wherever you go," says an article of "Advice to American Farmers about to Settle in New Countries," "a large kettle, in which you may make maple sugar in summer, and potash in winter. . . . Be careful likewise to preserve all the sugar maple, persimmon and chestnut trees you find on your farm. The two former will afford you excellent sugar and syrup." [7]

And so, like the Indians, from whom they learned the art, the first settlers gashed the trees, collected and boiled the sap, and made their own sugar in their own back yards. The more resourceful among the new settlers immediately started to improve some of the utensils with which trees were tapped and in which sap was gathered and boiled.

The first innovation introduced into the Indian method of sugaring was to substitute iron or copper kettles for vessels of wood, bark, or clay, which could not stand high heat and which were far more perishable. Their "troughs for receiving," or buckets, continued to be made of wood until a late period, as it was over a hundred years before tin and galvanized buckets came into general use. Their other sugar tools were gradually improved through the years.

The Indian way of gashing the trees and letting the sap seep down the tree or run out on bits of bark was recognized as wasteful of sap and tree, so augers were used to bore holes in which homemade "spiles" were inserted. Jeremiah Wilson, however, in his *Report of the Commissioner of Patents* still speaks in 1844 of incisions being made "with an axe in the tree, of about 3 inches deep, and from 6 to 12 inches wide." [8] As late as 1860 *The Canadian Settler's Guide* [9] reports the gashing of the tree as common practice. "Some cut a chip out across the bark, and cut two sweeping lines down so as to give the sap two channels to flow in; others merely gash the bark with a slanting cut, and insert the spill. . . . Some do not take much pains, and only stick a flat slip of shingle, slanting from the gash in the bark, to direct the flow of the sap to the trough." These spills, or spiles, says the author, were made of cedar "with a hollow sort of chisel." C. T. Alvord gives the dimensions of the tapping iron in olden times as being "about one foot in length, and made of iron in the shape of a carpenter's gouge, the cutting end being about two inches wide and usually made of steel." [10]

Michaux in 1810 reports augers three quarters of an inch in diameter, and "tubes of Elder or Sumac, 8 or 10 inches long, corresponding in size to the auger, and laid open for a part of their length." [11] These spouts were "made in long winter evenings with no other tools than a saw, a jack-knife, and a piece of wire with a handle on one end to remove the pith." [12] G. Imlay speaks of them as made of elderwood "to project from the tree 12 inches." [13]

Here is an elaborate description of the making of spouts, birch in this case being recommended. "The wooden spouts are made of hard wood, birch making the best. They are made by taking inch boards, sawing them into strips 1 inch wide, then cut into pieces the length of the spout, which is about 6 inches; these are then put into a lathe and turned round and smooth, one end of which is tapered down to a little less than half an inch in diameter; a hole about one-fourth of an inch is then bored through the entire length, and the spout is ready for use." [14] With even more detail, *Facts for Farmers* [15] gives the technique for making iron spouts "in half the time." "Take thin inch-and-a-quarter wide hoop iron, cut in lengths of 2 to 4 inches by your own hands with a small, cold-cutting chisel, using the end of a hard-wood block for an anvil. Now grind one end sharp before you make them into troughs, which you can do almost as fast as you can count, as follows: Bore an inch hole through a hard log and saw it asunder so as to leave half of the hole in one end; drive two nails upon one side, an eighth of an inch from the edge for a gauge; lay the flat piece of iron over this hollow, and a round bolt on it, and hit that with a stout hammer or an old axe. You can improve upon this by extemporizing a hand-press, both for cutting and shaping your spouts. You need not go to a blacksmith's, and you cannot make wooden spouts half as fast, and they will not last half as long." This seems a fearful task, of no mean dimensions, but apparently was tackled with intrepitude as just another home craft.

For containers to catch the sap, ash or basswood trees were felled in the late fall or winter, the trunks being sawed up into the desired lengths, the sections split and the halves hollowed out by ax or adz into rude shallow troughs. Bass or ash were selected because they split and worked most easily. The hollowed sections were then brought to the maples and stood on end with the cut side against the tree. At sugaring time these troughs were ready on the spot and only had to be put into position under the taphole. "Care should be taken as soon as the sugar season is over," says S. Strickland, "to set the troughs up on their ends, against the north side of the tree, which preserves them from being cracked by the sun in summer, or buried too deep in the snow in winter." [16]

Later, large-bottomed buckets were devised, which were set on the ground at the foot of the tree to catch the sap. But because the bucket at best was a foot or two below the gash or hole, much sap was lost, either by being misdirected or by being blown away by the wind. When the snow melted from beneath them, the buckets tipped and had to be propped up in clumsy fashion. It was figured the buckets could be hung, so "spikes were made by our blacksmiths, to hang the large topped unpainted wooden buckets on, and were driven into the tree 4 to 6 inches below the spout." [17] The bucket should thus be "hung up against the tree to prevent leaves being blown into it, to obviate the necessity of blocking up the vessel, as when set on the ground, or settling out of place as the snow melts, to avoid the loss occasioned by the wind blowing the dropping sap out at the side, and to be safe from the accidental visits of swine." [18] "Hanging the bucket on the tree is preferable to setting it on the ground. It saves hunting for a block or stone; the bucket is more conveniently emptied; the wind cannot blow the sap away as it drops, nor blow the bucket away; and, what is of most importance, the bucket can be covered." [19]

"When nails are driven in the tree to hold the buckets," says the *Country Gentleman,* "they should be drawn and saved for another year, and save the chopper and the sawyer some loud and harsh words, when the trees are used for wood or lumber." [20] In the same magazine, as a comment at a later date, Amos Fish, of Bethlehem, New York, writes: "A substitute for such nails to be driven into the trees to hold the buckets, and a safeguard against those loud and harsh words, which will save the edge of the axe and the teeth of the saw, (should the trees be used for lumber), may be found in the use of hooks made of round iron 5/16ths of an inch in diameter, the shank 2½ inches long, the end pointed, and a screwthread cut one inch in length, like that of a common screwbolt. By boring a quarter inch hole in the wood of the tree, one inch deep, these can be screwed in, easily removed, and laid aside for future use." [21]

The *Maine Agricultural Report* for 1862 gives the advantages and disadvantages of the various buckets in use at that time. "Every variety of vessel is used for receiving the sap as it flows from the tree, from the rude trough (hewn from the sapling pine or cedar), and birchen bucket, to the perfect machine-made shaker pail and glass vase. Anything will answer if it is but clean and sweet. Glass would be best, but it is too expensive; tin is good, but is also expensive; birch buckets are extensively used on account of their trifling cost, but are often leaky; are handled with difficulty when full of sap, and are not easily kept sweet. The shaker pail is used, but the top is too large, catching too much dirt when the winds shake the forest; sheds its hoops too freely when it has stood empty a day or two with a March wind blowing; and, if hung to the tree by its wire loop and nail, its flaring top gives it an outward pitch and lessens its capacity. Earthern vessels are easily kept clean, but are too heavy, and liable to be broken. The best thing on account of its low cost, lightness, durability, and well adapted form, is the mackerel half-kid, lacking its smallest head; its form is that of an inverted pail, consequently the hoops never fall off when it is kept right end up, its small top catches little dirt, is easily kept sweet by scalding, hangs well to a tree, and will last, with proper care, many years." [22]

From the 1858 *Maine Agricultural Report* we get the following direction. "Buckets for catching the sap are best made of pine staves, in form the frustum of a cone, bound with wooden hoops in preference to iron, and to contain about two gallons." [23] Solon Robinson comes forward with advice to make the article oneself. "Home-made pails can be made without much cost during the winter, if you have any genius for coopering, and will use the surplus heat of the stove or brick oven to season your stuff. Leave one stave long enough to bore a hole to hang upon the nail." [24]

From wooden buckets the next step was to tin. A primitive type, again homemade, is described by Robinson: "One old sugar-maker recommends making tin sap-buckets of a square form, of two sheets for the square sides and half a sheet for the bottom, with just taper enough to fit together when in store. The tin should be rolled around wire at the top, with a loop to hang by, or else with a hole under the wire large enough to hang over a wrought nail head or stub horsenail." [25]

From the receiving container, trough or bucket, the sap was carried in pails hanging from a wooden yoke. "The gathering pails were shaped like the tin ones we have now, but were made of pine, with two staves on opposite sides, some two or three inches longer than the rest, and had holes for pins, which passed through the wood bail and then through these holes, and were prevented from coming out by leather keys." [26] Patient oxen or horses hauled the gathered sap in tubs on sleds to the place of boiling.

The very largest containers, or storage tubs, were occasionally laboriously handwrought. Benjamin Rush mentions "store troughs or large cisterns in the shape of a canoe or large manger made of white ash, linden, basswood, or white pine." [27] "A trough that will hold four or five barrels can be dug out without any expense, for the man who is tending the first boiling can do the work," says Solon Robinson, but "a liquor cask will answer if it is brought home some weeks before wanted, and filled with water." [28] "For storage," says Harmon Morse, "they used molasses hogsheads cut in two in the middle." [29] As far back as 1825 these wooden casks were apparently used for storing sap. "Very large troughs are generally made of the trunks of trees, to receive the sap when it cannot be boiled so fast as it runs from the spiles. As the farmer's casks, however, are mostly empty before the time for making sugar comes, these will be found better than troughs, provided they be made very clean." [30]

Boiling shelters were few in the very earliest days and at best were only "calculated to turn rain." In fact, much of the boiling was done far from home, and the sugar makers camped out in the deep woods till the sap season was over. An account of such a trek and sojourn is given in Zadock Thompson's *History of Vermont.* [31] In the spring of 1777 Ezekiel Colby, John Nutting, and John Armand set out from Newbury, Vermont, each with a five-pail kettle on his head. With this load they traveled by pocket compass twelve miles through the wilderness to Corinth, where they made their sugar and returned home with it, and all the kettle paraphernalia, on their backs. Here is another similar instance: "Taking our large brass kettle with several small ones, some corn and beans for our sustenance, our bedding, and, indeed all our household furniture and utensils excepting the hominy block, we closed our cabin door, placing the customary stick against it . . . and packing our baggage on a horse proceeded four or five miles down the river to the sugar trees." [32]

The Society of Gentlemen, which in 1790 published their remarks "for the General Information and Benefit of the Citizens of the United States" on the subject of maple sugar, were particularly concerned about the lack of boiling shelters. "The exposed manner in which sugar has been usually made, in the back country, is attended with many inconveniences, especially in windy weather, when the ashes, leaves, etc. may be blown into the boilers, and thereby discolour the syrup, or injure its flavour; neither can the keeping up a proper degree of heat be always effected in an exposed situation. To remedy these inconveniences it is recommended that a back wall, for the fire place, be erected, 18 or 20 inches high, and to extend a sufficient length for all the boilers employed. This wall may be made of stones laid in clay or loam, where lime-mortar is not readily to be had. For saving the ashes, and the greater convenience in making and continuing a regular fire under the boilers, a hearth of flat stone, about three feet wide, should be made to extend an equal length with the back wall. And further to obviate the ill effects which too open an exposure is subject to, it is strongly recommended that sheds be erected, to extend over and cover the whole length of the hearth, and so formed that the smoke may pass off, and be at the same time a shelter from high winds, rain, snow, etc." [33]

E. A. Talbot, telling of the manner of sugaring in Canada, says, "A part of the estate is selected which contains the largest quantity of flourishing Maple trees nearly contiguous to each other; and a temporary hut is erected for the accommodation of the operators." [34] Another Canadian account pictures "a small shanty put up, of logs, and thatched with bark." [35] Timothy Wheeler, giving his remembrances of sugar making with his father, says, "No sugar-house or shed of any kind was ever thought of. The open firmament was our only shelter; storms of snow, rain and wind beat on us mercilessly as it did upon the trees around us." [36]

To brighten this picture, let John Burroughs tell of his pleasure in boiling. "Many a farmer sits up all night boiling his sap, when the run has been an extra good one, and a lonely vigil he has of it amid the silent trees and beside his wild hearth. If he has a sap-house, as is now so common, he may make himself fairly comfortable, and if a companion, he may have a good time or a glorious wake." [37] With a sugarhouse, says W. T. Chamberlain, "night boiling is not so bad as it might seem. A bunk is built in one corner of the sugarhouse, 3 feet high, with straw-bed, pillows and buffalo-robe or blankets; and two men divide the night, one boiling while the other sleeps. You will sleep soundly after gathering 30 barrels of sap." [38]

Before describing the early boiling rig, we should refer to the methods of tapping and gathering. In writing of the natural history of the coasts of North America, Nicolas Denys, in 1672, gives one of the first detailed reports of the operation. "A gash is made about half a foot deep, a little hollowed in the middle to receive the water. This gash has a height of about a foot, and almost the same breadth. Below the gash, 5 or 6 inches, there is made a hole with a drill or gimlet which penetrates to the middle of the gash where the water collects. There is inserted a quill, or two end to end if one is not long enough, of which the lower extremity leads to some vessel to receive the water. In 2 or 3 hours it will yield 3 to 4 pots of the liquid." [39]

In 1703 La Hontan has the tapper use, and leave, a knife in the tree. "This liquor is drawn by cutting the Tree 2 inches deep in the Wood, the cut being run sloping to the length of 10 or 12 Inches. At the lower end of this gash, a Knife is thrust into the Tree slopingly, so that the water running along the Cut or Gash, as through a Gutter, and falling upon the Knife that lies across the Channel, runs out upon the Knife, which has Vessels plac'd underneath to receive it. Some trees will yield 5 or 6 Bottles of this water a Day; and some Inhabitants of Canada might draw 20 Hogsheads of it in one day, if they would thus cut and notch all the Mapples of their respective Plantations. The gash do's no harm to the Tree." [40]

A dissenting opinion on this rough treatment is voiced by the Society of Gentlemen in 1790. "Although it has been found that the Sugar Maple tree will bear much hardship and abuse; yet the chopping notches into it, from year to year, should be forborne; an auger hole answers the purpose of drawing off the sap, equally well, and is no injury to the tree." [41] Another warning voice on the care of the tree sounds from a magazine of the same year. "It cannot be too often recommended to the sugar-makers, not to tap their trees with an axe, but to use a half-inch augre, which is a very useful tool to every farmer, and to plug up the hole at the end of the season." [42] This latter custom was practiced by some careful foresters at the end of every season. "The holes in the trees are filled with plugs cut from the small branches, on the principle, we suppose, that a hair of the same dog will cure the bite, and in two or three years scarcely a scar remains." [43]

Fear of destroying the trees by harmful tapping methods led Thomas Ashe to excoriate the practice. "This valuable tree, like every other valuable gift of nature to this Western world, is hastening to dissolution and decline. In the spring of the year sugar camps extend through the whole country; and the persons employed give the trees such great and unnecessary wounds that their whole virtue runs out, and they perish perhaps in a season. So violent has been the prodigality of the people of Kentucky, that they have nearly annihilated the maple altogether, never closing the wounds from which they drew the saw, though they well knew that the timber would perish from such treatment. Persons of better regulated minds tap the trees with an augur, insert a cane, draw off the liquor, and then stop up the flowing and the wound, by which means the trees recover their vigour, and afford fresh supplies from three to twelve years." [44]

Leander Coburn in Vermont's first *Agricultural Report,* [45] tells how in his father's sugar orchard "there were many trees badly injured, and some were hollow, from the effect of one year's tapping with an ax. The man that commenced on and cleared up the farm used to tap with an ax; he would cut some 4 or 5 boxes or gashes, one above the other, and then strike in his ax below these gashes and put in a spout as wide as the bit of his ax. The consequence was that in three or four years his sugar trees would be gone, and then he would move his boiling works to another place and commence with another stock of trees." E. A. Fisk, in Vermont's second *Agricultural Report,*[46] says much the same thing: "Trees were so plenty that no pains were taken in tapping them to preserve their lives. The ax was the instrument invariably used, and that with no sparing hands."

"If properly tapped," states the *American Agriculturalist* in an anonymous article, "the trees are not injured. This may be done with a 1¼ inch auger, slanting the hole downward to the depth of 1½ inches, so as to form a cup; or a square hole may be made with a chisel and mallet. Another hole should then be bored with a spike gimlet, slanting upward, so as to draw off the sap from the cup formed above, and into this hole a tube of elder or other kind must be closely fitted."[47] Here is an account of "boxing" with a chisel in preference to an auger: "I tap my trees with an inch and a quarter chisel; we cut into the wood of the tree about three quarters of an inch, in a sloping direction, so that the box (as we call it) will hold a spoonful or more. We bore so as to strike the lowest place in the box with a three-eighths of an inch breast bit. Spouts are made and sharpened to suit with the bit. A man who is used to it will box three hundred in a day—another man will bore and set the spouts. Some people tap their trees by boring into the trees with a half or three-quarters of an inch bit or auger; but I am persuaded that it hurts the tree much more than the chisel."[48]

Before we leave the old-time tapping of trees, here are three novel systems, which the practitioners maintained spared the trees. "Great quantities of this liquor may be extracted by cutting off some small branches and hanging bottles with the ends of the branches in the mouths of the bottles, into which the chrystaline liquor will distill."[49]

"An improvement has lately been made in the manner of tapping the sugar tree, which I hope will be widely circulated, that it may supersede the barbarous use made of the axe in tapping them. . . . About one of the small roots of the sugar tree, dig a hole large enough to set the vessel in, which is designed to catch the sap; saw off the end of the root, and it is accomplished. It is asserted that the sap will run more freely this way, than any other way yet discovered. Among the advantages attending this manner of tapping trees is this: the sap can be sheltered from animals, and from leaves and dirt, by placing a board over the hole. I hope farmers generally will make a proper application of this important improvement." [50]

Mackenzie's Five Thousand Receipts in All the Useful and Domestic Arts varies the root treatment slightly. "At the proper season for the running of the liquor, open the ground, and select a tender root, about the size of one or two fingers; cut off the end, and raise the root sufficiently out of the ground to turn the cut end into the receiver. It will emit the liquor from the wound as freely as by either of the other methods. When it ceases to flow, bury the root again, and the tree will not be hurt." [51]

Now to the boiling place. *The Canadian Settler's Guide* of 1860 gives the following directions to the immigrant for finding it and setting it up. "In the centre of his bush he should fix upon a boiling-place: a fallen pine, or any large tree should be chosen: if there be not one ready felled, he must cut one down, as he needs a good lasting back log against which to build his fire at the boiling time. . . . The boiling place is made by fixing two large stout-forked posts into the ground, over which a pole is laid, stout enough to support the kettles; iron-wood is good for this purpose; on this the kettles are hung at a certain height above the fire." [52]

The *Agricultural Report for 1862* describes a fireplace made of the butt ends of logs from a nearby tree, "the length of these depending on the number of kettles to be used. If only two are used, they would be about 6 feet long. These logs are placed on the ground parallel with each other, with a space between them wide enough to hang the kettles. At each end of the logs a crotched stick is set into the ground, and across these a pole is laid; from this pole the kettles are suspended. These are generally iron, and hold from 12 to 15 gallons. In boiling the sap, when the logs are burned up, others are cut from the same tree and rolled up to supply their places. If the tree did not supply logs enough for the season, and others could not be brought conveniently to the fire, a tree was cut in another place and the boiling place removed." [53] We have also seen mention of a single kettle being banked by logs on four sides and the fires made in the corners.

An inventive variant of any of the above methods was where a cauldron kettle "was hung up to one end of a long pole resting on a crotched stick set in the ground; this pole was so balanced that when the kettle was filled with sap, the other end of the pole would rise and let the kettle down to the fire; but when the sap was boiled down low, the kettle would rise out of the way of the fire. The advantage of having it hung in this way was that much less of foreign substances got into the sap while it was boiling; and if the person who was boiling the sap should be absent from the fire for some time, and the sap get low, it would swing up from the fire, and thus prevent it from being burned." [54]

The method of boiling in cauldron kettles was an endless affair and wasteful of time, labor, and fuel, while quality and color also necessarily suffered. It was difficult to take the finished syrup out of the unwieldy kettles unless the fire was low and plenty of help was around. So the tendency was to add more and more sap and boil the resulting syrup over and over again all day. As a German missionary wrote in 1789, "the sap is put into kettles and without any further addition, boiled upon a slow fire, till it becomes as thick as honey; then more is added and boiled down, which becomes of a still darker color." [55] "In those days," says Timothy Wheeler, writing of his experiences sixty years back, "we boiled the same sap from morning till night by constantly replenishing the kettle, thus wasting time and fuel and sacrificing quality." [56]

When more than one kettle was lined up, a slightly better technique could be used, that of ladling from pot to pot. An anonymous article in the *American Museum* puts it this way: "To carry on the business with the greatest advantage, there should be three kettles of different dimensions. These kettles should be fixed in a row, the smallest at one end, the middle sized next, and the largest at the other end. When there is a quantity of sap collected, put as much in the largest kettle as can be conveniently boiled in it. . . . Boil it briskly, till so much is evaporated, as that which remains may be boiled in the middle kettle. . . . As soon as the liquor is taken from the large, and put into the middle kettle, fresh sap must be put into the former. . . . When the liquor is sufficiently evaporated in the middle kettle, to admit its being boiled in the smallest, it must be put into the last, where it must be boiled, until it gets to a proper consistency to make sugar." [57]

More or less the same system is described by the Society of Gentlemen, with a further step of straining and preparing it for sugar. "When the liquor is reduced one-half in quantity, lade the second kettle from the end, into the end one; and when the contents of three or four kettles can be contained in one, then let the whole be laded into that, at the end; filling up the empty kettles, without delay, with fresh sap. As the liquor in the end kettle, removed from those which have been mentioned, becomes a syrup, it should be strained through a good blanket, or woolen cloth; and care must be taken, not to suffer it to boil so long, as to be too thick to be strained in this manner." [58]

The next step was for these same cauldron kettles to be set in rough stone bases or arches instead of being hung from poles. "The arch is not, properly speaking, an arch, or segment of a circle, but a parallelogram built of stone or bricks, of suitable height to contain the fire, and of such a size as to receive the pans upon the top, allowing one and a half inches of their bottom all around to rest upon the brick work." [59] Flat-bottomed pans of tin or iron were substituted for kettles. These exposed much more boiling surface to the heat. "This form of boiler is much better than the large caldron kettle, for the reason that when the latter is partially filled, the sides become heated by the flame flashing about it, and when it is again filled, or when the sap foams in boiling, it becomes scorched, giving the syrup or sugar a bitter taste and a dark color. No such results can possibly happen with the pans unless they are allowed to become nearly empty so as to leave some portion of the bottom bare." [60]

When flat-bottomed pans were first employed is hard to determine. They seem to have been used in some places long before they were heard of in others. *The Country Gentleman*, February 21, 1861, in answer to an inquiry as to the best boiling rig in use at the time, recommends a shallow home-made pan, adding, "We know of none kept for sale." The Washington *Agricultural Report for 1862* gives directions for the making of such a pan. "A good pan for boiling the sap is made of sheet-iron, by nailing the iron to a plank, so that the iron shall form the bottom and ends and the plank the sides, the sheet-iron being secured to the plank by two rows of closely-driven nails. Eight feet long, four feet wide, and six inches deep, are good dimensions, for the article, and if the arch or fire-place be made narrower than the pan, so it can be placed over it, it will be found a most useful arrangement for boiling the sap." [61] Mr. Harmon Morse, "an elderly gentleman from Johnson, Vt.," in adding his recollections to the eleventh *Agricultural Report* for Vermont, states that "when we got the Russian iron pan we thought we had reached the limit of improvement in sugar making." [62]

The first mention found of flow from one pan to another is made by Solon Robinson in 1866, when he explains the construction of the new rigs. "Build two straight walls as long as all the pans you will use, and a little less wide apart than the width of your pan so that the second will discharge the juice through a cock or spout closed by a valve or cheap gate. . . . A reservoir should be placed above the boiler, into which a faucet should be inserted, and the sap allowed to run in a constant stream, which a little practice will enable the operator to regulate to correspond exactly with the evaporation. A stop-cock should also be placed in the boiler to draw off the sirup." [63]

In 1874 A. M. Foster, in a Vermont *Report,* says, "There have been two or three pans invented to secure the evaporator principle, but with what success I cannot tell, not being acquainted with them." [64] In another Vermont *Report,* of

1886, Hiram Cutting says, "A few use evaporators, or pans so arranged that the sap flows in continuously at one end and comes out at the other as syrup. As they are more expensive and require more care than the pans, they are not very much used." [65]

W. J. Chamberlain, of Ohio, who wrote many articles on sugaring for the *American Agriculturalist* and who was apparently an enterprising and forward-looking authority on the subject, already had an evaporator in 1871, and praised it in the following words: "I speak within bounds, and from an experience of many seasons with good pans, and of the greater part of one season with an evaporator, when I say that it saves *half of the time, labor, and fuel,* and makes better sugar and syrup." [66]

A canny Vermonter, H. Allen Soule, had for years experimented with every new sugaring tool as it came along. In a letter to the State Board of Agriculture in 1872, he outlines aptly the various steps he took. "We formerly made our sugar in kettles, but were among the first to adopt pans. . . . We spared no pains with our product, and when we heard of improvements in methods of manufacture or in apparatus we investigated and adopted any which we found it for our interest to. We think we were among the very first to adopt the system of boiling shallow masses, and when the syphon system was introduced, we procured the apparatus and used it a few seasons. By this system the cold sap was all run into one pan, and being kept by the syphon connections at the same level in all, the syrup accumulated in the fourth or farthest pan. We do not hesitate to pronounce this as great an improvement upon the four pan system, as that is upon our original kettle system. Meantime, we were investigating the action and results of 'the evaporator,' and notwithstanding we were fairly fitted up with all the apparatus named above, we became convinced that our interest lay in discarding it altogether and putting in 'the evaporator.' We, nevertheless, determined to move safely, and we took 'the evaporator' only on trial the first year, but were glad to pay for it at the end of the season, and now, we say we know we can make more and better sugar, and with less labor, and much less fuel, in the 'evaporator' than by the four pan system." [67]

Speaking of the spout, the tin bucket, the pan, arch, and evaporator, W. O. Brigham says, "I consider these improvements to the sugar maker what the mowing machine, the horse rake, or our modern plows and cultivators are to every tiller of the soil; and as much superior to the old methods, as these agricultural implements are to the plough with the wooden mould board, or the old fashioned ways of raking or mowing. Should any of you be inclined to charge me with being too enthusiastic over these matters, or too easily carried away with every invention, I can at least assure you I am not an agent, but state things which in my estimation are facts." [68]

A wry account is given by A. M. Foster of his limping along, in the early days, with poor tools. "When I commenced sugar making I found I had 850 sap tubs, some split out and some just right to build fire with. The holders were left inside and out; nothing was in good shape for sap. The large gathering tub stood under the eaves in summer, and the low one was just right to scald hogs in. The pans were useful to set outside to put ashes in—and this was the rigging we had to use. The evaporator came around, but I was prejudiced against galvanized iron, and I struggled along about twenty years in this way." [69]

Before the days of thermometers and other precision testing tools, how did the early settlers know when the syrup was ready to take off? Most of the reports that have reached us are vague and indefinite: "Boil till the syrup is about half the sweetness of molasses"; "Reduce the sap by boiling about 95%"; "When the liquor becomes a syrup remove it from the fire"; "Boil until it is done"; "When it is reduced to a thick syrup, strain it"; "Merely boil until a sufficient degree of evaporation has taken place to convert the liquid into a thick syrup"; "Boil it as long as it can and not burn"; "When the sap is boiled to the right point, which experience teaches," etc., etc. These are not very precise directives. Very likely the tests were similar to many in use today, when practiced sugar makers, without using thermometers, test by the bubbles in the sap and by the way the syrup "aprons" from the dipper. Or perhaps the finished syrup was tested as two small boys of our acquaintance tested theirs, who tapped out and tended ninety-nine buckets in the spring of 1948. When we asked them how they knew when the syrup was done, they exclaimed, "Why, we tasted it."

Samuel Perley recommends simply reducing by boiling "until it is of suitable consistence to be used as a table syrup. . . . No uniform rule for the consistency of syrup prevails; each maker adopts a standard to suit his market, or his own private taste; or else, taking counsel of his cupidity he refrains from reducing it to a rich, honest, heavy syrup, so that he may have the greater number of gallons to market. Accordingly, much of that offered for sale will pour almost like water, where it should have the weight and consistency of good West India molasses." [70]

Jeremy Belknap, in his *History of New-Hampshire,* is equally vague on the process of turning the syrup into sugar. "When the syrup is to be granulated the boiling is repeated. . . . To know when it will granulate, a little of it is taken out and cooled, and when it appears to be in this state, the whole is poured into a cooler." [71]

Here is a more detailed description for testing the finished sugar. "Several tests are relied upon, some of which are as follows: *1st,* where the steam forcing its way up through the foaming mass, on reaching the surface, escapes by bursting its bubble with a slight explosion, similar to that observed upon hasty pudding when nearly cooked: *2nd,* when a small quantity, say a table spoonful, taken from the kettle and poured hot, upon a compacted snow-ball, after melting the snow a little, will lay upon it without diffusing itself through the ball: *3d,* when a drop taken hot from the kettle, on being let fall from the edge of the skimmer or spoon into one inch of cold water, will pass directly through the water without mingling with it, and rest upon the bottom of the vessel in the form of a flattened hemisphere: *4th,* when a drop taken

upon the finger on being touched by the thumb will draw
out a thread one-fourth to one-half an inch long: and *5th,*
when a small quantity taken into a saucer or spoon and
thoroughly cooled will granulate, so that it can be detected
by the eye, the taste, or when crushed between the teeth:
then it may be removed from the fire, for 'it is done.' These
tests, particularly the *3d* and *5th,* are useful to beginners as
aids in forming a correct judgment; but one long practiced
in the business seems, intuitively, to recognize the time when
the grain will form, and the boiling should cease." [72]

The *Country Gentleman* of February 20, 1862, in an
editorial, gives a singular direction for testing sugar. "The
way to know when it is done sufficiently to cake: take a twig
of a tree about a foot and a half long, dip it into the boiling
sugar to limber it; then tie a loop in the small end, leaving
the hole about half an inch in diameter. When you think it
is nearly done, dip this loop into the sugar and bring it up
quickly, and blow through the loop hole. When it will go
off in a ribbon eight or ten feet long, it is done. It will ribbon
a few feet before it is done; but wait a few minutes, then
try again till it will perform according to order. Take it off,
and stir it a short time; then pour it into your caking dishes,
and the work is done." Franklin B. Hough advises the following test: "A portion of the melted sugar is dropped upon the
side of a polished steel axe, where it quickly cools, and if then
brittle, it is thought to be done." [73]

To clarify the finished syrup, foreign elements were introduced into the syrup, which brought any extraneous matter
or impurities to a head. "In making good sirup the sap
should be reduced about one-thirtieth of its bulk, then
strained through flannel, and left to cool and settle for about
a day. After this, place it in the boiling pan, and add to every
gallon one beaten egg and a gill of milk to clarify it, care
being taken that it does not boil, till the scum has risen and
been skimmed off. Then boil carefully until it will harden
by placing it in cold water, when it should be poured into
vessels and the cakes placed in a box to drain. To have the
sugar perfectly white, lay a few thicknesses of flannel on top

of the cakes while they are draining; these absorb the coloring matter, and by having them washed daily with cold water
the coloring matter will wash out." [74] It was later proved to
general satisfaction that if clean metal utensils were used
throughout, and the sap strained in the bush, and kept
skimmed in the pan, and the syrup strained through flannel
or felt, no clarifying with eggs or milk was necessary.

As containers were scarce in the new settlements, it was
easier to store sugar than syrup, so a large proportion was
cooked down to sugar and kept in wooden tubs or pails or
in large blocks, which were melted down or hacked off as the
need arose. "The maple is the only sort of raw sugar made
use of in the country parts of Canada; it is very generally used
also by the inhabitants of the towns, whither it is brought
for sale by the country people who attend the markets, just
the same as any other kind of country produce. The most
common form in which it is seen is in loaves or thick round
cakes, precisely as it comes out of the vessel where it is boiled
down from the sap. These cakes are of a very dark colour in
general, and very hard; as they are wanted they are scraped
down with a knife, and when thus reduced into powder, the
sugar appears of a much lighter cast, and not unlike West
Indian muscovada or grained sugar." [75]

An Irish traveler in the late 1700's tells of finding this
sugar in a public house. "At breakfast I was surprised to see
our landlord bring in a large kebuck, as I supposed of cheese,
of about 20 pounds weight. I asked him, when did he make
that cheese? he answered, in spring last. I observed to him
that I had seen many a farm in my country who had three-
score of milk Cows, but never knew them to make a cheese
of that size at that season of the year. He said it took more
than that number of his Cows;—that he milked above an
hundred to make that cheese. This I could not divine, as I
knew he had only four milk Cows, which I saw that morning,
until he began to slice it down, when, to my great surprise,
I found it to be a loaf of maple sugar made in the form, and
of the colour of a cheese; which proved what he had said to
be true, as he had pierced that number of trees to make it." [76]

The refined sugar made today seems a tasteless, colorless article in comparison with the rank racy sugar of high color that was a product of the long boiling and the smoke and charcoal. Attempts were made to improve the product. A German traveler in this country gives his opinion of the sugar in 1788: "It is brown to be sure, and somewhat dirty and viscous, but by repeated refinings can be made good and agreeable." [77] In describing the process of making the prize-winning sample of sugar exhibited at the annual New York State Agricultural Fair of 1844, the committee who awarded the premium said they "have never seen so fine a sample, either in the perfection of the granulation, or in the extent to which the refining process has been carried; the whole coloring matter is extracted, and the peculiar flavor of maple sugar is completely eradicated, leaving the sugar fully equal to the double refined cane loaf sugar." [78]

The *Farmer's Every-Day Book* finds the flavor impaired by refining. "The sugar, in a brown state, has a peculiar flavor, very acceptable to those accustomed to it, though perhaps to some others objectionable. When refined, this peculiarity of flavor does not exist." [79] Says Hector St. John de Crèvecoeur, writing back to France in 1760 about maple sugar, "Some persons know how to purify it, and I am told that there are people at Montreal who excel in this branch. For my part, I am perfectly well satisfied with the colour and taste which Nature has given it." [80]

C. T. Alvord gives his explanation of the color and the flavor. "In boiling sap in kettles hung between the logs and kettles, and as the lower ends burned off, the tops of the small sticks would frequently fall into the kettles; leaves and ashes would occasionally be blown in by the wind; and when the sap was nearly boiled down to sirup it would burn on the sides of the kettles, thus giving the contents of the kettles an additional color. What the precise quality or complexion of the article thus made was, I shall leave the reader to imagine. In some instances the sirup was strained through hemlock boughs, and then boiled down to sugar, if a mixture made by boiling such a compound together could be called by that name." [81] Basswood and spruce also had a chance to add their essence to the maple. "In the old days a mat woven of narrow strips of basswood bark was placed over an extra kettle, and the sirup was strained through this mat, being dipped from the kettle with large wooden spoons. . . . If a kettle boiled too rapidly a branch of spruce attached to a stick was dipped into the froth. The motion was little more than a brushing of the froth with the spruce, but the bubbling at once subsided." [82]

Another addition to the flavor might well have come from the piece of fat that was hung over the boiling syrup. Catherine P. Traill, in her *Canadian Settler's Guide*, daintily draws back from this odious practice. "It is a common plan, but I think by no means a nice one, to keep a bit of pork or fat bacon suspended by a string above the sap kettles; when the boiling sap reaches this it goes down." [83] "The grease and flavor of the pork, which, with the sugar which would burn on near the top of the kettle when the sap boiled down,—to be knocked off when more was added, and the numerous cinders which fell into the sap with a fizz, together with the ashes drawn up by the draft around the kettle and eddying over into the seething foam—gave the peculiar *maple* flavor to the syrup and sugar of those early days." [84]

Maple sugar today is considered a luxury and a confection. In the early days of the settling of the American colonies it was almost a necessity to the isolated farmer, and often the only sugar on the family table. Pehr Kalm wrote, in 1751, "The common people in the northernmost English colonies, as well as the French in Canada, supply themselves with a large quantity of this sugar each year. Many farmers have whole barrels full for their own use. Practically every soldier in the French forts manufactures a year's supply of this necessity for himself in the spring. If you visit the French you will see no other sugar used. When milk is served it is heavily flavored with maple sugar, and the sugar bowl is placed on the table so everyone can sweeten his food according to his taste." [85]

Already, however, in 1812, white sugar was gaining favor

and Michaux comments on the preference for cane over maple. "When refined, it [maple] equals in beauty the finest sugar consumed in Europe. It is made use of, however, only in the districts where it is made, and there, only in the country. From prejudice or taste, imported sugar is used in all the small towns, and in the inns." [86] This, despite the fact that there was a tariff on the imported sugar, which made it dearer than the native. [87] In 1818 maple sugar is reported in Canada at "about half the price of the West-India sugar." [88] The tariff was taken off some of the sugar eventually, and in the 1880's cane and maple sugar were running an even race on price. Around 1885, cane sugar began to undersell maple; since then maple sugar has become a high-priced form of sweetening for all but those who could make it for themselves. Says C. P. Traill, in 1860, "There is little call for maple sugar, muscavado being quite as cheap. Still there are situations and circumstances under which the making of maple sugar may be carried on with advantage. There will always be a class of emigrants who, for the sake of becoming the proprietors of land will locate themselves in the backwoods, far from the vicinity of towns and villages, who have little money to expend, and who are glad to avail themselves of so wholesome and so necessary a luxury at no greater cost than their own labour." [89]

In 1890 a tariff act, known as the McKinley Bill, was made law with the hope of stimulating the production of native sugar. The act provided that after July 1, 1891, and until July 1, 1895, there should be paid to the producer a bounty of two cents a pound on sugars of high quality (testing 90 degrees or over by the polariscope) and one and three-quarters cents a pound on sugar of lower quality (testing less than 90 degrees but more than 80). It is reported that the impetus given by this act caused 2,600 Vermont sugar makers to take out license papers to make sugar in 1892, but the requisite formalities were not popular in the state, though it is reported that seven eighths of the sugar made in Vermont was "bounty grade" and though "in the matter of regulations the revenue officials claim that the rules for maple sugar producers are less astringent than those made for any other class of people who have to do with the treasury department, either receiving money or paying money into it." [90] Cantankerous Vermonters seemed to take no pleasure in enduring the inspections and regulations. "The maple sugar bounty has no friends among Washington officers. They claim that it has been ten times more bother and work to distribute $35,000 bounty among the 1,607 producers in Vermont, who succeeded in getting bounty in 1892, than in distributing $7,000,000 among a few large planters of Louisiana." [91] The hoped-for effect of the bounty was not forthcoming in the case of maple sugar and cane began by far to outstrip maple production.

Apparently the high hopes of the earliest enthusiasts who saw maple sugar flooding the home market, and even the world market,* were not to be realized. Yet maple had filled a great need, and in a time of scarcity had proved indispensable. While it failed to be the universal solvent and provider of sweetness predicted, it still serves a sweet purpose, and the following pious proposition of Coxe Tench, written in 1794, is as true today as it was then. "It is certain that every farmer having one hundred acres of sugar maple land, in a state of ordinary American improvement (that is, one third covered with judicious reserves of wood and timber, and two thirds cleared for the culture of grass and grain), can make one thousand pounds weight of sugar with only his necessary farming and kitchen utensils, if his family consists of a man, a woman and a child of ten years, including himself. . . . The operation in a family is as easy, as to make household soap or cheese, or to brew ale or beer, and as there is in this

*"Every part of the back country from latitude 42° to 36° produces an abundance of the sugar maple-tree as would be equal to furnish sugar for the inhabitants of the whole earth." G. Imlay, *op cit.*, P. 89.

"The United States will one day furnish the whole of Europe with this precious article, cheaper than the West Indies." J. E. Bonnet, *op cit.*, P. 44.

"Rush brought me to Mr. Jefferson the Secretary of State, he is as Sanguine as you or I about the Maple Sugar, he thinks in a few years we shall be able to Supply half the World." Letter from Arthur Noble to Judge James Fenimore Cooper, May 7, 1791.

country much more than twice the above quantity of sugar maple lands in situations not too southern, the only object that requires attention is to give, as fast as possible, generality to this simple, profitable, and comfortable manufacture." [92]

PART II

Sugaring: Its Present Practice

CHAPTER FOUR

The Sugar Bush

"I wish there were formed from north to south a holy coalition to accumulate the produce of that divine tree, if, above all it were looked upon as an impiety to destroy so useful a tree, either for burning or clearing lands."

J. P. Brissot de Warville, Nouveau voyage dans les Etats-Unis, *1791.*

"I have never seen a reason why every farmer should not have a sugar orchard, as well as an apple orchard. The supply of sugar for his family would require as little ground, and the process of making it as easy as that of cider."

Thomas Jefferson, Letter to Monsieur Lasteyrie, July 15, 1808.

"The sugar maple affording a luxury from its saccharine juices, and great convenience in its timber and fuel, has been so diminished by the progress of cultivation, that groves of this majestic and valuable tree, once over-spreading a large proportion of this State, are now found only on unfeasible, or mountainous land."

Nathan Hoskins, A History of the State of Vermont, *1831.*

"Were it generally known how productive are the groves of Sugar Maples, we should, I doubt not, be more careful, and not exterminate them from the forest, as is now too frequently done. . . . Groves in which they abound might be spared from the unrelenting ax of the woodman."
Charles T. Jackson, Report on the Geology of the State of Maine, *1839.*

"There is a human and poetic quality in maples, which is easily felt, and though the land would be worth more for its lumber than for its sugar, many farmers would no more part with their maple bush or orchard than with any precious heirloom."
Anonymous, *"The Green Mountains in Sugar Time,"*
Harpers, *April, 1881.*

GROUPS of maple trees, old enough to be tapped and handy enough to allow for economical sap collection, are called a bush, grove, or orchard. Without a sugar bush, no sap; without sap, no maple syrup and sugar. Anyone wishing to make a part or the whole of his living from maple-syrup production must therefore have the use of a sugar bush.

How many maple trees does it require to constitute a bush? The answer would probably be hundreds to thousands of trees if one could answer the question at all. Buckets, rather than trees, are taken as the measure of bush size, because of the great variation in the number of buckets that can be hung per tree. It is not economically desirable to make syrup unless about five hundred buckets can be hung for each adult who proposes to take part in syrup making. The usual unit of syrup production is a family, or a family plus one or two persons hired for sugaring. Allowing for some variation, one adult can take care of about five or six hundred sap buckets —tap them, hang them, gather the sap, and boil the syrup. If the sap is to be gathered with horses, under ordinary conditions a man and his team can collect the sap from twelve to fifteen hundred buckets.

Irrespective of the size of the sugar bush, the trees composing it should stand close enough to one another so that there is no excessively long haul in going from tree to tree. Maples scattered thinly over a big pasture, for example, do not make a good bush. Transportation, especially under snow conditions, is too expensive. But the maples strung along a highway often do make a good bush because the highway solves the transportation problem.

Also, the sugar bush must be accessible. "Like all other farm labor, that which is near the farm buildings being always most cheaply performed, so the labor of sugaring is very much relieved by having the orchard near home." [1] A neighbor of ours, whose bush is about a quarter of a mile from his barn, tells of one spring when the snow was particularly deep. He set out from barn to sugar house with his team and sled, spent the greater part of the morning wallowing through snow to his horses' bellies, got nowhere, and finally brought out his cattle, drove them from the barn to the sugar house through the snow, and was only then able to get his horses through the path that the cattle had tramped. Cattle usually "wallow" better than horses, especially when the horses are sharp shod and in danger of cutting themselves. Some horses get desperate after a little wallowing and lie down, harness, sled, and all.

We remember one snowy spring when two of us shoveled for the better part of a week, opening a road from the sugar house up into the bush. The highly necessary road was about a quarter of a mile long, and the snow was from four to seven feet deep. Each night it snowed and drifted. When we felt that we had a passable road we got out the team and a sled-load of buckets and covers. It took an hour to travel the quarter mile to the top of our road. The hill was steep. At the top one of the horses lay down and refused to get up. After trying everything else, we hitched the still-standing horse to the down horse with a tug chain, and pulled her down the hill on her back until she decided to try again. That night it snowed hard. Then the wind got up and drifted our shoveled road solid full. That was the spring we decided to put in equipment for bucket storage right up in the bush, plus a pipe system that would allow gravity flow of sap to the sugar house, thus eliminating the use of horses in any part of our sugar work.

However, we still need roads at appropriate intervals, and

since we rarely use horses, they should be truck roads. Over these we haul buckets at washing-up time. By this means we haul out the wood that results from necessary culling and thinning of growing trees and the removal of large broken limbs and the tops, which occasionally break off. "Roads first" is a good axiom for both construction and maintenance operations, and we aim to keep our roads as open as weather conditions will permit. Moses Mather, a sugar maker and road builder of no mean proportions, wrote in 1823, "After becoming acquainted with the situation of all the trees for use, roads were cut in all directions, nearly parallel to each other, and so near that no tree stands more than 100 feet from one of those roads." [2]

Men and materials must be able to reach the bush, even in bad weather. Accessibility of the sugar house is also very important. An old-timer, writing on husbandry in 1825, says, "When what are called good or bad seasons for making sugar are averaged, it is commonly considered an unprofitable business, unless the camp stands so near to the farmer's dwelling that he can gather the water without interfering with his other business, and boil it either in his house or yard." [3] Many sugar houses we have seen are so far up in the woods that the syrup when finished must be hauled out by back or by sled. Remember that one hundred gallons of syrup, in gallon cans, weigh about 1,200 pounds. Put your sugar house close to a negotiable road if possible.

Convenient groups of maple trees do not in themselves constitute a sugar bush. They must also meet climatic requirements. All maple trees run sweet sap in the spring. To make syrup production commercially feasible, however, the sap season must be of relatively long duration—at least three or four weeks.

Maple sap can be turned into edible syrup at any time from the first spring thaw until the leaf buds burst. The best or "first-run" syrup is made before the buds begin to swell. Syrup production is therefore possible in direct proportion to the length of time between the first thaw and the swelling of the leaf buds. The longer the time, the more sap and syrup.

Four conditions prolong the length of the sap season: (1) severe winters, with hard freezing that gets well down around the roots of the trees; (2) mountains, with their extremes of day and night temperature; (3) quantities of snow and ice on the ground, which tend to make the nights cold and keep the trees chill;* and (4) exposure to the proper points of the compass: in a cold country, to the south and west, and in a warm country to the north and east. If a bush lies around a knoll or hillside, so that part of it faces south and west and another part east and north, the south part may sometimes be tapped ten days before the north part. Ordinarily the trees facing south will start running sap before those facing north, thus prolonging the sap season for the entire bush. This should be taken into consideration in judging or using a sugar bush.

Land contour also plays a significant part in determining the productivity of a sugar bush. The sugar maple thrives on steep, rocky slopes. Frequently where boulders are so thick and soil so thin that adequate tree growth seems all but impossible, splendid specimens of sugar maple develop and live to a great age.

We have one sugar maple about two feet in diameter, perched on the edge of a granite ledge. From the lower side the ledge rises about eight feet above the surrounding slope. On the upper side the ledge is level with the soil, but juts out from the soil, to descend at a right angle to the lower level. We believe that this tree yields more sap than any other tree of equal size in the bush. We have a tradition that if buckets are running over anywhere in the bush, they will be found on Old Faithful. Incidentally, there is a current belief that maples growing among rocks yield sweeter sap than those growing on level topsoil. We have not been able to check the accuracy of this belief.

*Dr. C. T. Jackson, in 1839, makes the quaint recommendation "to heap snow around the roots or stumps of the trees, to prevent their putting forth their leaves as soon as they otherwise would, for the juices of the tree begin to be elaborated as soon as the foliage is developed, and will not run." *Report on the Geology of the State of Maine*, 1839. P. 167.

Sugar maples, or rock maples, as they are also called, thrive on rocky slopes. They cannot survive in swamps. Yellow birch, white and black ash, white maple, basswood, beech, and the soft woods will grow in swamps. Hard maple will not. There are several swampy places in our sugar bush. Invariably the hard-maple growth ceases at the swamp edge. This is noticeably true in sections that ordinarily produce great quantities of maple seedlings. At the edge of the swamp they stop growing.

Soil conditions have some effect upon maple-tree growth and sap production. Moisture, drainage, and plenty of organic matter should constitute the forest floor. As to the effect of fertilizers on tree growth and sap production, we assume that liming would prove advantageous, especially on granite soils. We save our wood ashes, from both house and sugar operations, and scatter them through the sugar bush. Thus far neither our experiments with fertilization nor those of our neighbors have been extensive enough nor continued long enough to yield noticeable results, and we have been unsuccessful in getting information on this point from agricultural colleges, forest services, or agricultural departments.

We did, however, come across certain information on the subject written by Hiram A. Cutting in two *Vermont Agricultural Reports*. "Like all other crops, maples may be fertilized. Potash or ashes I have found not only increases the growth, but greatly increases the amount of sap flow, also the quantity and quality of the sugar. Gypsum (land plaster) also increases the sap flow, and all manures seem beneficial. ... I find the greatest benefit from fertilizing just as the leaves begin to fall in autumn ... A tree tested for the season after potash fertilization averaged about seven per cent sugar content and produced twenty-four pounds of sugar." [4] "If ashes are sown in the orchard at the rate of 10 bushels to the acre, the increase in sugar will be readily perceptible. ... A man in Barnet sowed about 10 bushels of ashes per acre in his sugar orchard, and was satisfied that the yield of sap was double in consequence." [5]

Concerning the effects of contour, rock, and soil upon

maple reproduction we might make three observations: (1) some sections of our Vermont countryside produce and re-produce hard maple with no more apparent effort than a well-fertilized garden produces a crop of weeds; (2) neighboring areas, where conditions are quite similar, produce a scant growth of maple, or no growth at all. For example, we have slopes and knolls apparently similar in all essentials. On some of them hard-maple saplings crowd each other for sunlight, water, and nutrition. On others there are few or no hard maples. (3) The only test we know thus far is a purely pragmatic one. Go over a wooded area, observe where hard maple grows abundantly, and accept nature's verdict as to sugar-bush availability.

Does one plant cultivated sugar maples or just let them grow? There are planted sugar bushes in some parts of the United States. We have read of them but have never seen one. In 1784, Crèvecoeur reports, "By way of imitating in some respects my provident father, who so religiously saved this small sugar plantation, I have cleared about a half acre of land abjoining it, on which I have planted above seventy young maples, which I have raised in a nursery . . . I propose to enlarge this useful plantation as fast as I can raise trees big enough for transplantation." [6] Isaac Weld, in 1799, recommended the advantages of a planted bush. "As the oaks and other kinds of trees were cut away for different purposes, maple might be planted in their room, which would be ready to be tapped by the time that the old maple trees failed. Moreover, if these trees were planted out in rows regularly, the trouble of collecting the sap from them would be much less than if they stood widely scattered, as they do in their natural state, and of course the expence of making the sugar would be considerably lessened. Added to this, if young maples were constantly set out in place of the other trees, as they were cut down, the estate at the end of twenty years would yield ten times as much sugar as it did originally." [7]

Nurseries grow fruit and nut trees, which are set out at one or two years of age and which produce a crop in anywhere from three to nine years. Sugar maples reach tappable size, under the best of conditions, in about forty years. A fruit farmer does not object to waiting five or even ten years for a crop, but it takes a hardy, farseeing individual with capital, patience, and longevity to wait forty or fifty years for his first harvest.

Here are some old-timers with the long view. Ethan A. Greenwood writes to *The New England Farmer,* March 31, 1832, regarding the planting of sugar-maple trees: "And why should men delay to plant and cultivate all sorts of good trees because they may not live to see them fully grown? What can a man do better on the face of the earth than to cultivate and beautify it? While ever ready to depart, the lover of beautiful trees should act as if he expected to live a thousand years. . . . I have set within the last three years, on both sides of the road which passes the distance of a mile through my farm, upwards of four hundred of these trees. . . . Although I shall not live to see them grown very large, yet somebody else will; and I hope that whoever may successively occupy the same place hereafter, will not only see them of large size, but have taste and feeling to enjoy their beauty and preserve them for their usefulness." Says Dr. Jackson, "It would certainly be one of our most beautiful pledges of regard for posterity to plant groups of maples in convenient situations, upon our lands, and to line the roadsides with them. I am sure that such a plan, if carried into effect, would please the public taste, in more ways than one." [8] "All good citizens, who are desirous of doing good deeds, and of being remembered by posterity hereafter, we would recommend to transplant a goodly number of sugar maples round their dwellings. . . . Be not discouraged by looking forward, and say it will be a long time before you can have any benefit by sugar. You must remember the timber is growing every year, and wait with patience, and be assured the other part will not fail." [9] Joseph C. G. Kennedy, superintendent of the 1860 census, tells of the "sage injunction of the dying Scotch laird to his son: 'Jock, when ye hae naething else to do, ye may be aye sticking in a tree; it will be growing, Jock, when y're sleeping.' " [10]

"Wise men were they who set hard maples along the boundary lines of their farms in earlier days. They now have avenues to be proud of. And they have also a source of revenue, for these low-branched, isolated trees give abundant flow of sap in the early spring." [11]

All of the sugar bushes we have ever seen have been self-seeded. The hard maple produces a huge crop of winged seeds every two, three, or four years. These seeds are blown about and finally covered by the autumn leaves. The next spring, in favorable locations, the forest floor is carpeted with tiny maple seedlings. Since the maple is tolerant of shade, the seedlings survive, under a complete foliage cover. The seedlings grow so quickly and so thickly that within five or six years it is all but impossible to go among them with gathering pails.

While we are on this subject it may be noted that when a hill pasture goes back to brush, berry bushes grow first, followed by pin cherry, poplar, white birch, shad, soft maple, basswood, and ash, in that order. At the same time, if cones are available, softwood seedlings get under way. The soft woods grow slowly during the first four or five years. Consequently they have a well-established brush cover to filter the sunlight and give them the shade they relish. Up to this point no hard maple appears in the picture. After the quick-growing deciduous and evergreen trees have made their start and grown whips twelve or fifteen feet high, hard maples make their appearance, grow slowly and steadily within this cover, and sooner or later top it and dominate it.

Since there is a wide variation in the sugar content of sap from different trees (from as little as 2 per cent to as much as 12 per cent) we are convinced that if the volume of maple business justifies the development, a time will come when maples will be raised for the high sugar content of their sap. Sugar bushes will thus be developed by planting rooted cuttings or by grafting or budding on native-grown seedlings. The Department of Botany of the University of Vermont has two men, James W. Marvin and Fred H. Taylor, working on the problem of domesticating wild sugar maples. They hope to raise a pedigreed strain that will become productive in about twenty years, yield about four times as much sap, and have a high sugar content. For the time being we must content ourselves with native, wild, hard maples.

The first sugar bush we took over was located along a series of rocky knolls and slopes lying at the base of a four-thousand-foot mountain. The land sloped mainly to the southwest. The bush had been used for a great many years— we never found out exactly how many. It contained about 800 tappable trees. Some of them were more than three feet in diameter. The majority of them were from eighteen to thirty inches in diameter two feet above the ground.

The bush also contained: (1) a considerable amount of beech and some yellow birch; (2) a scattering of softwoods, especially hemlock in the swamps; (3) a large amount of brush, from seedlings to saplings of three or four inches in diameter; and (4) a great surplus of hard maples, with a scattering of soft maples, which, as we have already mentioned, are not so advantageous in quantity or quality of sap. The bush was on the edge of a mixed forest that surrounded it east, north, and west. Hardwoods predominated in this forest; among the hardwoods were quantities of hard maple.

The first question we faced was that of establishing and maintaining a pure maple stand or of tapping maple trees scattered through a mixed forest. Early sugar makers tapped hard maples all through the woods, wherever they could find them. Modern sugar bushes are generally clear stands with everything but hard maple eliminated.

In ordinary farming, monoculture has given way to crop rotation. But in dealing with maple trees, which have a life span of a century or more, crop rotation for an individual producer is out of the question. The maple farmer must decide between a clear stand of maple and a mixed forest. We decided in favor of a clear maple stand.

We are not yet sure that this decision was entirely wise. Theoretically we accept the principle of crop rotation. In practice we noted three things about this fairly old bush: (1) older trees were developing many dead limbs and in places were dying off; (2) young trees were not growing rapidly, especially in the heavily tapped section that lay immediately around the sugar house; (3) there were places, especially near the sugar house, where maple presumably had stood the longest, where there were no maple seedlings and saplings, even on ideally situated rocky slopes. Were these not all indications that the essentials of maple reproduction had been eliminated from the soil? Professor Marvin, chairman of the Department of Botany at the University of Vermont, answered a letter we wrote him on the whole general subject. "Another interesting point that you raise has to do with the effects of a mixed forest in contrast to a pure stand of maple. Conifers seem to be beneficial in a young stand of maple; that is, there are some records that maples planted with pine grow better than maples planted in a pure stand. However, so far as the effect on trees big enough to tap, I have very little to offer. Certainly, spruce or hemlock in a sugar bush shade the trees and make it difficult to work the bush, and from that standpoint have a nuisance value."

Our first step in developing the bush was to take out all the brush and softwood. Brush makes it difficult to move about easily with tapping equipment and gathering pails. During a heavy sap run, when speed is essential, brush probably reduces gathering possibilities by 50 per cent.

Brushing out should stop at the inside of the bush. When we reached the last tappable tree in any area, we cut brush for another six or eight feet to give room for movement around the tree, and then let the brush grow, especially on the north side. A good brush barrier will act as a windbreak and snow fence all in one.

Softwood in the sugar bush cuts off sunlight. Sunlight is vitally essential to sap flow, especially in the early days of a sap season. First-class sap runs, early in the season, often occur entirely on the south side of the trees. There are sunny days in March when the south side of trees will thaw out and yield a plentiful run of sap, while scarcely a drop will run on the north side. On such a day a single thinly branched hemlock or spruce, so located as to shade the south side of a tree, will cut off direct sunlight and thus prevent sap from running. Any considerable amount of softwood, under such circumstances, would restrict or prevent the early sap runs.

Our third step was to cut out everything but hard maple. This is called "weeding" in forestry vernacular. Since a weed is a plant out of place, in a pure stand of hard maple, any other tree, even a valuable one like white ash, is a weed.

Weeding cannot be done all at once, because it would leave big open spaces that would admit wind and too much sunlight into the bush. In our bush there were several large units of beech, for example. One very large beech top shaded almost a quarter of an acre. In such cases we culled out a tree here and there, went back the next year and culled again, and finally in the course of six or eight years got the last of the weed trees in the district removed.

Finally we began thinning the maple. An ideal sugar bush should have a foliage cover so complete that no direct sunlight penetrates to the forest floor. There are two reasons for this. First, the more complete the forest cover, the more the available sunshine is absorbed by the foliage; it is by means of the leaves, and as a result of sunshine working in the leaves upon elements drawn from the soil, that sap is enriched and trees grow. Second, the forest floor should be a soft spongy mass of humus and of decomposing leaves, twigs, branches, and bits of bark. This humus sponge will absorb and hold great quantities of moisture. It also provides an important part of the nourishment for tree growth. Where sunlight penetrates the sugar bush a sod forms, which retards moisture absorption and allows part of a rainfall or of melting snow to run off, instead of being absorbed and held by the humus sponge on a well-preserved forest floor. Since an adequate supply of moisture is one of the most essential elements in sap production, it is easy to understand the importance of moisture conservation.

With our aim thus defined, we began to thin. Hard maples, grown in the open, frequently develop a limb spread of fifty feet. Such trees almost invariably yield large amounts of rich sap. Twenty such trees would cover an acre. Twenty-five acres of such trees would probably be worth fifty acres of closely spaced, spindle-topped trees. If maple trees are crowded together they develop narrow, spindly tops, with a small leaf area and cramped roots. Such trees do not grow rapidly and are subject to fungus and other inroads. Sap yield and quality seem to be directly proportional to leaf area, so it is important to have the maximum of leaf area per tree. "The total yield of sugar from different trees is roughly proportional to their summer leaf areas." [12] Therefore the goal toward which bush thinning aims is the least number of trees that will yield a complete leaf cover. Maples often grow to enormous heights, and the girth of a white maple in Maine has been reported as twenty-three feet in circumference. Such a tree might carry its trunk fifty feet before branching, and reach a height of over a hundred feet in all. Timothy Dwight writes of a maple he has known, "cut for the keel of a vessel, which measured eighty-eight feet in length after it was hewed." [13] Uncountable leaves would make such a tree a valuable sap giver.

In our bush the maples were too close together. The bush had been developed by farmers who wanted quantity of maples, and who therefore let the trees stand as close as they could and still survive. This seems to be an all-too-common practice. People often want to drain the source of supply without thinking of future generations. We have seen a number of sugar bushes in which mature trees were less than twenty-five feet apart on the average—that is, seventy or eighty trees per acre. We know of a comparatively young bush in which there are more than one hundred trees per acre.

We began thinning out the hard maples, cutting diseased and broken trees and trees that yielded small quantities of sap. Still there were too many maples. In the older parts of the bush where crowded trees had diameters of about two feet there was not much we could do beside taking out the culls. Where the trees were younger, however, averaging eight to ten inches in diameter, we followed a simple rule laid down by the agricultural colleges—keep the best trees.

Cut the poorer trees until there is a space of from ten to twelve feet between the standing treetops. The assumption is that healthy trees will fill such a space in about five years, when a new thinning should be undertaken.

Another matter must be kept in mind. There is some evidence that length of trunk plays a part in sap yield. John Burroughs went so far as to say that "in the production of sap, top seems far less important than body. It is not length of limb that wins in this race, but length of trunk. A heavy, bushy-topped tree in the open field, for instance, will not, according to my observation, compare with a tall, long-trunked tree in the woods, that has but a small top." [14] Trees with longer trunks are presumed to furnish larger runs of sap. Since culled-out sugar maples with long trunks also produce saw logs, there is a double argument for leaving trees rather closely spaced until they have developed a trunk at least twenty feet long. After butting for tapholes, such a trunk will provide a twelve-foot saw log.

Thinners must also have an eye to replacement trees. Mature maple trees often die off in a peculiar fashion. A fungus will find an entrance into the tree through a woodpecker hole, a rotten limb socket, or some other aperture. The fungus then works horizontally across the tree. This type of behavior was first called to our attention when one of our finest and most productive maples, three feet in diameter, broke off about twenty feet above the ground. At the breaking point, the wood was completely decayed. The butt was sound. Since that time, two other maples, slightly smaller in diameter, have behaved in the same way, breaking off fifteen or twenty feet from the ground while the butts were still solid. A neighbor had the opposite experience. He had a splendid maple almost rotted off at the butt. He cut it and took a sound sixteen-foot log out of the tree.

When a big maple goes down, it leaves a space forty or fifty feet in diameter, through which the sun can reach the forest floor. If all of the neighboring trees are mature, the opening will not be filled in by top growth. To meet such contingencies, we leave replacement trees—saplings here and there that can fill in, if and when a big tree is lost. If a bush is well thinned, such saplings will be encouraged to develop wherever there is a chance of losing a mature tree.

It is important to have trees of all ages in a sugar bush, from young seedlings and saplings to trees of a century or more. Early in a cold spring, small trees thaw out and produce sap days and even weeks before the big trees run freely. "Young, thrifty, thin-skinned trees start up with great spirit, indeed, fairly on a run, but they do not hold out, and their blood is very diluted." [15] A sugar bush that contains both small and large trees can therefore take advantage of severe weather early in the season. Furthermore, if a sugar bush contains both small and large trees, it will yield sap indefinitely, since there will always be a new crop of trees to take the place of mature trees that die off, as all maples eventually do.

In describing our sugar bush we noted that while it was limited to a few hundred rather mature trees, it was surrounded on three sides by a mixed forest that included maple. We therefore began to extend the area of the bush by cutting out everything except the maple.

There was one area, along the edge of the bush, that contained some softwood and a dense stand of yellow birch, soft maple, beech, pin cherry, ash, and poplar. The hard maples ranged from saplings to trees eight or ten inches in diameter. We weeded and thinned this area, leaving a stand of hard maples close enough together so that ten or twelve feet remained between the tops. The stand had been dense. The maples were tall and rather spindly. With ten or twelve feet between tops, the trunks of the trees were fifteen to twenty feet apart. Six years later the hard maples left standing had grown rapidly, the trunks had a diameter of twelve to fifteen inches, and the tops had filled in so solidly that they were crowding. So we went through the area again, singling out the least desirable trees, and again leaving ten to twelve feet between tops.

A neighboring area, also adjacent to the bush, was filled with bull spruce. A bull spruce tree is one that has grown in the open and has therefore developed huge lower branches, sometimes fifteen or twenty feet long, which could never have grown in a dense spruce stand. A bull spruce log is all but useless for lumber because of the great number of big knots at the base of the low branches. There were about 125 or 150 of these bull spruces, scattered over four or five acres. There were also many small spruces, some balsams, and a scattering of poplar, pin cherry, and white birch. We also found five hard maples, about a foot in diameter, and an immense number of hard-maple seedlings and saplings.

It took parts of two winters to get out the spruce and everything except the hard maples. The spruce logs went to the sawmill. The long limbs and the tops made sugar wood. At the same time we thinned the hard maples so that saplings one to two inches in diameter stood eight or ten feet apart. The next winter we had a bad ice storm. The thinned saplings, which had grown in a dense stand, were not sturdy enough to support the weight of ice. We lost about a quarter of them. The porcupines took a few more. (These lumbering beasts find the bark of young maple very succulent and often girdle tree after tree.) But now, after seven years, we have an almost solid stand of young hard maple, ranging up to eight inches in diameter. Another year or two, and we plan to go through this area again, leaving ten to twelve feet between tops and giving the young trees a maximum chance for growth.

A third area, adjacent to the sugar bush, contained beech, maple, and other trees with diameters up to forty inches. Here we cut everything except maple and thinned the maples to stand about thirty feet apart, or with tops ten to twelve feet apart.

In a fourth area, there was a dense stand of pin cherry, poplar, white birch, white ash, and hard maple. Few of the trees were over six inches in diameter, but because of the dense stand they were very tall and spindly. In this case we left a rather thick stand of hard maple and a considerable number of white ash. The white ash is valuable and grows rapidly. We figured that before the maples were large enough to tap, the white ash would be salable. Meanwhile the ash would help to protect the maples against ice storms and wind damage.

Ordinary forest practice can be applied to the development of a sugar bush. The trees should be so spaced that maximum tree health and growth are maintained. Poorly shaped trees should be eliminated. Sturdy, vigorous growers should be retained. Mature sugar maples (thirty to forty-eight inches in diameter) should stand from thirty-five to fifty feet apart, or from thirty-five to twenty trees per acre.*

Thus far, we have said nothing about the disposal of the weedings and thinnings. Very large trees may be taken out of a mature bush either because they are culls, or because they stand too close together. Extending the bush into new-forested areas will involve heavy selective cutting. In either case the trees taken out in the process of weeding and thinning may be disposed of in any one of five ways. (1) They may be girdled and left standing, or cut and stacked up and left to rot and fertilize the bush; (2) they may be cut into saw logs; (3) they may be cut into wood pulp; (4) they may be cut into cord wood; or (5) they may be cut into sugar wood.

When we cut a tree, in the sugar bush or the wood lot, we take out a log if the trunk is large enough. Then, if the tree is yellow birch, beech, maple, or ash, we convert the remainder of the body into four-foot cord wood, which must be reasonably straight and free from bad knots and at least three inches in diameter at the top end. Big limbs make cord wood. Everything else, down to about one inch diameter at the top end, goes into sugar wood. We turn poplar, elm, white and gray birch into sugar wood, as such trees are not acceptable for cord wood and not always as logs.

We never leave anything in the sugar bush except small branches and saplings, and wood so rotten that it is useless for fuel. Everything else is worked into logs, wood pulp, cord

* "In districts which have been cleared of other trees, and even of the less vigorous sugar maples, the product of the remainder is, proportionately, most considerable." C. W. Johnson, *Farmers Encyclopedia*, Philadelphia: Carey & Hunt, 1848. P. 791.

wood, or sugar wood. If the mill or market is at any distance from the sugar bush, nothing less than a truckload of these items is worth handling. It takes about one thousand feet of logs, three cords of pulp wood, or three cords of cord wood to make a truckload. On lesser amounts, the cost of handling comes so near to equaling the net return from the operation that it pays to put everything into cord wood for home use, or into sugar wood.

We expect to make one thousand gallons of syrup in a good season. If sap is sweet, we will need forty to forty-five cords of wood fuel. If it is less sweet, we will need a larger quantity of fuel. We never buy coal or fuel oil, but depend exclusively upon our fireplaces and stoves for heat in the house. To keep these home fires burning, we require from twelve to fifteen cords of wood per year. Consequently, the ratio between the amount of house wood and sugar wood needed in any year is one to four or five. We sell a little cord wood and swap some for labor performed on the place.

Virtually all of our wood is cut to three- or four-foot lengths in the woods and then hauled to the house woodshed or the sugarhouse woodshed. If a tree or limb is under four inches in diameter at the small end, it goes into sugar wood, unsplit. If it is larger than four inches and can be split easily by two men with axes, it again goes into sugar wood. Our experience leads us to believe that sugar wood should not be more than four inches across or have an end area of more than fifteen square inches. When wood is larger than that, it is heavy to handle and burns more slowly than smaller wood.

We are under the impression that it is not truly economical to handle wood smaller than three inches in diameter at the top or small end. Since we aim to have our bush clear, so that we can move freely through it with gathering pails, we pile all the brush in hollows. This practice helps to even up the forest floor, and at the same time makes it easier for the autumn leaves to pack in on top of the brush, and, with the aid of the winter snow and ice, to press the brush into a compact mass that will rot quickly and thus be converted speedily into the humus that supports tree growth. Actually, we cut sugar wood out of anything that is an inch or an inch and a half at the small end.

When we go into the sugar bush to weed or thin we take a two-man crosscut saw, a pulp saw and our axes, a maul, saw wedges, and splitting wedges. When we take down a tree or sapling, we first trim it. Then, if it can be cut into three- or four-foot lengths with not over two clips from an ax, we cut it that way. If it is larger, but less than four inches in diameter at the butt, we throw it in a heap. At the end of the half-day or day, one person saws these poles into four-foot lengths with the pulp saw. (As an aid in this operation, we use a saw-buck made of two-by-four spruce with a two-inch hole bored at the intersection. Through this hole we put one end of an eight-foot pole. Such a sawbuck is kept on a woodpile near each cutting operation, and stored in the woodshed when not in use.) A larger tree is felled, trimmed, and cut into three- or four-foot lengths with the two-man crosscut, down to the four-inch diameter limit for the pulp saw. If the butt pieces split easily, two men with axes turn them into sugar wood. If they are hard to split, we use a maul and wedges to turn them into house wood.

If we are hauling the wood out of the bush on the same day it is cut, we toss it in heaps along the road. If we are leaving it in the woods, we lay down pieces of wood (runners or skids) to keep the wood off the earth, and stack the wood conveniently near the road.

During the average sap season, there are often entire days or even consecutive days when everything is frozen hard and no sap runs. In anticipation of such an eventuality, we select two places in or near the sugar bush—one near the sugar house and one farther from it, where we plan to cut wood until sap flows again. If we have an entire day with no sap, we go to the far place. If it seems probable that sap will run that day, we go to the near place and cut sugar wood until there is sap to gather and boil. Thus we utilize our extra time to advantage and get out a supply of sugar wood for the following season. In light sap seasons like those of 1947 and 1948, we cut as much sugar wood as we used in the evaporators.

One problem remains to be mentioned—the grazing of animals in the sugar bush. Many sugar bushes were grazed in the past on the theory that grazing animals kept down the brush and thus avoided the periodic brush clearings that are necessary if sap gatherers are to move freely through the bush.

Browsing animals do keep down certain types of brush. But one of their favorite forms of nourishment is young hard maple.* Where a bush is grazed over a long period it contains virtually no hard maple seedlings or saplings. Consequently there are no replacement trees, and as the older trees disappear, the bush carries less buckets and yields less sap.

Grazing animals harm the bush in another way. Their hoofs cut into the soft floor, destroy fern growth and other forest floor covering, beat the earth hard, and make paths along which rain and melting snow first run and then begin to cut and erode.

We will quote from three authorities, from olden times to fairly modern times, who are justifiably concerned over the widespread practice of grazing. John Evelyn, in a famous book on *Sylva, or a Discourse of Forest-Trees*, pleads: "It were to be wish'd that our tender and improvable Woods should not admit of Cattle, by any means, till they were quite out of reach." [16]

Horace Greeley stoutly maintains: "My first care, on getting possession of my farm, was to shut cattle out of the greater part of the woods, where they had been free to roam and ravage throughout the two preceding centuries that this region had felt the presence of civilized man. Pasturing woods is one of the most glaring vices of our semi-barbarian agriculture. Cattle browse the tender twigs of delicate, valuable young trees, while they leave the course and worthless unscathed. I have, today, ten times as many of the Sugar Maple,

* "Its small branches are so much impregnated with sugar, as to afford support to the cattle, horses, and sheep, of the first settlers during the Winter, before they are able to cultivate forage for that purpose." Anonymous, *The Book of Trees*. London: Parker, 1852. P. 44.

White Ash, etc., coming on in my woods as there were when I bought and shut the cattle out of them." [17]

F. B. Hough, in his *Report on Forestry*, states that "a sugar bush ought not to be pastured, as cattle destroy the young growth, and the ruin, although it may be remote, is certain." [18] Every book or pamphlet we have read dealing with the care of the sugar bush opposes grazing. We therefore take it for granted that animals will be excluded from a well-kept sugar bush.*

An even more barbarous practice than grazing a bush is the cutting down of a fine stand of sap-yielding maple for the quick and easy money there is in it at a time of keen demand, such as 1943–1949, when maple was being bought for as much as $25 a thousand feet on the stump. A forcible writer has aptly said: "Timber trees declare a dividend only at death, and there is constant and strong temptation to their destruction. The Sugar Maple declares annual dividends and the tree survives." [19] A tree that contains five hundred board feet of lumber would sell for around ten dollars on the stump. Ten dollars at the going rate of bank interest would yield about twenty-five cents per year. A tree this size would carry at least two buckets which in the ordinary year would yield a half a gallon of syrup, representing a gross annual return at present syrup prices of around three dollars. In five years or so the trees would earn their lumber price and would continue the same annual yield for an indefinite period. It seems a wise policy to retain the tree and reap an annual crop rather than cut down the faithful producer of sap and syrup.

The rules we have laid down in this chapter, if carefully followed, should provide the prospective syrup producer with a usable bush. We believe they represent the generally accepted practices among the most thoroughgoing and care-

* Well-regulated animals should also be kept from the bush—as the following quotation feelingly describes the effect on them at saptime: "Wild and domestic animals are inordinately fond of maple juice, and break through their enclosures to sate themselves; and when taken by them in large quantities, it has an exhilirating effect upon their spirits." D. J. Browne, *Trees of America*, N. Y.: Harpers, 1846. P. 87.

ful sugar producers in New England. There is always room, however, for improvement. In the words of an old-time traveler: "How far a careful cultivation in plantations may still increase the quantity and enrich the juices drawn from this valuable tree, remains to be ascertained by experiment. The presumption, however, is in favour of still greater advantages from cultivation and art. [20]

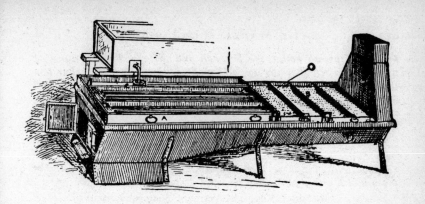

CHAPTER FIVE

Sugar Tools and Equipment

"Concerning the maple-sugar, it may here be remarked that no cultivation is necessary; . . . neither the heavy expense of mills, engines, machinery, or a system of planting. . . . The whole of the buildings and other articles necessary for carrying it on, are to be obtained at so trifling an expense, as to be within the reach of any person of common industry, whose conduct in life can entitle him to the most moderate credit."

Anonymous, An Account of the Soil etc. in the Back Parts of
North America, *1791*.

"The manufacture of maple sugar is an article of great importance to the state. . . . The business is now carried on, under the greatest disadvantages: without proper conveniences, instruments, or works: solely by the exertions of private families, in the woods, and without any other conveniences than one or two iron kettles. Were the workmen furnished with proper apparatus and works, to collect and boil the juice, the quantity of sugar might be increased, during the time of making of it, in almost any proportion. And it might become an article of much importance in the commerce of this country."

Samuel Williams, A Natural and Civil History of Vermont, *1794*.

"Let one who has used the modern improvements of the most approved pattern, go back to the mode of our fathers; let him have the caldron

kettle, the potash kettle, the five pail and three pail kettle hung on poles, and watch them by day and night, with nothing to shelter him from storms; let the wind blow and fill the boiling sap with ashes and dust, and his eyes with smoke, let him mount his snowshoes and bring in all his sap to the 'boiling place' upon his back, and if he finds poetry in it, I think he will say, I prefer prose hereafter."

E. A. Fisk, Report of Vermont Board of Agriculture, *1874.*

"A good outfit for sugaring pays twice, once in the increased value of the product, and again in the pleasure derived from it."

A. M. Foster, Report of Vermont Board of Agriculture, *1874.*

ANYONE who has at his disposal a sufficient number of sugar maples to justify the commercial production of maple syrup, and who intends to produce more than a household amount, must get tools and equipment peculiar to the industry. We have pointed out that the early maple producers made most of their own equipment and were therefore all but independent of outside sources for the supply of sugaring tools. Nowadays the maple industry is supplied by concerns that specialize in sugar-tool production.

Tools and equipment used in present-day sugaring may be divided into six groups: (1) those used in obtaining sap from the tree; (2) those used in handling sap from tree to sugarhouse; (3) those used in boiling down the sap; (4) the fuel supply and woodshed; (5) the building in which the sap is boiled down; and (6) equipment used in converting syrup into sugar.

Tools for Obtaining Sap

Tapping tools are simple. They consist of a brace and bit and a light hammer or hatchet. We use a breast drill instead of the ordinary brace. We prefer the breast drill because it is somewhat faster and the motion is less tiresome than that of the common brace. The size of the bit varies slightly according to the size of the spout used. The regular tapping bit is usually seven sixteenths of an inch in diameter, about five inches long, and rather fast cutting.*

Sap is obtained from the tree by boring a hole, inserting a spout, and hanging a covered sap bucket on the spot. In the olden days, as told in chapter three, spouts were made of elder, sumac, birch, or balsam wood. Maple producers now use metal spouts. They are about three inches long, made with a tapered shank that is driven into the tree, a channel through which the sap runs from taphole to bucket, and a hook on which the sap bucket hangs. The ideal spout should not corrode, should allow free flow of sap, exclude all air from the hole, be strong enough to hold a full bucket, and yet be as slight as possible so as not to damage the tree unduly.

Many years ago sap buckets were made of wood. Later they were tin. While both wooden and tin buckets are still in use, most new sap buckets are now galvanized iron. Each type has its advantages and disadvantages.

The wooden bucket when exposed to sunlight heats up less than metal. The sap is therefore kept cooler and the danger of fermentation is correspondingly reduced. This is a very important item in maple sugaring, because syrup made from fermented sap is darker in color and less delicate in flavor than syrup made from fresh sap. Frozen sap does not ferment. As the temperature rises, the speed of fermentation increases. Sap dripped into sun-heated metal buckets begins to ferment almost immediately. Maple producers who use wooden buckets and keep them clean can probably make fancier syrup than those who use metal buckets. This is notably true during a warm spell, when the metal bucket heats and sours more quickly than the wooden bucket.

* The 1946-1947 sap season saw the advent of a power-tapping rig consisting of a light gasoline motor, mounted on an aluminum frame and attached like a knapsack to the back of the tapper, a flexible shaft, and a chuck to hold the tapping bit. The rig weighs 35 pounds. While it is moderately expensive, we believe it would reduce the costs of tapping, particularly if it could be used co-operatively by a number of sugar makers in the same area. For most sugar makers the machine would lie idle 364 days a year, since the ordinary sugar lot sets from 1,200 to 2,500 buckets, and with this power rig the whole lot could be tapped out in a day.

Wooden buckets are subject, however, to several grave disadvantages. First, they dry out when not in use and therefore must be soaked before they are tight. Even with soaking, they are likely to leak for a day or two after sap begins to run. Second, in order to preserve them and keep them from drying out, they are usually painted. Most paint contains lead, and the lead from the paint is dissolved in the sap, traces of it appearing in the syrup. The danger of lead poisoning from this source compels the producer to use a nonlead paint or else abandon wooden buckets. Third, wooden buckets are bulky to handle. Metal buckets "nest" together so that it is an easy matter for one man to carry a roll of twenty-five buckets. Wooden buckets do not nest. Consequently, if a man handles eight to ten at a time he is doing well. Fourth, the storage space required for wooden buckets is far greater than that required for metal buckets. For a few buckets, this is not a matter of great consequence, but when buckets are numbered in thousands, storage space is a serious item. Fifth, a wooden bucket must have a metal clip fastened to it before it can hang on a spout, whereas the metal bucket hangs directly on the spout through a hole punched under the rim. This metal clip on the wooden bucket sticks up like a sore thumb and is forever in the way, and also can be broken off and lost.

Leander Coburn gives his preferences for the tin bucket, or "tub" as he calls it, over the wooden. "I think that tin tubs are much better than wooden ones, for tin tubs are easier kept clean and sweet. The sap will penetrate the wood of the wooden tub, and sours and dries during the last part of sugaring; and another advantage tin has over wood is, you can gather the sap earlier in the morning from the tin tubs than you can from the wooden ones."[1] His last point becomes, however, a reason for the subsequent general shift from tin to iron. It was found that the tin bucket heated in the sun more readily than the galvanized and thus resulted in earlier sap fermentation. The tin rusted more easily. Furthermore, tin buckets were less sturdy and therefore dented far more often than galvanized.

Modern galvanized buckets usually hold fourteen to sixteen quarts. In early days eight to twelve quarts was the commoner range. Occasionally they were larger, and then were called "Sunday buckets," to hold the sap that would likely run over while sugar makers were at church on the Sabbath.* Today's buckets are gradually tapered toward the bottom, with a two-inch collar at the top, against the bottom of which the rim of the bucket next below will fit, and thus prevent sticking when the buckets are pulled apart. The earlier metal buckets lacked this collar around the top. This made them fit so tightly that it was often necessary to use a hammer or mallet to separate them. During tapping, if buckets stick badly when being scattered, it may require the time of an extra person to get the buckets apart. A prospective syrup maker will do well to see that any buckets he buys have such a cuff or collar.

Buckets should most certainly have covers. Twigs, bark, leaves, bugs, rain, or snow might otherwise get in. Rain and snow in the buckets are serious liabilities. At best they will dilute and color the sap. At worst they will fill with water and split the buckets in zero weather. W. J. Chamberlain, writing in the *American Agriculturist* for February, 1871, is most emphatic on this point. "I cannot emphasize too strongly the advantages of using covers. I have seen a soft, damp snow, falling when the wind blew, plaster itself up and down the south side of the trees while the sap was flowing briskly; and then, as it thawed more and gathered thicker, suddenly slide for twenty feet above the bucket, carrying dirt and bits of bark with it, and fill the uncovered buckets full of slush. And I have known some of my neighbors, whose buckets were uncovered, throw away barrels of such stuff—snow, dirt, and sap—or boil it with more than its worth of fuel, to get a black inferior syrup, while those who had the covers, gathered as nice a lot of sap as any in the season. Or if it is a rainstorm, the rain trickles down the trees, carrying with it

* "These buckets are large, for I had them made for Sunday buckets. I never gather sap on Sunday." Mr. Carleton, *Vermont Agricultural Report*, 1894. P. 139.

dirt and stain into the sap. Syrup or sugar of the first quality can never be made from sap and rain-water. It is easier to *keep* out the dirt, insects, and rain, than to *get* them out. Then, too, a cover counteracts the bad effects of heat and cold. The sap is not so liable to sour during warm days, nor to freeze solid in very cold nights. I consider hanging the bucket on the spout by a hole beneath its wire rim, and then covering it, as the greatest single invention in sugar-making. Much as I prize my new evaporator, I would rather give it up and go back to the pans than give up the covers and go back to boiling sap and water!"

A fifteen-quart galvanized sap bucket and cover weigh about four pounds. A thousand buckets therefore weigh some two tons. Two tons are child's play for a good team of horses in fine weather and on hard roads. But late in February, with deep snow honeycombed by spring thaws, moving tons of metal through the sugar bush may be an arduous affair. Most sugar makers store their buckets in the sugarhouse. In the spring they break roads and haul them on horse-drawn sleds —100 to 150 buckets per load, up into the bush.

This operation, for us, would involve hauling many of our four thousand buckets half a mile and elevating them four hundred feet above the sugarhouse. We met this problem by building a series of concrete bucket storage boxes at appropriate intervals through the bush; filling the boxes with buckets, covers, and spouts before snow came, we thus had them in place for tapping time. The first day of sugaring we go to a bucket box with toboggan or sled, shovel off the snow, open the box and scatter the buckets—moving them in almost every case downhill. No roads to break. No bother with horses. Under ordinary snow conditions one man with a toboggan scatters the buckets and covers at the rate of about one hundred per hour.

Added to the convenience of having the buckets already up in the bush, ready to be scattered at the beginning of the season, this way of storing them fulfills the novel requirements of Solon Robinson, who in 1866, in his book *Facts for Farmers*,[2] recommended that buckets "should be stored dry, in a dry place, in piles bottom up, and be kept good for your grandchildren."

Tools for Handling Sap

Holes have been bored, spouts driven, and buckets hung. Sap has dripped in sufficient quantity to justify gathering. How shall the sap be moved from tree to sugarhouse? There are two methods: one is to carry it, either by hand, horse, or tractor. The other is to let gravity take it.

Sap is heavy. Like water, it weighs about a pound to the pint, eight pounds to the gallon. A sixteen-quart bucket or pail full of sap weighs about thirty-five pounds. Thirty-five pounds does not sound like a great weight for a strong man. Across an even floor, and for a minute or two, it is of no consequence. But in the woods, with snow, ice, swamps, rocks, fallen branches, and growing brush, up and down hill, carrying a bucket full of sap in each hand throughout an eight- or ten-hour day is a chore even for a sturdy fellow.

Sap was lugged by hand originally, from tree to boiling place. The "carry," which frequently covered a quarter or a third of a mile, was eased by a wooden yoke fitted across the shoulders, with a thong or rope that held the bucket on each side.

The next step in carrying sap was to let a team of horses or oxen do the work. On level ground a low-hung wagon or a sled was fitted up with a tub, and thus the sap was moved to the sugarhouse. But most sugar bushes are hilly. Some are so steep, rough, and rocky that a wagon is at a great disadvantage. Therefore a sap sled was built. Sometimes it was a stone-boat pulled with a chain. Sometimes it was a single bobsled, fitted with a tongue. Sometimes it was a dray, the front end of which was mounted on a single bob, with two poles dragging behind.

The tub or wooden tank of earlier days has been replaced by a metal gathering tank holding five or six barrels of sap. The tank is equipped with a strainer on top and a pipe connection on the bottom through which the sap can be run into the storage tank at the sugarhouse. A tractor (until recently, oxen or horses were used) is hitched to the vehicle bearing the gathering tank. With tractor haulage, the storage tank may be larger. In our neighborhood, where the terrain is rough and steep, almost all gathering tanks are mounted on one-bob sap sleds, fitted with a tongue and drawn by horses.

Drawing sap to the sugarhouse creates two problems. The first is snow; the second is mud. The syrup producer who hauls his sap must begin the season by breaking out roads through the snow. To do this he picks a warm day, hitches his horses to an empty sled, and wallows his horses along the customary roads. If the snow is too deep for the sled, the horses are unhitched and wallowed alone until the road is broken. A bad ice crust will cut the legs of the horses. If the crust is sufficiently heavy it may have to be broken by hand or with an ax. Where snow conditions are unusually difficult the syrup producer sometimes has a caterpillar tractor run through the roads. This procedure is particularly useful in handling hard crusts.

Once the roads are broken, sap haulage is a simple matter while snow lasts. Thawing brings mud, and since most sugaring is done under thawing conditions, mud is even more of a problem than snow.

Mud slows up gathering operations. Sleds drag hard on mud. Equipment is wracked and broken in consequence. Worst of all, horses and men both wear out. Our bush slopes moderately toward the sugarhouse, which is below the entire sugar bush. The loaded sap sled therefore moves down rather easily. Once it is emptied there comes the real problem—getting it back up the hill for a refilling. It is this climb that takes the life out of both horses and men. The back trip, with the empty gathering tank, may take two or three times as long as the trip down with a load.

Given a moderate amount of sap in the buckets—with each bucket, say, a quarter to half full—two men with two pails each should be able to fill a gathering tank in ten to fifteen minutes, depending on the distance the sap must be carried. Each man takes one side of the road, empties the sap from the buckets into his carrying pails, and dumps his full pails into the gathering tank.

Then comes the time consumer. The driver must take his load to the sugarhouse, empty it, and get the empty tank back into the woods. With a moderate length of haul, it will take from two to five times as long to take the gathering tank to the sugarhouse and back again as it did to fill the tank.

The helper will probably stay in the woods, gathering sap from the more distant trees and assembling it along the roads, ready for the next load. Such a procedure speeds up the time of gathering, but it cannot reduce hauling time. Hauling may be entirely eliminated by using pipes.

The General Question of Piping Sap

Pipes have been used for a long time to get sap from the bush to the sugarhouse. The earliest contrivances were wooden troughs.* A later development was inch tubing of the type used for speaking tubes in buildings before the days of the telephone. Gutter spouting and iron water pipe came after that.

Sugarhouses were frequently built at the bottom of the slope on which the sugar maples were located. The gathering tank was then drawn in on the upper side of the sugarhouse, a trough or a three- or four-inch gutter spout was laid on stakes from the gathering tank to the storage tank, and the sap run in by gravity.

The next step was to extend this feed pipe up into the sugar bush, so that instead of taking the gathering tank all the way to the bottom of the hill, the tank dumped into a long line of trough or spouting farther up in the bush. A small tank was then attached to the upper end of the feed line, and the sap was run down when needed.

At some point in this evolution of sap piping, an inventive mind developed a bright idea. Instead of allowing the sap

* An early pipe, or spout, system, as it was then called, has been described in detail by C. T. Alvord in his *Report* for 1862, *op. cit.*, p. 402.

to drip from the spout into a bucket, why not let it drip directly into a spouted pipe and then be conducted by this same pipe to the sugarhouse, thus eliminating all gathering? The idea led to the development of the tree-to-tree pipe system. The earliest record known of such a system is given by Paul D. Evans in his book, *The Holland Land Company*,[3] in which an elaborate handmade wooden tubing is described. It was devised and installed by Gerrit Boon in 1793, but had to be abandoned because of excessive warping and cracking.

The unit of pipe finally evolved was a piece of inch tin pipe, four feet long, with hooks on one side. These pipe sections were sleeved together and hung on wire that was strung through the sugar bush and left permanently in place. The wire was laid to grade so that all of it would drain toward the sugarhouse. Trees were used where possible to hold the wire in place. Where the wire was wrapped around a tree, three or four edgings were slipped under the wire to prevent it from growing into the tree. Where no trees were available, stakes were used. A gooseneck spout was devised that drained directly into the pipe system and the sap trickled from bush to sugarhouse in a steady stream. After the pipe was put in place, one man, operating the evaporator, could handle the entire system.

It was freely predicted that this development would revolutionize syrup making. The equipment was produced in quantity and was installed by a number of producers.

Physical difficulties presented themselves. First there was the difficulty of keeping the wire in place, particularly when the pipe was strung on it. The supporting wires maimed the trees. Ice storms loaded the pipe and wire, and broke them down. Masses of snow and ice, dead limbs, and branches fell from the trees, wrecking the system. Worst of all, deer, running through the sugar bush in the dark and not seeing the wire and pipe, would smash into it where it was fairly close to the ground or leap through it where it was high, and sweep away entire sections of the system. Until the break was discovered and repaired, the sap would run away into the ground.

There was another difficulty—storage of the accumulated sap, which frequently runs day and night. With buckets, the night run is stored on each tree. A thousand four-gallon buckets would store perhaps one hundred barrels of sap— the equivalent of four or five ordinary storage tanks. With the pipe system there is no storage at the tree. A unit of two thousand spouts, in the course of a good night's run, would overflow the storage tank several times over.

Storage of pipe was also a problem. After every season the whole pipe system had to be taken down, cleaned, and stored away; every spring it had to be brought out again and re-strung.

Still another difficulty arose from the heating of the pipe. Tin heats up quickly in sunshine. The pipe, up in the air above the snow and earth, absorbs sun heat on a bright day and heats the sap the moment it drips into the pipe. Where the pipe lines are long (in an ordinary bush setting two thousand buckets and covering, say twenty-five acres, some of the pipe lines would have to be at least twelve to fifteen hundred feet long), by the time the sap reaches the sugar-house it is warm if not hot, and ripe for fermentation unless it goes immediately into the evaporator and is cooked down.

In subfreezing weather, sap often drips slowly at midday from south-side tappings and freezes as soon as it enters the pipes, which fill solid with ice. Aside from the difficulty in regard to pipe damage because of expansion, there is no practical way to thaw this ice out, and when the next sap run comes, the pipes will be clogged and the sap lost.

Performance had failed to measure up to promise. By the time we became interested in syrup making, in 1935, and were investigating various ways of setting up a sugar bush, we could find only one example of a tree-to-tree pipe system —that of a neighbor in East Jamaica. After visiting the plant and talking with the operator, we found, or were told, so many disadvantages that we decided against installing the system.

That left us in a quandary. In theory it was cheaper to let sap run itself down to the sugarhouse than it was to carry it.

If the tree-to-tree system did not work, was there any one that did? When we came into possession of the bush, the farmer who was operating it on shares was running sap over considerable distances in four-inch galvanized gutter spouting and also in half-inch galvanized water pipe. The gutter spouting had to be staked and wired in position. Even then it leaked. The half-inch galvanized pipe was so small that it did not drain out a storage tank as fast as two men and a team could gather and dump in. This system was obviously ineffective.

We need not burden the reader with a list of all our blunders and partial successes in working out a pipe system that would entirely eliminate the transportation of sap in gathering tanks and that would move sap directly, by gravity, from bucket to sugarhouse. They were numerous, and some of them were costly. Instead, we will describe the net result of our experimenting—a pipe system that cuts the cost of sap gathering by at least one half and does away with the necessity of owning or hiring, stabling, and handling horses.

Our sugar bush lies across the face of a south-by-south-west slope. The land is broken up by sags and gullies in which there are swamps and streams. We set out to cover this slope with a pipe grid consisting of pipe lines approximately one hundred feet apart. As it worked out, the grid comprised two long base lines, the longest about half a mile, into which emptied a series of branch lines spread out somewhat like a fan, with the handle at the sugarhouse.

After a good deal of discussion, we decided to lay our pipe grid with three-quarter-inch pipe, and the first few thousand feet laid down were of that size. Three-quarter-inch pipe was slightly cheaper than inch. It was much lighter to handle, and fittings, of which we would require quite a number, cost about two thirds as much as inch fittings. Within two years we had stopped buying three-quarter and had begun buying inch pipe. There were two reasons for this: first, three-quarter-inch pipe was not large enough; second, it was not strong enough.

Half-inch pipe had been almost big enough to drain a tank

into which two men and a team were gathering. A three-quarter-inch pipe, with double the capacity of a half-inch, was not big enough to take care of the sap delivered by two men gathering along our new pipe lines. That is not wholly accurate. Where the three-quarter pipe was on a steep slope, two men could not keep it full, but where it lay on a gradual slope, two men, gathering from buckets that were half full or better, could keep the pipe solid full. Often they had to stand for minutes with full pails of sap, waiting for the sap to clear from the pipe.

The most serious limitation on the three-quarter pipe was its inability to stand up under ice pressure. In our region thaws and winter rains freeze into heavy ice crusts. A new snow will fall, then a thaw or a rain may form a second crust. At times these ice crusts are as much as six inches thick, and we have seen as many as four of them, one above the other, with layers of packed snow between.

Leaves, litter, and snow prevent our forest floor from freezing deeply. If heavy snows come early, the ground does not freeze all winter. Consequently the underside of the snow blanket keeps thawing a little and with each thaw the ice crusts settle. Where they settle on a three-quarter-inch galvanized pipe lying on stones with a three-foot span between the stones, the pipe will bend down far enough to make a pocket in which sap will lie and freeze and enough to pull pipe fittings apart and cause leaks.

Inch pipe, under the same conditions, will resist ice pressure on a five-foot span. The conclusion was forced upon us by experience. From then on we bought inch pipe only, took up the three-quarter-inch pipe on our main lines, and used it on spur lines.

Experience taught us several other sharp lessons. For example, we began laying our pipe as straight as the ground permitted. We soon discovered that inch galvanized pipe expands and contracts from summer heat to winter cold by about one inch in one hundred feet. A long, straight pipe, laid on stakes over a sag, and exposed to full winter cold, had been known to pull the unions apart on particularly cold nights. The answer? Lay the pipe in a series of long, gentle S curves that can take up the pull and slack of contraction and expansion.

We made another adaptation to our severe climate by connecting every fifth length of a long pipe line over difficult terrain with heavy-duty radiator hose, clamped into place with hose clamps, allowing about an inch play between pipes. We have protected the rubber against mouse and porcupine attack by a metal sleeve made of old tin cans.

We have very hard freezes during sugaring. Sometimes the temperature gets down to zero. Since sap freezes almost as readily as water, the sap pipe must all drain out every night. Otherwise it may freeze and burst. That means it must all be laid with a definite downward grade toward the sugarhouse.

We began putting up our pipe in the form of a grid, with about a hundred feet between lines. Whenever we came to a sag, we put in stakes three or four inches in diameter, drove twenty-penny spikes into the stakes, rested the pipe on the spikes, and thus got beautifully graded lines, because the nails could be driven at any point required for leveling. That was all very well in the autumn when we put up the pipe. In winter the ice load bent down the supporting spikes as though they had been common nails. We countered by sawing the posts off, or partly off, at the proper level and laying the pipe on top of the stakes. But stakes rot off quickly in the damp forest floor. Besides, it soon dawned on us that the pipe lines should follow the sags, most of which had been eroded by running water and were therefore naturally graded.

By following the sags, our pipe could lie almost entirely on the ground, or on stones where there were irregularities. We made one further improvement by digging through slight rises in the ground and laying the pipe in this open trench. The pipe therefore lay even with the ground in the hollows. The closer it lay to the ground, the warmer it was in the cold weather and the cooler it was in the hot weather. The pipe contracted and expanded less and was less likely to freeze up or to heat sap on warm spring days.

Laying pipe in the sags had one additional advantage—all the sap that was gathered and lugged to the pipe was carried downhill. That may sound unimportant, but under snow conditions it makes a vast difference whether a sap gatherer ploughs through snow uphill or downhill.

Sags do not run regularly, so our decision to follow the sags with our pipe lines compelled us to put in short spur lines whenever the sags ran so far apart that the sap had to be carried more than fifty feet. Fifty feet was an arbitrary figure. We selected it because we considered fifty feet a reasonable maximum distance for lugging full sap pails. Consequently we had to find a means of pouring sap into our pipe lines at least once in each hundred feet.

The first step was easy. At the end of each fifth length of pipe we put a T connection. Into the vertical opening of this T we inserted a piece of three-quarter-inch pipe about sixteen inches long. We called these standpipes. Each end was threaded and we put pipe caps over the top end, thus excluding dirt and preventing sap running down from higher levels from escaping.

We might note in passing that the pipe caps were also tight enough to exclude air so effectively that the sap was airbound and held in the pipe. We overcame this difficulty by boring a one-eighth-inch hole in the top of the pipe cap at the upper end of each line. When sap is poured in lower down the line, the air whistles as it rushes through these small holes.

Our next job was to get the sap into the standpipes. We tried a funnel at first, but a funnel small enough to fit into a three-quarter pipe was so small that the sap ran out too slowly. After experimenting with several schemes, we took twenty-quart galvanized concrete pails, chiseled an inch hole through the bottom at the center, soldered a three-quarter-inch pipe standard to the bottom of the pail, screwed the whole thing onto the standpipe, and thus had a twenty-quart funnel with a three-quarter-inch exit.

In practice we found that where the standpipe fitted into an inch pipe line, a man could go to the twenty-quart funnel with two fourteen-quart pails of sap, pour in the first, and by the time he was ready to pour the second pail, the contents of the first pail had run out sufficiently to allow the second pail to be emptied into the funnel.

One other problem arose. Sap often contains bits of leaves, pieces of bark, and small twigs. These are strained out at the sugarhouse, but they clogged the pipe lines. After some experimenting we found that a round galvanized foot tub with a diameter of about twelve inches and slightly tapering sides, would fit into the top of our funnel sufficiently to hold it steady. At the same time its sides extended several inches above our funnel, thus increasing the holding capacity of the funnel by nearly half. In our first experiment of turning the foot tub into a strainer, we used an eight-penny nail and punched the bottom full of holes. The result was that the sap ran from the foot-tub strainer faster than it ran out of the funnel. Thereafter we used a six- or four-penny nail, punched much smaller holes, and by experiment determined just how many holes would let the sap run into the funnel as fast as it ran out. The resulting combination of funnel and strainer had a total capacity of nearly thirty quarts and easily took the contents of two sixteen-quart gathering pails, poured almost simultaneously.

We now had a pipe line every hundred feet and an entrance into each line every hundred feet. In theory, therefore, no tree was more than fifty feet from a standpipe and many stood beside standpipes.

We should like to make two further comments on this pipe system. The first concerns the standpipes. The second concerns inspection.

We wire each standpipe to a short, sturdy stake about two inches in diameter. When snow is deep, these standpipes disappear completely. We therefore set a six-foot marker pole, about two inches through, three feet uphill above the standpipe, and beside the pipe. The top of this pole is painted with a red strip to help mark it in the snow. When we do our first gathering in the spring we know just where the standpipes are even if we can't see them. This marker stake has another use. We drive a six-penny nail shoulder high into each one and hang the standpipe cap on the nail while pouring is in progress. This reduces likelihood that anyone will go off with the cap in his pocket, leaving the standpipe open to cascade sap when poured in from above.

In laying out the pipe lines we put a union at the end of every fifth length of pipe. We also put a union at the end of the first length on each side line. The unions are marked by eight-foot poles set two feet below the union and not painted. The standpipe markers and the union markers outline the course of the pipe lines even in deep snow. Under heavy snow and in case of difficulty we can quickly locate unions and intersections for any necessary repair work.

Once each year, in the autumn, after the foliage is off the trees and the ground foliage has been frozen down, we go over all pipe lines, replace old stakes and markers, examine pipe fittings, and generally check the system before it is snowed under. When sugaring begins in the spring it is quite impossible to do any checking unless the snow is shoveled off from the pipe. In emergencies we have shoveled as much as six or seven feet of snow off pipes in an effort to check stoppages. Any reader who has attempted to handle such a volume of snow will appreciate the magnitude of the task. The time to check the pipe lines is during mild days before snow falls.

Pipe costs vary. We figure that a mile of pipe will take care of eight hundred to one thousand buckets, with medium-sized trees spaced approximately fifty per acre. A mile of pipe with fittings usually costs about the same as one thousand buckets, covers, and spouts. This does not allow for the cost of laying the pipe. If this is done in spare time in the autumn it is not an important item, and once down it is down. If the ground is not too rough, two experienced men should lay five hundred to eight hundred feet of pipe in an eight-hour day. Our experience indicates that the saving on gathering costs will pay for the pipe in from three to five years.

We have been using our pipe system for about fifteen years. The first five years were experimental. The last ten have proved the efficacy of the scheme. We have tried to sum up here the results of our experiments because we are convinced that the plan can be applied to advantage in many a sugar bush.

When sap is running freely, two experienced men using our pipe system can keep a three-quarter-inch pipe more than full of sap. Two men and a team, where the haul is not too arduous, will gather thirty to fifty barrels of sap in eight hours. A five-by-sixteen-foot evaporator (the size we use) will boil down about five or six barrels of sap per hour. Since the evaporator holds about seven barrels of sap at any one time, either pipe or horse gathering can easily overrun an evaporator. In order to handle excess sap, every sugarhouse is equipped with at least one storage tank, with anywhere from ten- to fifty-barrel capacity.

There is another reason for the storage tank. The modern evaporator, when once heated up, cannot be cooled off quickly. As it is operated with about an inch of liquid in the front pan, the pan will be burned in the course of a very few minutes unless a sufficient supply of sap is kept ahead. Most sugar makers wait to start their evaporators until they have at least eight or ten barrels of sap in the storage tanks. The moment the sap supply falls below this amount, they begin to reduce their fire, so that by the time the available sap is exhausted, the evaporator will be cool or cold.

The most convenient size for a storage tank is twenty to thirty barrels. The tank should be set almost level, with just enough slope to drain completely. It should be roofed or equipped with a hinged cover. In any case, it must be cleanable. We usually wash our storage tanks at the end of each sap day.

Tools for Boiling Sap

We have described the implements used in obtaining and handling maple sap. We must now comment on those that are used to convert sap into syrup: the evaporator, the fuel supply, and the sugarhouse.

Early sugar makers set up their boiling apparatus in the

woods near their maple trees, boiled in an open cast-iron kettle, cut the wood that was immediately at hand, and protected themselves, if at all, by a rude shelter.

Maple syrup produced in the United States today is made almost entirely in a specially designed evaporator, located in a specially built sugarhouse. The fuel supply is lodged in a woodshed.

There are several makes of evaporator on the market. The principle of all is the same—to spread the sap out in a thin film, bring it into the closest possible contact with the source of heat, and convert it rapidly into maple syrup. They consist of two parts: a bed frame or "arch," which holds the fire, and conducts the flames and gases to the base of the stack; and the pans, which rest on the arch and hold the boiling sap.

Early evaporators were built on a brick arch, hence the word "arch." The present-day arch consists of a firebox, with heavy grate bars at the bottom, an incline up which the flames are conducted toward the chimney, and a rear flat section at the back, occupying about half of the evaporator, into which the back pan nestles. The firebox rests on the ground. The bulk of the evaporator is held a couple of feet off the floor by iron legs.

The arch is made of heavy galvanized sheets. The firebox is lined with firebrick; the balance of the evaporator with firebrick or common brick. If water is kept out of the arch, and if the bricks are kept in good condition, with a firm pointing mixture between them, the arch will last for many years—sometimes thirty or forty.

The sap pans are made of galvanized or tin sheets of moderately heavy gauge. Copper is also used, but rarely. The size necessary would of course vary with the size of the bush. It is suggested by the makers of evaporators that ten square feet of boiling surface is adequate for every hundred trees tapped.

In our evaporators the front pan, which rests directly over the fire, has a flat bottom and eight-inch sides. The back pan, which covers the remainder of the arch, has a corrugated bottom, with corrugations six inches deep and half an inch wide. There is something more than an inch between corrugations. Sap runs down into these corrugations. The flames and hot gases from the fire pass between them. Thus a half-inch column of sap is subjected to heat from two sides and the boiling process is greatly expedited. The pans are five feet wide. The front pan is seven feet long, the back pan nine feet. The arch, including the base on which the smokestack rests, is seventeen and a half feet long.

The evaporator, as it comes from the manufacturer, has a large draft in front and an opening under the firebox for removing ashes. The end of the arch toward the stack is quite open. Therefore the fire in the firebox sweeps unhindered up the smokestack. If the stack is tight, a furious draft is generated.

The evaporator pans are built with partitions, so that the sap flows in at one corner of the back pan, through an automatic regulator, and then is directed by the partitions toward a corner of the front pan where syrup is drawn off through an exit gate. Both sides are equipped with such gates so that the syrup may be taken off on one side or the other.

Near the evaporator, on a low platform, we have two settling tanks made of galvanized sheets. Each tank will hold around thirty-five gallons of syrup. Each is equipped with a frame, holding three felt filters. The finished, hot syrup is carried from the evaporator to the settling tanks, passes through the filters, and is then drawn off through a molasses gate into bottles or cans. We feel these settling tanks are invaluable, not only in filtering our syrup to sparkling clarity, but as very convenient storage places for the finished syrup, which otherwise stands around the sugarhouse in pails.

The Fuel Supply and Woodshed

Various means are used to heat the sap—wood, coal, coke, oil, gas, steam. We have never heard of an electrically heated evaporator. It seems unlikely there is such. In a district where wood is scarce, some other fuel may be cheaper and certainly would be less cumbersome. In our district, where wood is still abundant, it is by all odds the simplest and cheapest means of heating sap.

Slabs from the nearby sawmills are often used. We do not favor them because they pack down in the firebox and make it difficult for the air to pass through the solid mass of burning wood. We greatly prefer limb wood or split body wood, with perhaps a little dry slab wood split up for kindling. By mixing limb wood and split body wood, we get a fire that does not pack closely.

There are two requisites for good sugar wood. The first is that it should be dry, as dry wood goes about one third further than wet. It is obvious that if green wood is used, a proportion of the heat generated must go to the drying of the moist wood. The second consideration is that it should be of the proper size. As to bulk, it should be easily manageable. We are of the opinion that wood four-by-four inches is large enough. Larger pieces just stuff up the firebox and tame down the fire. Smaller wood necessitates a constant refurbishing of the fire and opening and closing of doors, which in its turn tones down the fire. Wood of the four-by-four size, if it is slightly crooked or irregular, does not pack tightly and leaves openings through which the flames may pass.

Our evaporator fireboxes are four feet long. Until recently we cut all of our sugar wood to four feet. One of our neighbors who has been experimenting with three-foot wood claims that it can be crisscrossed in the fire, thus providing better draft. C. T. Alvord, in the *Agricultural Report for 1862*, says, "If the wood is too long it will clog up the back part of the arch with coals, so that the heater will not work well. My own opinion is, that one cord of wood (running measure) two feet long, will boil as much sap as a cord four feet long." [4] An elaborate method of using short wood has been explained in detail in a Canadian government bulletin.[5] "For rapid boiling, part of the wood should be cut short enough to go across the fire box. When firing it is well to lay a stick crosswise at each end and then lay a single layer of wood on the top of these sticks; then another pair crosswise and another layer on top, continuing until the box is within eight inches of being full, then close the doors. The fire box should be deep enough and the wood fine enough to allow for three or four tiers of wood and still leave space under the pan. This is important, as it allows the fire to roll over and over, giving off the utmost heat to the pan. In firing the fuel should be thrown in very rapidly so as to keep the doors open as short a time as possible, as the inrush of cold air when the doors are open quickly cools the pan and delays the evaporation."

For the 1948 season, along with our usual cordage of four-foot wood, we cut some twenty cords of three-foot wood. The wood was cut in the early spring of 1947 and thus had a year to dry. We used it alone, we mixed it with four-foot wood, and we also used four-foot wood alone, to complete the test. Our conclusions were: (1) that the three-foot wood can be crossed more easily in the firebox, thus keeping the mass of burning fuel more open to draft; (2) that once in the firebox the three-foot wood can be poked and shifted about more easily; (3) that the bulk of the flames are kept nearer the firing door and thus travel farther under the evaporator before reaching the stack; and (4) that the mass of charcoal that piles up at the back of the firebox on a long boiling day, clogging the draft and raising the new wood up to the bottom of the front pan, is far less with three-foot wood than with four-foot wood. As a result of this experiment we plan to cut at least half of our sugar wood to three feet.

One cord of reasonably good, dry wood should boil down twenty to thirty barrels of 2- to 3-per-cent sap and produce fifteen to twenty-five gallons of syrup. A sugar bush that sets 1,600 buckets, in an average season, would make three hundred to four hundred gallons of syrup and would therefore require fifteen to twenty cords of wood. (Our wood cords are 128 cubic feet.) We always plan to have ahead fifty cords of wood. This, we feel, could net us around one thousand gallons of syrup.

The same Canadian government bulletin above referred to has this to say about storing sugar wood. "Whatever wood is used should be cut the previous winter, piled out of doors

during the summer to dry well, and stored before autumn
rains commence in the wood shed adjoining the sugar
house." [6] There are not too many woodsheds up our way.
Wood is cut as and when needed and piled up outside the
sugarhouse. We felt that dry wood was an imperative, and
therefore sufficient woodshed room a necessity. Beside an extension of the sugarhouse roof to accommodate dry wood, we
planned an auxiliary wood-storage unit. Fire hazard made it
undesirable to enlarge the wood volume under cover beside
the sugarhouse. We therefore decided to build another wood-
storage unit fifty feet away from the sugarhouse. As we con-
templated the possibility of adding a new sugarhouse to the
unit at some later time we planned the new woodshed
parallel to the sugarhouse, as part of a "C" rectangle open at
one end toward the road. There is a sled-and-truck road all
around the buildings.

If the new woodshed was to be fifty feet from the sugarhouse, how would the wood get across? We discussed a concrete runway, but it was not practical because the sugarhouse
was higher than the woodshed. We also discussed a temporary
wooden track along which our wood trucks could be pushed.
Finally we hit on the idea of removing the metal top from a
rubber-tired wheelbarrow, replacing it with a light woodrack,
and moving the wood with this device. The scheme worked
excellently, even on top of snow, which was soon packed into
a path. In open weather, the pickup truck was used to take
over the wood.

It might be of interest, and of use, to describe the type of
building we put up to house our wood. We had already experimented with roofed but open-sided woodsheds, and we
decided to build such a one for this purpose, 18 by 28 feet,
set on concrete piers. We built forms for the piers, set them
level, bedded a piece of metal in the center of each, put a
7-foot peeled spruce log upright on each concrete pier, strung
7-by-7-inch hewed plates on top of these peeled logs, braced
each peeled log to the plate with two 45-degree braces, fastened the plates across with heavy round poles for tie beams,
anchored the four corner posts to the concrete piers with

4-by-½-inch steel plates bedded in the concrete, built the roof structure with peeled spruce pole rafters, nailed on spruce 6-inch boards, two deep, 16 inches from center to center, and put on a corrugated galvanized roof over the whole. This building, which may sound formidable in one sentence, is an easy and cheap type of construction, yet lasting, sturdy, and good looking.

The Sugarhouse

Sugarhouses are built to shelter the operator, protect the evaporator, provide storage space for sugar tools, and sometimes cover space for the wood supply. Against sugarhouses (on the north side, to keep the sap cool) are placed the storage tanks, usually near an elevation from which sap can be poured from the gathering tubs or run in by pipe.

Vermont and other agricultural colleges and experiment stations issue bulletins with directions for sugarhouse construction. We read the bulletins, visited a number of sugarhouses, and then built our own version. Twelve years later, after much practical experience with sugaring, we built a second sugarhouse and made some decided improvements over the first attempt.

Most of the sugarhouses in New England are wooden, put up with no great eye to beauty or even durability. They are sheds to house the boiling. The old sugarhouse on our present sugar lot was located on low ground and separated from the town road by fifty feet of swamp. Each spring, for years, whoever sugared there waded back and forth across this swamp, the horses wallowing in it up to their bellies. We decided to remedy this. Three wide planks built us a culvert at the low point in the swamp. Poplar poles served for corduroy. On these we piled small stones, followed by gravel. A few hours' work, and we had completed a truck road as well as a sled road across the swamp. Our farmer-helper friends rode over this viaduct as cheerfully as heretofore they had sloshed through the swamp.

The sugarhouse itself stood on the edge of the swamp. It

was a small rectangular wooden building with boards hanging loose on the sides and a roof in none-too-good condition—such a sugarhouse as is seen frequently in many parts of New England. Its sills were set up on loose stones. It was windowless, with a large solid swinging door at one side and two holes cut just below the peak of the roof at each end to allow for escaping steam. The building was floorless, and in wet spring weather was washed by a small stream, part of which flowed in front of the building and the other part directly through it. A few loose planks enabled the rubber-booted boiler to slop around without getting too wet. In freezing weather the floor was a sheet of ice. There was no woodshed. Wood was piled in front of the sugarhouse. In rainy weather it had to be carried across the small water course that separated the woodpile from the sugarhouse, and went into the evaporator dripping wet.

We are convinced that the first requisite of a good sugarhouse is that it should be as fireproof as possible. On our first sugarhouse we built ten-inch concrete sills and laid our wooden sills on these concrete foundations. In the second sugarhouse the concrete sills are eighteen inches high. Thus we are assured that no wood is near the floor and the chance of burning embers getting out of the firebox and contacting timbers is reduced to a minimum. On the sills we built a wooden framework with the plates at least seven feet above floor level, studs at appropriate distances, pole rafters and doubled strips of six-inch boards laid horizontally on the rafters, sixteen inches from center to center. Over the whole, sides and roof, we lay corrugated galvanized roofing. With this construction there is almost nothing to catch fire, and the entire outside is metal and therefore fireproof.

The next most important requisite of a good sugarhouse is a concrete floor covering the entire area and extending, in the form of a forty-eight-inch runway, at floor level, into the attached woodshed. The cement floor provides a level base on which to set the evaporator (and the evaporator must be level to give good results); makes it easy to move around the evaporator and the sugarhouse on a smooth floor; and provides facilities for pushing wood on a hand truck from the woodshed to the evaporator. A concrete floor may become slippery if syrup is spilled, and sometimes, on cold mornings, it is icy cold, but the advantages outweigh these features.

A sugarhouse should be roomy. For our 5-by-16 evaporator we build an 18-by-28-foot sugarhouse (forty feet with the woodshed). This provides ample space all around the evaporator, and allows for settling tanks, a bench for putting up syrup, a stove to heat water, and one or two wood trucks, each holding about a quarter of a cord. These trucks, on four-inch ball-bearing castors, even when heavily loaded, can be easily pushed on the concrete runway to the adjoining woodshed, and on the same runway out to the auxiliary woodshed. In the push of a big day's boiling, firing is speeded up enormously if the operator can get the wood in a slack moment and have it at hand, on a movable base, at the point and time wanted.

One of our neighbors built a track from the sugarhouse into the woodshed, mounted his wood truck on flanged wheels, and ran it back and forth on the tracks. Such tracks are rigid. They have generally been abandoned in warehouses and factories in favor of rubber-wheeled trucks moving freely on concrete floors. We are thus following the best contemporary practice in the handling of heavy materials.

A sugarhouse should be well lighted. In our first, we put in too few and too small windows. In our second we trebled our window space and noticeably eased the job of syrup making. We are now of the opinion that it is hardly possible to have too much window space. Many of the old sugarhouses still in use in Vermont allowed for no windows at all. The orginal sugarhouse on our place when we bought it had a large door, which was left swinging open in the wind to give light, and an open hole of nine by twelve inches at about shoulder level near the front of the evaporator.

A sugarhouse should have one big door, opening on the wood supply. This door should be at least five feet wide to admit wood trucks. There should be another door, at the other end of the sugarhouse, giving access to the storage tank. There are many times when it is necessary to get to the storage tank quickly.

A sugarhouse should have a handy water supply. A brook or spring nearby is invaluable. S. F. Perley says, "The sugarhouse, if the nature of the ground will admit of it, should be placed . . . if possible, near a spring or brook; for if water is lacking, dirt will abound, and cleanliness is an important item in sugar making." [7]

A sugarhouse requires a ventilator to carry off the steam. The ventilator should be located directly over the evaporator and should be at least as large as the evaporator, to give greatest service. On our first sugarhouse the ventilator was a cupola 5 by 12 feet—too small. On our second, it was 6 by 18 feet and worked much better. The cupola is five feet high, roofed like the sugarhouse, and has six metal-covered frames, three on each side, which are hinged at the bottom, drop down onto the sugarhouse roof, and are pulled back into place by sash cords running through pulleys.

One matter in connection with the sugarhouse bothered us. Our evaporator came with a heavyweight twenty-two-inch galvanized stack, in six-foot sections, twenty-eight feet high in all. If we left the stack out all year it would tend to rust through very quickly. So the practice was to put it up and take it down each year, an operation that required from four to six able-bodied people and that was fairly dangerous to manage.

"Why not a permanent concrete stack?" we asked ourselves. We wrote around, but could find no record of a sugarhouse with a concrete stack, so we planned one. We dug an 8-foot foundation, put our 22-inch stack in as a core, used two sets of 18-inch forms bolted at the corners for outside forms, and built the stack 3 by 3 feet square outside. In our forms we set up two ¾-inch galvanized pipes, in 6-foot sections, in each corner, connected these pipes together with two strands of barbed wire strung horizontally every 9 inches and wrapped around the pipe, then poured the stack, 3 feet at a time. Incidentally, we used medium-soft concrete and pushed into it about 40 per cent of its volume in small fieldstone, 3

or 4 inches in diameter. This practice cut the cost and increased the strength of the stack.

The concrete stack was added years after we had built
the first sugarhouse. In the new sugarhouse we built the
concrete stack at the same time. The connection from evaporator to concrete stack came from the manufacturer built to
our specifications. Neither stack has given us any trouble.
Once up, they are there until an earthquake or a bomb
wrecks them. They draw well and are among the most
satisfactory features of our setup.

We have spoken of two sugarhouses and one may wonder
why two were thought necessary. We put up the additional
one, first, because there were various improvements we
wanted to make; second, we put it up as insurance. A sugarhouse fire, in the early part of a syrup-making season, might
cost us our entire crop. Furthermore, in rush times, with
heavy sap runs, one loses much sap no matter how hard one
pushes the evaporator. We therefore decided to build a completely new sugarhouse, equip it fully with an exact duplicate
of our other tools (which again safeguarded us in case of the
burning of pans or other misadventures), use it as the regular
boiling place, and treat the older sugarhouse as an alternative and reserve unit, to be used only in cases of heavy runs
or of damage to the new sugarhouse.

If any of our readers feel that we seem to be putting more
into the business than we can possibly get back, we refer
them to our chapter in the last section, entitled "The Money
in Maple," and to two writers of the last century, careful and
canny Yankees. Moses Mather, writing in the *American
Farmer* of May 29, 1822, describes his *four* evaporators of
sheet iron, each six by twelve. "Last season three of these
pans were used, and the present only two were in use, in
consequence of the moderate flowing of the sap." He uses
a light one-horse sled to gather sap and "an extra sled has
been kept in case of necessity." "I have used from four to
five cords of wood to a thousand pounds of sugar made,
which is cut and put under cover, a year before used. . . . It
was first calculated that sugarmaking on so large a scale as

I had adopted, would require six or seven hands; but incredible as it may appear, five hands managed my work last year with ease; and this season, from the moderation with which the sap has overflowed, four hands only have been employed."

The second writer from whom we quote is A. M. Foster. "I frightened our folks by building a sugar house forty feet long. I built a plant that cost me $1000 and I have been adding to it since. I have a copper evaporator fourteen feet long that I have used 15 years . . . There is some work and expense in rigging up for this, but the argument I have to offer for it is—it pays. I like to make sugar, but I don't like to make sugar well enough to do it unless it pays." [8] "The more expensive the utensils, the better they are cared for, and the closer the sap is kept gathered up and boiled, the more it costs to make sugar. But the value of the sugar is enhanced, and the expense will all come back, and more with it, in the long run." [9]

CHAPTER SIX

Maple Sap and Sap Weather

"For the trees to give their water in abundance there should be at the base of the trunk a certain amount of snow, which keeps the water fresh. It should freeze during the night and the day should be clear, without wind and without clouds; because then the sun has more strength, which dilates the pores of the trees, and which the wind closes, —so much so that it stops the running."

Joseph François Lafitau, Mœurs des sauvages Amériquains, *1724*.

"That maple sap might run in abundance, there should be much snow on the ground—that it freeze the night before—that the heavens be serene—and that it should not be too cold in the day."

M. L'Abbé de la Porte, Le Voyageur Français, *1749*.

"Frosty mornings and bright sunshine are necessary to produce copious exudations."

G. Imlay, A Topographical Description of the Western Territories of North America, *1792*.

"The influence of the weather in increasing and lessening the discharge of sap from trees is very remarkable. Dr. Tonge supposed, long ago, that changes in the weather of every kind might be better ascertained

120

*by the discharge of sap from the trees than by weather glasses. I have
seen a journal of the effects of heat, cold, moisture, drought, and thun-
der, upon the discharge from the sugar trees, which disposed me to
admit Dr. Tonge's opinion."*

E. Jones, The Acer Saccharinum, *1832.*

*"A sap-run is the sweet good-by of winter. It is the fruit of the equal
marriage of the sun and frost."*

John Burroughs, Signs and Seasons, *1886.*

MAPLE trees shed their leaves each fall in a riot of autumn
color. In the spring maple-leaf buds swell and burst
first into a feathery light green, and later, as the leaves mature, into a mass of dark green foliage. While the leaves are
on the maple, the wood is relatively dry. The bark adheres
strongly to the wood. If a branch is broken by the wind, or
if the tree is wounded by ax or saw, no sap makes its appearance. But while the tree is leafless and dormant, sap
flows freely from branches, trunk, and roots. An English
writer, speaking of spring and "the growing, sap-stirred
world," calls it "that divinest of all moments in the year,
when in man and brute, and as yet leafless tree, the sap once
more stirs." [1]

Cut a maple sapling, prune a branch from a maple, or
rub the bark from the body of a maple tree during its leafless
period, and if weather conditions are right, there will be a
deluge of sap. Loggers, cutting maple in the early spring,
reset their saws to accommodate to the new conditions, as
sap flows in such quantities that it converts the sawdust into
a sticky mass and retards sawing. After a spring ice storm,
in which maple branches have been broken by the load of ice,
a walk through the woods on a frosty morning will show sap
icicles hanging from the ends of broken limbs. One morning,
late in the autumn, we were digging sand from a sand pit
located on the edge of a grove of hard maple. The sand was
frozen when we began. We cut it away in big chunks, tearing
off the rootlets sent out by the nearby maples. As the sun got

higher, the sand thawed and sap began to drip from the severed roots, so that those of us working under the overhanging bank thought at first that rain was falling. These experiences bring us face to face with sap action in maple trees, and of trees in general.

Plants, like animals, depend for their life and growth on nourishment taken into the organism, digested by it, and distributed to its various parts. Unlike animals, who take their food in either solid or liquid form, plants handle mostly liquids. In both plants and animals, however, water is the chief medium in which nourishment is carried from one part of the organism to another. "Without water there can be no life. The living portions of all organisms are permeated with water; it is only when in this condition that their vital processes can be carried on." [2] Animals move water through the alimentary canal and the blood vessels. Plants move water through lines of connected cells. This continuous flow is called the "transpiration stream."

"As the watery fluid absorbed by the roots contains salts, oxides, and other non-volatile substances in solution, these on evaporation are left in the plant and gradually increase in quantity. This accumulation of mineral salts is absolutely necessary for the plant, for the nutrient water taken up by the roots is so weak in mineral substances (it contains but little more solid matter than good drinking-water), that the plant would otherwise obtain too little food if it were only able to take up as much water as it could retain and make use of." [3] "During the whole vegetative period, a sunflower or cornplant evaporates as much as 440 pounds, or a barrel, of water. Of the total amount of this water, the plant assimilates but an insignificant fraction." [4] "An average oak tree in its five active months evaporates about 28 thousand gallons." [5]

Tree sap, then, is water that carries certain minerals taken by the roots from the soil and certain organic substances manufactured by the leaves from sun and air. These mineral and chemical compounds, dissolved in water, provide the nourishment upon which roots, trunk, branches, and leaves depend for their life and growth.

There is a wide variation in the amount and nature of the minerals and chemical substances carried in the sap of different trees. "Maple sap is essentially a dilute solution of sucrose, carrying also small amounts of proteids, of mineral matter, more especially lime and potash and of acid, mainly malic acid." [6] The sugar in maple is synthesized by the leaves drinking in sunshine in the summer and producing starch, which is stored in the tree for the next season. This starch is the food of the plant, and in spring, with the further action of sunlight, it is converted into sucrose and in turn to invert sugar.

Maple sap contains, on the average, about 3 per cent of sugar, though it may go as low as one per cent or as high as 12 per cent. The percentage, of course, varies from tree to tree, from sugar grove to sugar grove, from one part of the season to another, and from season to season. "The first run of sap in the fall and the last in the spring has the smallest percentage of sugar in it. As the sap season advances toward the maximum flow, sometimes occurring in March and sometimes in April, sap increases in sweetness, and from this point it lessens until the close of the sap season." [7]

Albert P. Sy, in an important article on *The History, Manufacture and Analysis of Maple Products*,[8] speaking of the physiology of the maple, says, "A tree containing 150 gallons of sap would carry about 37 pounds of sugar, taking three percent as the sugar content of the sap. Such a tree if it yields three pounds of sugar, would give up only about eight percent of its total sugar." "Even during a so-called good season considerably less than one-tenth of the sugar in the tree is secured by ordinary tapping processes." [9]

The sugar from maple trees is identical in properties and composition, when equally refined, with cane or beet or sorghum. A Canadian bulletin points out the most significant difference between the product of raw maple sap and of other saps containing sucrose. "In the natural juice of sugar cane and beet root, the sucrose is associated with other substances in solution, as is the case with sucrose in the sap of the maple tree. The difference is that these other substances, if allowed to remain in the juice while this is concentrated by evaporation to the consistency of syrup, cause the product to have a disagreeable flavor, in the case of cane and beets, while in the case of maple sap, the characteristic flavor is pleasant and the resultant syrup is in demand on that account." [10] Both cane and beet-sap products must be lengthily and elaborately processed before they are palatable. Maple syrup and sugar are whole sap; a simple process of boiling, eliminating the excess water, with a very small proportion of malate of lime being removed by filtering through flannel or felt, is all that needs be done.

"First-run sap," that is, sap procured early in the season while snow is still deep and nights are cold, produces syrup and sugar that is light amber in color and delicate in flavor. Writes John Burroughs, the naturalist, "The first run, like first love, is always the best, always the fullest, always the sweetest; while there is a purity and delicacy of flavor about the sugar that far surpasses any subsequent yield." [11]

As the season advances, the weather becomes warmer, the leaf buds begin to expand, and the sap becomes "buddy." It is then slightly tinted in color, somewhat unpleasant to the taste, boils heavily like asphalt, and in the process of boiling gives off a strong racy odor. Syrup made from buddy sap tastes like burned bacon. Lafitau, in 1724, makes an observation about the last run. "The trees," he says, "stop giving when the sap begins to have more consistency and to thicken. One notices that very soon, because not only do the trees give less but the water that comes is more viscous, and though it has more body than the first run it will not crystallize as easily, nor make as easily into cakes of sugar, and it only makes a sticky and imperfect syrup." [12]

Fermentation is another factor entering the picture. As the snow melts, as nights get warmer and days hotter, microorganisms develop in the sap spouts and buckets, and the slow-dripping sap begins to ferment almost as soon as it leaves the tree. "Maple sap as it occurs within the tree is free from bacteria and other micro-organisms. As the sap flows from the tree it becomes infected, in the taphole, spouts and buckets, with wild yeast, spores of moulds, and countless number of bacteria. This infection becomes increasingly heavy with the advance of the sugar season and is the cause of the 'souring' of sap." [13] Also, the changes in the tree's organism at the turn of warm weather may release certain compounds seemingly necessary for the buds but not conducive to finely flavored syrup. Such sour sap will produce dark colored, strongly flavored syrup that, at its best, is on a par with the South's sorghum or the flavor of Mexico's pinnochio sugar, and at its worst cannot be grained into sugar and is usually sold to tobacco firms, or used in households for flavoring and sweetening baked beans. Rescalding spouts and rewashing buckets will retard the growth of the organisms and temporarily check fermentation. But the sap that runs after the buds begin to swell is so inferior and so scanty in volume that it is not worth the fuel required to boil it.

Sap Movement

Anyone who sets out to make a living from maple needs at least a rudimentary knowledge of sap hydraulics. The common saying that "in the spring, sap rises" is only partly true. Experiments have shown that sap flows from both below and above and across tapholes,[14] and that the pressure is inward and absorbing at some times and outward at others.[15] Even the most learned among the plant physiologists cannot give a complete explanation of sap movement. Consequently, the layman who sets out to study the subject encounters plenty of difficulties.

Our first venture toward understanding sap movement was to ask botanists with whom we were acquainted about the life processes in trees. Their replies were much the same: "The question is a difficult one. We are not certain. There is not much known." We consulted numerous books on plant physiology. Interspersed in every section on our subject we found such sentences as: "The factors which bring about the lifting of water in large quantities to the tops of tall trees, sometimes more than three hundred feet above the ground, are very hard to determine." "As to what causes this movement there is still much question." "The evidence that has been obtained is in no way conclusive in many respects." "There is much need for more experimental data before this important question can be settled." "The manner in which the water is transferred from the cortical cells of the root to the xylem elements and then forced upward is not known." "The nature of these forces and even the cells concerned in the process have not, as a rule, been established with any degree of certainty." "It must be admitted that this problem, like so many others in biology, has not as yet reached a satisfactory solution." There were theories a-plenty, and "almost as many hypotheses as to how water goes up a tree as there are scientific men who have studied the question," but apparently no certain knowledge.

A distinguished Indian physicist, Jagadis Chander Bose, says, "the ascent of sap has been the most elusive problem in plant physiology," and not explicable on the mechanistic grounds ordinarily advanced. Bose, who regards all plants as living conscious organisms, argues that plants possess a circulatory system, and their sap movements correspond to the blood pressure of animal bodies, that "the propulsion of sap in plants is found to be essentially a process of peristalsis, in which a wave of contraction squeezes the sap forward. A succession of such peristaltic waves maintains the continuous ascent of the sap." [16] As long ago as 1790, Samuel Deane wrote in the same way of sap—as "the fluid contained in plants, which is drawn from the earth and atmosphere, by which plants are augmented, and rendered fruitful. It answers the same purposes as the blood and other juices in animals." [17]

Nicolai A. Maximov, eminent botanist of the U.S.S.R., writing of the translocation of substances in tree trunks, speaks of the "ascending stream" carrying water and minerals and the "descending stream" carrying chiefly organic substances. "In some instances, the ascending stream may carry organic substances. This occurs during the spring, when the sap flows and the reserve substances stored in autumn, in the wood and bark of the roots and stems, are digested rapidly and, penetrating in large quantities into the vessels of the wood, are carried upward to the opening buds under the influence of root pressure, which is very intense at this time of year." [18]

Dr. F. W. Went, plant physiologist of the California Institute of Technology, propounds his theory in the June, 1946, *Sunset* magazine, in an article ingeniously called, "Plant Plumbing." "When one cell has access to water, the neighboring cell passes its surplus water on to the next cell. This could explain water movement in small plants like mosses, but when a million cells intervene between the source of water in the soil and the transpiring leaf cells, this 'bucket brigade' would not be very effective. In all larger plants, long 'water vessels' connect the water-absorbing root cells and the water-transpiring leaf cells. This pipe system does not change the principle of water movement from a cell saturated with water to another one with less water, but only makes it more efficient. The difference between the plumbing system of a house and that of a plant is that water is pumped to a house and its individual faucets by pressure, whereas in the plant it is the cells which suck the water in. Water movement in a plant is caused by suction, rather than by pressure."

The most lucid interpretation for our purposes comes from a Vermont leaflet written by Walter H. Crockett. "The immediate cause of the flow from the taphole is sap movement under pressure towards the point of least resistance. Its exciting cause seems to be temperature fluctuations back and forth over the 32nd° F. line, causing alternation of pressure and suction, a pumplike action. The ultimate and absolute cause can hardly be this or any other physical one, but is probably a function of the living cell. Increase of water content and rising temperature produce pressure, pressure induces sap movement, and sap movement means sap flow which comes usually from tissues directly above and below the taphole." [19]

So far in our reading we have collected the following

theories on sap flow: peristaltic action, osmosis, capillarity, atmospheric pressure, cohesive power of water, adsorption, transpiration, root pressure, gas pressure, chemical ferments, electrical attraction, local action of living cells. No wonder Darwin himself spoke of sap flow as "that most nebulous of subjects."

There are, however, several acknowledged facts about sap movement in trees that the following points illustrate. The elongated, connected cells that make up the wood of trees provide a series of parallel tubes through which sap passes from rootlet to leaf. This process is more active in the sapwood than it is in the heartwood.

The sugar maple contains an immense preponderance of sapwood. It is quite a common experience to cut a sugar maple twelve inches in diameter and find the heartwood no larger in diameter than an ordinary man's thumb—perhaps three quarters of an inch. The tree at this stage (thirty to fifty-five years old, depending upon surroundings) is still virtually all sapwood.

Tree leaves breath out, vaporize, or transpire the surplus moisture which has carried plant food up from the roots. Leaves are chemical factories where inorganic material is changed into living factors through the action of sun and air on the chlorophyll. The chlorophyll breaks up the carbon dioxide into carbon and oxygen and unites the carbon with water to form grape sugar. The latter turns to starch and is stored for future use. So tree leaves, using sap, sunshine, and air, manufacture the plant food upon which the survival of the tree depends. Both the growth and health of the tree are determined by the area of its foliage. A thrifty maple tree, fifteen inches in diameter, and fifty feet high, had 146,250 leaves in 1890 and 162,500 ten years later. The total leaf area was 8,846 square feet in 1890 and 14,930 square feet in 1900.[20]

Three widely varying sources give us the same rule of thumb for a good sugar season, leaf condition, and coverage. "The carbohydrate foods (starch sugars, etc.) are all manufactured in the green leaves under the influence of the sunlight. It is important to emphasize this fundamental point, because the sugar content of the sap depends upon the conditions of the preceding season as to sunlight and leaf development." [21]

"It is a well established fact that the sugars, starch and other carbohydrates stored in the maple are formed during the growing season, May to September of each year. It follows therefore that if conditions and moisture during this interval are favorable an increased growth of, and storage in, the tree would result and that if suitable conditions obtained the following spring, a large flow of rich sap would be secured. . . . The formation and storage of sugar in the maple tree is dependent on sunshine and moisture conditions of the previous summer. The ultimate source of the sugar is the carbon dioxide of the air, and the chlorophyll of the leaf and the sunlight are the agencies that build starch and other carbohydrates into plant tissue. A large leaf area on well exposed trees results in increased sugar storage and richer sap." [22]

To Timothy Wheeler we are indebted for an Indian rule for predicting the character of the sugar season. "If the maple leaves ripen and turn yellow, and the buds perfect themselves so that the leaves fall off naturally, without a frost, then there will be a good flow of sap the following spring; but if there is a hard frost that kills the leaves and they fall off prematurely, before the bud is perfected, then we may look out for a poor yield of sap. In other words, the flow of sap will be more or less abundant in proportion to the ripeness of the tree before the frost of the previous autumn." [23]

The water content of maple trees varies seasonally. The Vermont Agricultural Experiment Station checked a tree for variations. In summer, when transpiration is active, it was 27 per cent; in December, 31 per cent, in mid-March, 36 per cent. All of these measurements were made in the same tree. It also varies in different parts of the wood. On December 13, the outer tissues contained 37 per cent of water, while the inner tissues contained 24 per cent. Then, until March 11, water content decreased in the outer tissues and increased in the inner tissues. On June 9 the two were about equal. An average taken during April and May was for roots, 29 per cent; trunk, 30 per cent; branches, 34 per cent; twigs, 37 per cent.[24]

Maple sap, during the sugar-making season, exerts a pressure from a negative or suction pressure of two pounds per square inch to a positive or expulsive pressure of twenty pounds per square inch. "It fluctuates in a general way with the rise and fall of temperature during the day and night."[25]

Experimenters at the New Hampshire Agricultural Experiment Station recently cut off a dormant sugar maple, set it in a barrel of water, and subjected it to alternate freezing and thawing. The tree yielded sap. The top was then cut from a sugar maple and the body set topside down in a barrel of water and subjected to freezing and thawing. Again it gave sap. The body of a sugar maple was laid horizontally, a rubber pipe filled with water connected with the severed butt end and subjected to freezing and thawing. It likewise gave sap. Only when the severed tree was stood on a rock and subjected to freezing and thawing did it fail to give sap. These experiments suggest that trees cells can draw their water directly from a source of supply, without the intervention of roots and that the water may be drawn through the cells from the bottom up or from the top down.

One further point should be made about sap movement —its wide variability. Sap may start to run in the morning as soon as the temperature has reached the thawing point. It may flow freely for hours, or, in extreme cases, for consecutive days and nights. It is much more likely to flow for a brief period—perhaps two or three hours, taper off gradually or stop suddenly and not flow again until the next day or until some weather change has occurred—wind shift, freezing, precipitation. A sugar orchard with every spout dry at noon may begin to run and run freely at ten minutes after noon. The sap starts at the same time in a large number of trees having the same exposure to weather conditions. This point we will discuss in more detail before the end of this chapter.

Sap Weather

The most important single factor in sugaring is the weather. Those who wrest a living from nature—farmers, herdsmen, woodsmen, fishermen, hunters—are keenly weather conscious, because the pursuit of all of these occupations is determined to a considerable degree by the weather. Among the weather-conscious farmers, sugar makers rank high in the list, because sap production is tied tight to weather.

Sap is available in quantity only after severe freezing. It cannot run when the thermometer reads below 30 or 32 degrees. It stops running when the mercury rises to around 50 degrees. It will not run when the trees are in leaf. With autumn and early winter out on account of the low sugar concentration in the trees (the sugar accumulations having been devoted to summer tree growth), the sugar maker is limited to the few warmish days or weeks that intervene between the breakup of winter and the burgeoning of spring.

With these facts in mind, readers might enjoy a chuckle at the expense of an anonymous English author who put several unrelated facts together and produced the following account of a salubrious harvest drink made from maple sap. "During the Summer, and in the beginning of Autumn, the maple-tree yields a thin sap, not fit for the manufacture of sugar. It is used as a pleasant drink in harvest; and in Connecticut, the ancestors of the present race of farmers have in many cases left a single maple-tree in each field, probably intended as a shelter for their cattle, but which now produces a refreshing drink for the weary reaper." [26]

We noted in the previous section that the water content of maple wood is highest in spring, and that sap movement was more or less dependent upon an alternation of cold and hot weather. We likewise called attention to the fact that edible syrup must be made before the leaf buds swell. Add all of these factors together, take down your physical geography, and you will note that maple syrup can be made commercially in very limited areas.

So far as we know there is no maple syrup or sugar industry

today in Europe, Asia, or Australia, their weather cycles not
being conducive to the lengthy flow of sap. Timothy Dwight
writes, "The great distinction between the Climate of New-
England, and that of European Countries lying in the same
latitudes . . . is the peculiar coldness of its winters. . . . The
changes from heat to cold, and from cold to heat, are more
sudden, and violent . . . The changes throughout most parts
of Europe are less sudden, and not so excessive." [27]

Charlevoix, writing of the maple's wondrous properties as
he found them in America, says in a letter to the Duchesse
des Diguières, in 1744, "Our maples might possibly have the
same virtue, had we as much snow in France as there is in
Canada, and were it to last as long." [28]

Also writing of the possibilities of procuring sugar from
the European maples, J. P. Brissot de Warville exclaims,
"What a revolution would come to pass if the maple could
be naturalized throughout all Europe! It has been tried with
success by M. Noailles in his garden at Saint Germain." [29]
(We could find no further trace of M. Noailles' experiment.)

Many large estate owners in eastern Bohemia became interested in *Ahorn Zucker,* or maple sugar, in the late 1700's.
There are reports that in 1785 trials were made in Sweden
to procure sugar from the sap. In 1794, Graf Zichy is said to
have planted twenty thousand trees. "The Chamber of the
Mark at Berlin has lately been at great pains to promote the
manufacturing of sugar from plants indigenous in Germany.
Some experiments were made for that purpose with the juice
of the maple, which was refined in a sugar bakehouse, and
found to be equal to loaf sugar. . . . Attempts are being made
in Brandenburg to cultivate this tree, and seeds have been
ordered from America." [30] Heinrich aus Schweidnits, of Bres-
lau, reported in 1799 that he got "17 liters of beautiful syrup
from 28 trees." In 1800, in Austria, Fürst Liechtenstein put
in thirty thousand trees, and in 1809 built in Eisgreb a central boiling place to take care of eight separate domains. In
that same year, Dr. Adam Steinreiter was given one hundred
guilders by the Prague Patriotic-Economic Society to further
his researches in maple products. Nikau, in 1811, wrote of

forty-nine domains existing, with two thousand to twenty thousand trees.

At the time of the Napoleonic Wars, sugar was scarce in Europe on account of the British blockade of supplies from the colonies. The Continental governments urged and helped farmers to become self-sufficient for their sugar crop. Sugar-beet and sugar-maple growing was encouraged and promoted. Edmund O. von Lippmann, in his monumental work *Geschichte des Zuckers*,[31] goes with great detail into these systematic attempts at tapping and boiling in Bohemia, Austria, Germany, and Sweden, which however were finally abandoned. It was found that the mild, short European spring made maple-syrup production commercially unfeasible. With Napoleon's defeat at Waterloo and the opening of the blockade, cane sugar again became available. A beet of high sugar content was developed at a far lower cost than sugar could be obtained from the maple tree. The sudden and great fall in the price of sugar caused by the Peace of 1815 crippled for good the budding maple-syrup industry in Europe.

Maple-syrup producers require a relatively long spring. Otherwise the cost of equipment and of tapping out exceeds any possible return. The spring must be broken up into cold nights and warm days.* The best syrup is made while the ground is snow covered or while the day and night temperatures are low enough to prevent sap fermentation. These factors are all present in mountainous northern country. Finally, the sugar maple must grow vigorously. It seems to thrive on rocky, steep slopes, and grow badly or not at all on low land or in swamps. Rough, broken country is the natural habitat of the sugar maple. The maple industry should therefore be found in hilly or mountainous country, where the sugar maple grows freely and where a long, cold, changeable spring intervenes between winter dormancy and the swelling of leaf buds.

Hard maple is an ornamental and useful shade tree that

* "The almost sudden transition from cold to heat appears essential to the production of the article." J. Bouchette, *The British Dominions in North America*. London: Longmans, Green & Company, 1832. Vol. I. P. 371.

is distributed over a very wide area. The maple-sugar industry, however, is concentrated in a narrow segment of eastern
North America. Vermont is the state in the union whose
name invariably is coupled with maple syrup and sugar. It
has more of the necessary conditions in soil, altitude, and
weather for maple growth than any other. It has granite soil
where rock maples thrive; it is largely mountainous, or at
least hilly; its winters are severe and its springtime delayed
and lingering. Ira Allen proudly lauds the weather of his
native state in his *Natural and Political History of the State
of Vermont.*[32] "The climate," he says, "is friendly to the population and longevity; the air is salubrious, nothwithstanding
it partakes of heat and cold in high degrees, which gradually
make their approaches." He would hardly have agreed with
the old farmer who lived close to the state line on his Vermont farm, and who being told by the surveyors that he
didn't live in Vermont at all, but on the New York side,
replied, "Well, thank the good God Almighty—I couldn't
have stood another of them Vermont winters." New York,
Pennsylvania, Ohio, Michigan, New Hampshire, and Maine
in the United States, and Ontario and Quebec in Canada, are
the other main districts where the weather is right for making
quantities of maple syrup.

Sap flow needs not only long, cold springs. It is primarily
dependent upon thaws. This holds true of the big spring
thaw when ice breaks up in the rivers and snow begins to
sink under the heat of a northward-moving sun. It also holds
for the many little thaws that take place when night temperature drops to 20 degrees and midday temperature reaches 38
to 45 degrees.

Every person who has lived in a cold, mountainous region
knows the smell and the feel of the first spring thaw. Sugar
makers feel the sugar weather in their bones. They scan the
south horizon at dawn, get the wind direction and velocity,
watch the thermometer rise during the first two hours after
sunup, and announce, "Sap'll run today. Guess we'll tap out
a few."

When we began sugaring in southern Vermont, such was

the general procedure. No one tapped until sap began to run. If a sugar maker began tapping and found no moisture in the tap holes, he stopped tapping. The assumption was that sap flow was dependent on "sugar weather." What is sugar weather? In general, and subject to some comment that we shall reserve for the section of the next chapter devoted to tapping, sugar weather comes when winter breaks up and dormant maples make their preparations for putting on a new vesture of leaves. In the words of the French botanist and explorer, François André Michaux: "The sap begins to be in motion two months before the general revival of vegetation." [33]

John Burroughs, the American naturalist, puts it differently: "The moment the contest between the sun and frost fairly begins, sugar weather begins; and the more even the contest, the more the sweet. . . . It seems a kind of see-saw, as if the sun drew the sap up and the frost drew it down; and an excess of either stops the flow. Before the sun has got power to unlock the frost, there is no sap; and after the frost has lost its power to lock up again the work of the sun, there is no sap." [34] Duhamel also points to the sun's effects. "If it has frozen rather hard during the night, the sap will flow next day, but not unless the ardor of the sun is superior to the force of the frost." [35]

The simple and obvious formula for sugar weather that is widely accepted—a 20-degree night followed by a 45-degree midday—is generally true, but it is subject to limitations. For example, a 20-degree night may be followed by a shift of wind to the southeast, a rise in temperature, and a rain. In that case, sap flow will fall off when the wind has gone back into a cold quarter and there has been a frost. Under such circumstances the sap run would last from eight or nine A.M., when the spouts thawed out, to perhaps noon, when the rain began. If it were a very cold rain, mixed with ice particles, the sap flow would probably continue while the rain lasted. If it were a warm rain, sap would stop running at about the time the rain began or shortly thereafter.

If a 20-degree night and 45-degree midday is accompanied by

west or northwest winds, and if the sky is patched with fluffy, cumulus clouds that prevent the sun's heat from warming up the trees too much, sap will run well into the afternoon and may even run until freeze-up, at or shortly after sundown. Should this freeze-thaw weather formula be repeated, sap will run freely each day for a limited number of days. If the forest floor is dry and there is no precipitation, there will be little sap flow, even with the 20-degree-night and 45-degree-day temperatures. This was notably true in 1946 when a long period of delightful, clear weather with cold nights and moderately warm days resulted in about half of the normal syrup crop in our area.

Our best sap runs have not come out of 20-degree-nights and 45-degree-days. Quite the contrary. Take two examples —one from 1943 and one from 1942. On March 23, 1943, we had a 19-degree temperature at seven A.M., west to northwest winds. The night of the twenty-second–twenty-third was semi-overcast. It cleared during the morning of the twenty-third, was 31 degrees at one P.M., and 27 degrees at 7 P.M. Sap ran on the south side of the trees for a time during the afternoon. The twenty-fourth began with a yellow sunrise and a temperature of 23 degrees at seven A.M., with winds still northwest. It was overcast all day. In midmorning the wind shifted to the southwest. It was 38 degrees at one P.M. and 40 degrees at seven P.M. March twenty-fifth had a sky filled with cloud masses. High winds blew the previous night and all day— northwest in the morning, southwest in the afternoon. It was 41 degrees at one P.M. and 36 degrees at seven P.M. Temperature was 33 degrees at seven A.M. on the twenty-sixth, wind north. It had been misty all night, 30 degrees at three A.M., 36 at five A.M. At one P.M., it was 52 degrees and at seven P.M. 47. This was the first really warm day of the spring, with fleecy clouds, warm sunshine, winds variable, east to northwest. The next day, the twenty-seventh, the wind was west and the temperature 47 degrees at seven A.M., with a clear sunrise. There was a bright blue sky till two P.M., when it became hazy and overcast. The temperature was 45 degrees at one P.M. and 36 at seven P.M. The following day, March 28, it turned cold, and no sap ran for four days. During the March 23-27 period sap ran almost continuously, day and night, although there was practically no freezing during the four-day period. The run gave us 202 gallons of syrup, or exactly one fifth of the total for the season, which extended from February 23 to April 24, a total of sixty days.

The sap run just described took place during relatively clear, warm weather. It was misty and cloudy for a good part of the time, but there was no precipitation. The barometer remained relatively constant. Compare with it a sap run during a period of cold, misty, cloudy weather—March 15-19, 1942. The snow was very deep in the woods. On March 15 it snowed six inches, with easterly winds. It was 25 degrees at one A.M., 30 degrees at one P.M., 34 degrees at four P.M., and 30 degrees at seven P.M. The barometer began falling the next morning, dropping from 29.85 on the morning of the sixteenth to 29.12 on the morning of the nineteenth. There was a thunderstorm the night of March 16-17, with gusty winds, rain, and sleet. When the run began, the buckets were all snow capped. Sap dropped on the fifteenth after eleven A.M. On the sixteenth it began dropping at ten A.M. At two P.M. it was running hard, and continued till after nightfall. On the seventeenth, sap ran from noon until nightfall of the eighteenth, a period of thirty hours. Much of the time the sap was coming through hollow icicles that had formed on the spouts. It stopped running only when the spouts froze up. From March 16 till the twentieth we made 208 gallons of syrup, or 22 per cent of our total crop for the forty days of the 1942 season.

Obviously, the 20-degree-night and 45-degree-day, sunny-days and cold-nights formula for sap weather is very far from telling the whole story. "A curious circumstance in regard to the flow of the sap of the maple-tree in early spring" is mentioned by James Johnston in his *Notes on North America*.[36] "After a frosty night in April, the snow still being on the ground, the sap will flow freely after sunrise, *if the wind be west, north-west, or north*. But if the wind be south, the sap comes sparingly; and if, while it is flowing freely, the wind change to the south, the flow will diminish, and gradually cease altogether. Of course, this curious fact must be connected with the quality of the wind, and the aspect of the sky when it is blowing. The April mornings are remarkably clear when the wind is northerly; and, consequently, the light and heat thrown upon the tree, and any other influences, chemical or actinic, which the sun's rays bear with them, are proportionately great. The wind itself, also, is cold and very dry. The south wind, blowing from the Gulf stream, though warmer, is moister, is attended also by clouds and mists, and usually ends in rain. The heat, light and surface evaporation, being therefore less when the south wind blows, the flow of sap to supply the latter may decrease in consequence. It is possible, however, that the chemical influences of the rays of the morning sun may enter as a sensible element into the case." Wind, cloud, mist, rain, snow, sun all play a part, and sometimes a decisive part, in providing weather conditions auspicious for sap flow. The maple tree is like a sensitive plant affected by every slight change in weather. Even what is not noticeable to the outward eye has its effect on the flow of sap.

In the season of 1947 in our section, almost every standard condition for sap runs was present, but there were no storms —no wind, rain, or snow. Sap flow was slow and unsatisfactory. When sugar makers met each other their invariable greeting was, "If it would only storm!" A lady traveler visiting the United States in the 1820's gave an inadvertent description of ideal sugar weather. "The close of the winter, for one may not term it the spring, is here decidedly the least agreeable season of the year. Siberian winds to-day, and Indian heats to-morrow, and then driving sleets the next day, and so on, from heat to cold, and cold to heat, until the last finally prevails, and all nature bursts into sudden life, as by the spell of a magician." [37]

In the disastrous sap season of 1945, "the worst in a hundred years," as the gossip said, the snow was deep on March 1 and it looked like good sugaring. On March 3 the temperature was 31 degrees at seven A.M. At eight A.M. it began to rain; at three P.M. it was 54 degrees, at seven P.M., 40 degrees. Between March 4 and March 15 the seven-A.M. temperatures fell below 20 degrees only three times. Winds were west and northwest. On March 15 at seven A.M. it was 47 degrees; at noon 62. At five P.M. it was raining. The snow was all but gone. There followed two weeks of balmy summer weather. On April 3, yellow violets were out all through the woods; willow catkins were furry, and apple and maple buds were bursting. Spring sugar weather had lasted a fortnight and the syrup crop was about one third of normal. Contrast this 1945 season with 1943, when we had our first warm day on March 26, had repeated snow storms until April 20; had to use snowshoes in the bush up until April 23, and made more than three times as much syrup as we made in 1945.

Two neighborhood slogans for sap weather seem to stand the test of time: "If the trees go into winter with wet feet, there will be a good sap season," * and "Sap runs before a rain and after a snow." We are here tempted to set down an accumulation of old saws and speculations on sap runs that we have collected through the years. Sources are too varied and occasionally too local to recount. We pass these maple maxims on, contradictory or mutually corroborative, as they came to us.

"Sap runs better by day than by night."

"Sap run during the daytime is sweeter than that run at night."

"Sixty-three per cent of the sap is said to drop before noon."

"After three P.M., as the sun declines, the dripping sap lessens, even when there is no change of temperature."

"The darker the evening the sooner sap will stop."

"There is a slight increase in sugar content as the day advances."

* "There is reason for supposing that a deficiency of moisture would retard the formation of sucrose; first, because a normal water content is essential to the elaboration and transport of the constituents in the organism, and further, an excess of water is indispensable to the formation of the carbohydrates." H. W. Wiley, Bulletin No. 39, U. S. Dept of Agriculture. P. 51.

"The nearer the occurrence of a freeze or snowstorm that sap is caught, the sweeter it is."

"Sap caught at a low temperature is sweeter than that caught at a high temperature."

"The more intense the cold, the greater the quantity of sugar in the sap."

"A layer of snow and frozen ground over the roots of the trees is always favorable to the highest yield."

"Good sap weather requires that the opposite ends of the maple tree should be affected by opposite degrees of temperature."

"During clear weather more sap is produced than during cloudy weather."

"An open winter with plenty of thaws indicates a good sap year."

"A cold and dry winter foretells a better season than a changeable and humid season."

"The better the sap season the better the sugar."

"The more sap the more sugar."

"Quantity and quality do not go together."

"Light, heat and cold are the main factors in sap flow."

Scientists' and natives' information about sap movement and sap weather is meager, especially in its theoretical aspects. Experienced sugar makers will guess, and often correctly, how sap will run under a given set of circumstances. On the whole, these guesses are about as dependable as any guesses concerning the weather.

Sap Yields

People always want to know how much sap a single tree will yield. It is not easy to give a satisfactory answer. Burroughs has put it well: "Trees differ much in the quantity as well as in the quality of sap produced in a given season. Indeed, in a bush or orchard of fifty or a hundred trees, as wide a difference may be observed in this respect as among that number of cows in regard to the milk they yield." [38] "Some will produce," says C. T. Alvord, "as many pailsful as others do quarts." [39] "The quantity and quality of sap varies with the situation of the trees, their age and size, the nature of the season and of the preceding season, the meteor-ological conditions and the methods of tapping." [40]

When a tree is tapped on a bright March day, with wind west and temperature around 40 degrees, we have seen sap drop 300 times a minute. Later in the season, during a good run, we have counted 120 to 150 drops per minute. These rates, extended through an ordinary sap day, would yield six to twelve quarts of sap in a single bucket.* But, as has been noted, the rate of sap flow varies greatly, even in a single day. A tree may run 150 drops a minute at ten A.M. and not a drop at three P.M. If a taphole has struck new wood, and if the tree is a good sap tree, a fifteen-quart sap bucket may be filled in one twenty-four-hour day. At the same time, within a few feet, another bucket may contain only three or four quarts.

In terms of syrup, thirty-five quarts of sap will yield about one quart of syrup. Again, however, there is a wide variation. We have known times early in a good season when it took only twenty-five quarts of sap to make one quart of syrup. Later in the season, we have encountered a ratio of about eighty to one.

We keep our records as gallons of syrup per bucket for the entire sap season. In 1942, our best season in this respect, we made 0.339 gallons of syrup per bucket. That is, for every three sap buckets we made one gallon of syrup. In our worst season, 1945, the yield was 0.100 gallons per bucket, so that for every ten sap buckets we made one gallon of syrup. Ordinary syrup seasons have ranged from 0.17 to 0.26 gallons of syrup per bucket, or about a fourth of a gallon of syrup.

There are many record yields of maple sap and sugar there-from. Samuel Williams, in 1794, related how "a man much employed in making maple sugar found that for twenty-one days together, one of the maple trees which he tended, dis-

* Dr. C. T. Jackson hands on the following report: "I have known trees of one foot to yield 30 quarts of good sap in 24 hours." *Op. cit.*, p. 330.

charged seven gallons and an half of sap each day." [41] In his authoritative *Report on Trees and Shrubs,* G. B. Emerson narrates, "Mr. Lucius Field, of Leverett, informed Mr. Colman, the agriculture commissioner, that in one season he obtained, from one tree, 175 gallons of sap, which, if of average strength, would have made 43 pounds of sugar." [42] A contemporary writer, Lawrence Southwick, in the *New England Homestead,*[43] reports that "there are records of individual trees yielding from 250 to 300 gallons of sap in a single season. I know of several instances where one tree produced sufficient sap to make five gallons of standard syrup."

The *Brattleboro Reporter* of June, 1806, notes that "Captain John Barney of Guilford last year made from eleven maple trees upwards of sixty pounds of clear white sugar, and from the same trees the present year seventy-four pounds and one gallon of molasses. Captain Barney . . . gathered the sap himself, is in his 77th year, having lived to see the above trees grow from twigs to be thus fruitful."

Alexander Reed sent in a testy letter to the editors of both the *American Farmer* [44] and the *New England Farmer* [45] on the subject of sugar records: "I question much whether any tree in the United States can exceed one that grows on the farm of Amos Walton, of West Bethlam Township, in this county. The product of this tree for the last three years was as follows; spring of 1822, 35½ pounds; spring of 1823, 24 pounds; and this spring 29½ pounds, with a small portion of molasses each year. I had the statement from a member of the family. I am well acquainted with them, and know them to be very respectable. The tree is not of the largest kind, but has a very bushey top. It stands near the head of a spring, without any other trees near it." Solon Robinson, in *Facts for Farmers,*[46] gives two record instances: "A sugar orchard of 100 trees, belonging to William Searls, Eaton County, Mich., yielded one spring 950 lbs. of sugar, at the rate of 9½ lbs. to a tree. . . . From a moderate-sized tree, standing in open ground in front of the residence of the Rev. David King, of Vernon, Trumbull County, Ohio, his wife made 34 lbs. of very fine sugar one season. It is thought if all the sap had been carefully saved it would have given 40 lbs."

H. W. Wiley, at the twenty-eighth meeting of the American Association for the Advancement of Science, 1879, referred to his boyhood, when on his father's farm they tapped a tree, which, "in honor of its excellence," they named "the sweet tree." The percentage of sugar was found to be 4.30.

Since the average yield of sugar per maple tree tapped in the United States is around two to three pounds of sugar,* two explanations for these prodigious yields should be mentioned. One is the phenomenally high sugar content in the sap of some few trees. The other is high lighted by the two following examples of tapping. The first is from Michaux. "While I resided in Pittsburg, the following curious particulars appeared in the *Greensburgh Gazette:* 'Having introduced,' says the writer, '20 tubes into a Sugar Maple, I drew from it the same day 23 gallons and 3 quarts of sap, which gave 7¼ pounds of sugar: 33 pounds have been made this season from the same tree.' " [47] The second example, quoting Timothy Wheeler of Waterbury Center, Vermont: "The more spouts put into a tree, the more sap is obtained and the more sugar is made." Then he speaks of a tree "tapped with ten spouts, and fifty pounds of sugar were made, but it killed the tree." [48]

That is the story: "We made a wonderful record, but our overtapping killed the tree." "There are careless and avaricious growers who bore their trees in several places at once, or before the proper season, and then the trees, like overdriven creatures, fail and die of exhaustion." [49] It is possible to take an immense quantity of sap from a sugar maple in one season, but the record yield may kill the golden goose and end the life of the tree.

Length of Season

Any time from the middle of February to the first of May sap will run in the maple trees. Some years the season drags on into May, at other times it is over in March. A Canadian

* "An ordinary mature and thrifty maple will produce about 12 gallons of sap, or 3 pounds of sugar per season." Bulletin No. 59, Department of Agriculture, Bureau of Forestry. P. 35.

report says, "It often happens that only eight or nine days
are propitious to this part of the settler's labours." [50]

An interesting record was made in Lowville, New York,
by Benjamin Davenport, who kept records from 1830 to 1850
showing the dates of beginning and ending of the sugar season, as observed on the same farm.[51]

Year	Begun	Ended	Days of Duration
1830	March 20	April 19	31
1831	" 14	" 18	36
1832	" 15	" 18	35
1833	" 23	" 12	21
1834	February 22	" 5	43
1836	April 17	May 2	16
1838	March 13	April 26	45
1839	" 20	" 24	36
1842	" 15	" 17	34
1844	" 11	" 9	30
1846	" 19	" 7	20
1847	" 26	" 26	32
1848	" 23	" 10	19
1850	April 2	" 9	8

Figures from 1880 to 1900 are recorded by A. H. Bryan
and W. F. Hubbard in a Washington bulletin.[52] We kept
parallel figures from 1937 to 1947, with an extra item of interest—the percentage of syrup made in March and that made
in April.

Year	First Day Boiled	Last Day Boiled	Total Days	Per Cent in March	Per Cent in April
1937	March 20	May 3	45	17	83
1938	" 14	April 19	37	62	38
1939	" 25	" 23	30	14	86
1940	" 18	" 30	44	4	96
1941	" 17	" 17	32	35	65
1942	" 6	" 17	43	74	26
1943	Feb. 23	" 29	66	46	54
1944	March 13	" 20	39	28	72
1945	" 14	" 11	29	92	8
1946	" 3	" 15	43	85	15
1947	" 13	" 26	45	33	67

Even though some seasons seem particularly long and others exceptionally short, this does not mean that the former is a good season and the latter a poor one. A dozen or so good sap days, even in a long season, are a fair average; during some years there are no real "runs" at all. The short season may have the good runs and the long season may drag on interminably with stubborn weather that never breaks right.

There is a point already raised earlier in this chapter, on the sugar content of the sap as the season advances, which should be brought up again in relation to the length of the sap season. As the days and nights get warmer and the first buds begin to swell on the trees, the sap changes, first faintly then radically, in flavor and finally even in color. Sap soured by heat will become yellow, or milky, or greenish. Before this point is reached the wary sugar maker should stop boiling, take down his buckets and pull his spouts. When the quality of the syrup drops perceptibly, no matter how long or short one has been sugaring, then is the time to close up operations. There is a story told of Timothy Wheeler in which he urged "closing up the sugar making before any black, strong sugar was made, that we should be tempted to sell for what we could get for it. He said that in one sense a successful preacher and a successful sugar-maker were alike. They both knew when to stop." [53]

On the whole, the shifts and changes in North American weather seem to be suited to the growth, development, sap, and sugar yield of the hard maple. It seems its very variability and sharp contrasts are part of our heritage that make sugaring possible. An English author scratches his head over our weather: "In the New England states, the extremes of heat and cold can neither be conceived by an European, nor accounted for by an American." [54] A later wanderer in America laments, "In the month of February, 1820, I was mid-leg in snow, and over-head fevered with a burning sun! Hence it is a climate so oppressed with terrible extremes, makes mere threadpapers of the living." [55]

Mark Twain, the famous humorist, would have concurred with all these opinions. He is known to have said, "If you don't like the weather in New England, just wait a few minutes." At the annual dinner of the New England Society in New York City on December 22, 1876, he made a speech on the weather. He found the New England climate worth special mention. "There is a sumptuous variety about the New England weather that compels the stranger's admiration —and regret. The weather is always doing something there; always tending strictly to business; always getting up new designs and trying them on the people to see how they will go. But it gets through more business in spring than in any other season. In the spring I have counted 136 different kinds of weather inside of four and twenty hours." Perhaps this is part of the secret of our sap weather.

CHAPTER SEVEN

Making Maple Syrup

"Maple-water, which is the sap of that tree, is equally delicious for Frenchmen as for the Savages who in the Springtime take their fill of it . . . With a small hole, which they make with a hatchet in the maple, they can distill ten or twelve pots. That which seems to me remarkable in the maple-water is that, by boiling, it is reduced to a veritable syrup and becomes as sugar, of a brown color."

Chrestien Le Clerq, Nouvelle relation de la Gaspésie, *1691.*

"I was regaled here with the juice of the maple; this is the season of its flowing. It is extremely delicious, has a most pleasing coolness, and is exceedingly wholesome; the manner of its extracting is very simple."

P. F. X. de Charlevoix, Journal d'un Voyage fait par Ordre du Roi dans l'Amérique Septentrionnalle, *1744.*

"The March winds had blown themselves out. Rainy April had set in. Over all New England the signs of the new season were thickening. Maple-sap was flowing freely, and the woods and maple orchards were filled with sounds of industry."

Henry Ward Beecher, Norwood, Village Life in New England, *1868.*

"The most delightful of all farm work, or of all rural occupations, is at hand, namely, sugar-making . . . Huge kettles or broad pans boil and foam; and I ask no other delight than to watch and tend them all day. . . . I sympathise with that verdant Hibernian who liked sugar-making so well that he thought he should follow it the whole year. I should at

*least be tempted to follow the season up the mountains, camping this
week on one terrace, next week on one farther up, keeping just on the
hem of Winter's garment, and just in advance of the swelling buds, until my smoke went up through the last growth of maple that surrounds
the summit."*

John Burroughs, Winter Sunshine, *1881.*

THE recipe for strawberry jam begins, "First find your
strawberries." Before the sugar maker can turn out maple
syrup, he must have maple sap. The sap will run from any
break or cut that extends to the maple sapwood, but the
"sugarous liquor," to be useful in syrup production, must be
collected in containers and taken to a central point for boiling. We must tap the trees and gather the sap before we can
make the syrup.

Maple trees are "tapped" by boring a one- to two-inch-deep
hole with brace and $3/8$ or $7/16$ bit at some point within four
feet of the ground, inserting a metal spout, hanging a bucket
on the spout, and slipping a cover over the mouth of the sap
bucket. Such a process, applied to half a dozen trees, is a
minor affair. When buckets are hung by hundreds or thousands, however, it becomes quite an undertaking.

The first step in the tapping-out process is to get buckets
and covers distributed to the tappable trees. This distribution involves some knowledge of the sap-running capacity
of each tree plus a critical eye to the size of the treetop, the
number and position of possible dead limbs on the tree, signs
of rot or of bark destruction by maple borers.

We have some simple premises upon which to judge bucket
distribution: never tap a tree with a diameter of less than
twelve inches two feet above the ground; a twelve-inch tree
takes one bucket, an eighteen-inch tree two buckets, a twenty-
four-inch tree three buckets, and a thirty-inch tree four
buckets; never tap a soft maple if a hard maple is available.
Our corresponding reasons for these rules are (1) a young
tree needs all possible nourishment for its growth, and what

sap one gains in tapping too young a tree one loses in later years; (2) it is obvious that a tree should not be overtapped so that it will not be worn out; (3) the sap of the soft maple has about half the strength of sweetness of hard maple, stops running earlier in the season, and gives a darker color to the syrup.

We move our buckets from the storage boxes on a toboggan if the snow is soft—on a light sled if there is a good crust. We aim to have the storage containers so located that the buckets will always move downhill. Unless snow conditions are very bad, one man will take sixty buckets and covers on a toboggan or forty buckets and covers on a sled, select a line of trees, and distribute a bucket and a cover wherever a hole should be bored.

The bucket should be set upright, within easy reach of the tree but far enough away to leave room for the tapper to move about. A cover should be set upright beside the bucket. When a tapping team is working on snowshoes or when the ground is rough or steep, it saves much time to have bucket and cover within arm's reach and not chucked haphazard and covered with snow.

A tapping team consists of either two or three people. The tapper sets the pace for the team. He walks up to a tree, examines it for previous tapholes and for signs of decay, scans the branches above to get if possible under a sound limb, which is a good sign of growth,* or over a vigorous root, selects a place, and bores a hole one to two inches deep,† sloping slightly upward so that the sap may drip easily. The hole is usually bored as low on the tree as one can conveniently bend and keep the bit level. The reasons for this are

* "There is more sap on that side of the tree which has the largest and most limbs, as that is the side which is forming the most new wood and will require the most nourishment. This side of the tree is usually the south side, and is best for tapping as it will yield the greatest amount of sap." W. W. Ashe, *Possibilities of a Maple Sugar Industry in Western North Carolina,* Geological Survey Economic Papers, 1897. No. 1, p. 15.

† "I have tapped up to six inches in depth. . . . The best and lightest colored sugar is made from sap coming from the white, or sap-wood, and the darkest-colored product comes from the sap of the duramen, or darker heart-wood." Timothy Wheeler, in *Garden and Forest,* April 19, 1893.

various. If one tapped high in deep-snow seasons, one would be left barely able to reach the bucket when the snow melted. As the height of the snow level most likely varies every season, this ensures a wider vertical latitude between tapholes.

Three experimentalists in the nineteenth century give us their advice on where to tap. Timothy Wheeler reports: "I have tapped trees at various distances from the ground up to 38 feet from the ground, and down in roots 15 feet from the base of the trunk, and made sugar from all these places." [1] "Trees tapped nine inches from the ground," says Hiram Cutting, "produced double the amount of sap that was obtained from tapping three feet higher, while the sap was considerably sweeter." [2] Hough, in his *Report on Forestry,* declares, "I have this season tried an experiment by placing five buckets in a vertical line upon a tree, at intervals 4 feet 6 inches. The lower one, at 3 feet from the ground, gave at least twice as much sap as any of the others, and would run at times when those above it did not." [3]

Solon Robinson, in *Facts for Farmers,*[4] quotes a New Hampshire man who writes in 1857: "I tap with a three-fourth-inch auger four feet from the ground and hang the bucket by a ring, on a hook driven into the tree so close to the spout that the wind will not waste the sap. I tap at this hight [sic] that cattle can not disturb the bucket." This brings to mind a statement found in Michaux: "Wild and domestic animals are inordinately fond of maple juice, and break through their enclosures to sate themselves; and when taken by them in large quantities it has an exhilirating effect upon their spirits." [5]

Here we are again tempted to list a series of sayings on tapping which have come to us sundrywise. These are farmer's axioms, some of them contradictory, but all proved to their own satisfaction.

"The lower you tap the more the sap."

"The higher you tap the sweeter the sap."

"The older the tree the sweeter the sap."

"Sap is sweeter from trees which have been previously tapped."

"Sap early in the season and late in the season is the sweetest."

"Trees differ as much for sugar as cows differ for butter."

"Younger trees are more sensitive to changes of weather."

"Shallow boring yields better quality, less quantity."

"Deeper borings yield darker sugar but greater quantity."

"A tree will run the most sap on the side where it has the coarsest bark."

"A tree that leans will run the most sap if tapped on the lower side."

"Trees by a brook or spring run much sap."

"Isolated trees yield not only the earliest and most sap, but also the sweetest."

"One pound of the first run is often worth two of the last."

To look up, when tapping, is as necessary as to look at the base of the tree. Maple trees are tall, and their branches begin far above one. Moving among the trees in the spring, intent on the business of tapping, one tends not to look up but to go straight ahead with the work in hand. When we first began sugaring, some of the local people who were working with us played a time-honored joke by placing a bucket and cover at the base of a sturdy, good-sized maple which happened to be topless. We went up to the stub, picked out a good place, tapped it, and hung the bucket. The top had broken off the previous winter and the wood was still green and seemed to tap perfectly. After we had been duly laughed at we made a point thereafter of looking over each tree, top and bottom, before tapping it.

A friend, and a newcomer in sugar making like ourselves, was also taken for a ride by the local fellows who let him tap out a certain tree in his bush year after year, and they religiously hung the bucket on it after him. "Ed," he finally said to one of his helpers, "what's the matter with that maple tree? It's a likely looking one, yet it didn't run last year and it doesn't run this." "Nope," said Ed with a friendly leer, "and 'twon't never run. 'Tis a bass wood." So it's well also to know your trees when tapping.

An old taphole must always be avoided in making a new tapping, because the old hole converts a band of sapwood into heartwood and thus greatly reduces its sap-yielding capacity. These bands of heartwood are slightly wider than the taphole, extend into the wood to the depth of the taphole, and run from four to ten inches along the grain of the wood above and below the hole. A new tapping in this strip of heartwood will yield a small quantity of sap early in the season; after that the sap stops running. The first year after a taphole is bored it shows up clearly—almost as clearly as when it was new. In fact, an inexperienced spout driver, who does not stay right beside the tapper, will put his spout into a last year's boring unless he is careful. To watch below for the fresh chips from the bit is a good idea.

The old-timers used to put plugs in the holes after the season was over. This, they thought, tended to help the tree heal. We find that the second year the taphole begins to grow over. If the tree is a healthy one, by the fourth or fifth year, the taphole is overlaid by sapwood and new bark. After that it is difficult or impossible to detect the presence of the old taphole by outside inspection. In the course of time taphole and heartwood become part of the tree. We have found marks of old tapholes in old trees covered by a foot or more of first-class sapwood.

We have wondered and it has often been asked of us, if tapping does not hurt the tree and if we are not grossly exploiting them by leaching them of their life's blood. Bacon, in his *New Atlantis,* speaks feelingly of "the tears or wounding of trees," and elsewhere we have found mention of "the wide-brimmed maple with bleeding veins of liquid sugar," "the ceaseless drip of its watery blood," etc., etc. It is certain, of course, that the tree is deprived of nourishment that would otherwise be there for its use and that this is exploitation. The trees must work the harder to make up for what we take. On the other hand, we clear the ground beneath them so that there is less competition from crowding neighbors and therefore more moisture and nourishment for them to draw on. The real test as to injury to the trees lies probably in the fact that groves of maple have been known to flourish and to increase in girth and size even after being tapped for over a century. "The fact that large trees have been tapped for fifty and a hundred years without being killed in the process, and that, when compared with trees of the same age not often tapped, they are found to elaborate sap in larger quantity and contain more nutritive material, points to the conclusion that, with care, the injury to fair-sized trees is immaterial." [6] Duhamel states that "one does not notice that a tree is exhausted by the sap that it furnishes if one merely makes only one incision in each tree: but if one makes four or five with the intention of having a large quantity of sap, then the trees waste away, and the following years they yield much less sap." [7]

This same warning, to tap with care, is given in a 1795 volume: "In order that the trees may continue productive, they require to be tapped with extraordinary care. The fissures must be neither too deep nor too wide, so that no water may settle in them after the juice is extracted, and that the wood may close again in the space of a twelvemonth." [8] An article in *The American Farmer* [9] praises the constant tree for withstanding man's assaults in tapping. "The almighty Fabricator of the Universe has in his infinite wisdom and beneficence bestowed on this precious tree a tenacity of life truly wonderful. Though every year assaulted by the axe, the auger, or by fire, it clings to existence, and yields to its ungrateful possessor a luxury and necessary of life."

The tapper may bore for an inch through new wood, as shown by his white shavings. This is the new growth. He may yet come upon an old taphole or the band of heartwood above and below the taphole. Beyond this first inch the shavings may turn dark. The bit has entered heartwood and the tapper has struck an old tapping. The hole will never yield a full quota of sap and usually will dry up early in the season. The tapper may similarly strike a decay spot in the tree, which made no showing on the outer bark. In either case he will do well to abandon the hole and bore a new one.

The tapper must also decide on which side of the tree to bore. In general, it is good practice to have about half of the buckets on the north and east sides of the trees and about half on the south and west. Buckets on the south and west will run on cold days. Buckets on the north and east will run on warm days. Since early sap is likely to make the best syrup, sugar makers tend to hang buckets on the warm side of the trees and thus get the maximum of sap in the first part of the season.

If he is quick and apt, and if he uses a breast drill and a sharp bit, even when working on snowshoes the tapper can bore from 80 to 120 holes in an hour. A good bit will bore one thousand holes before it gets dull. With the power-tapping rig mentioned in chapter five the tapper could easily bore two hundred holes an hour. With the motor running, the actual boring of a hole does not take over two or three seconds.

The tapper is followed by a spout driver equipped with a stout carpenter's apron, the pockets of which will hold from seventy-five to eighty spouts (a bucket is the usual carrier, but the apron leaves both hands free), a hammer, or, better still, a light hatchet. The spout driver inserts the spout in the hole, with the bucket hook down, and drives it gently until the spout responds with a solid thud to additional hammer taps. If the spout is driven too lightly, wind or a heavy load of sap will loosen it or even pull it completely out. If it is driven too hard, the inner bark splits and the sap leaks out around the spout. It should be driven in straight so that later the sap gatherers can automatically hang the bucket back on the hook.

On old trees, where the bark is more than half an inch thick, it is likely to be so spongy that the spout will not be firmly held. On such trees, the spout driver should blaze off enough of the outside bark (but just enough) to ensure the spout gripping the solid wood of the tree. It is here that the hatchet comes in handy.

If the tapper is slow and the spout driver is quick, there will be time for the spout driver to pick up the waiting bucket, hang it on the spout and attach the cover. If the tapper is fast, the spout driver should be followed by a third member of the team, who hangs the bucket and puts on the cover. Hanging the buckets is an easy operation that is usually performed by a youngster or some person not able to do the heavier work.

Tapping out is one of the most thrilling and exciting of farm occupations. Winter is over. The sun moves northward. Spring shows herself in faint, indefinable signs—a warmer sun, geese honking overhead, a softening of the snow crust, a few tiny snow fleas, minute objects but the first signs of new life born in the spring. The year lies ahead, with the primary fierce activity of sugaring.

A telling description of the push of tapping is delightfully depicted in a child's book, *The Golden Almanac*.[10] "It is rush, rush, rush, once the sap has started to rise. Drill, drill, drill. Put in spout, put in spout. Hang on pail, hang on pail. Put on cover, put on cover. And start all over with more and more trees. There may be dozens, hundreds, even a thousand trees for one family to tend. It may be long after dark before they can stop to go home to dinner and to bed."

It may not be out of place here to point out the remarkable similarity in the eager action of maple sugaring in New England and cane sugaring in the South. The following illustrative quotation could be a description of New England in March. "The sugar crop has to be gathered in Louisiana within ninety days, or else it will be destroyed by the cold; as a consequence, from the moment the first blow is struck, everything is inspired with energy. The teams, the negroes, the vegetation, the very air, in fact, that has been for months dragging out a quiescent existence, as if the only object of life was to consume time, now start as if touched by fire. The negro becomes supple, the mules throw up their heads and paw the earth with impatience, the sluggish air frolics in swift currents and threatening storms, while the once silent sugar house is open, windows and doors. The carrier shed is full of children and women, the tall chimneys are belching out smoke, and the huge engine, as if waking from a benumbing nap, has stretched out its long arms, given one long-drawn respiration, and is alive." [11]

Now we come to the question: when to tap? We found a well-established and widely accepted formula being practiced: tap when you can get sap in the spout. According to this formula there should be no tapping until the breakup of winter has begun. In practice this meant that tapping started with the start of the first sap run. Since it takes several days to tap out, and since the average early run is not likely to last for more than two or three days at most, this practice meant that the sugar maker lost most if not all of the first run. For several years we accepted and followed this formula for determining the time of tapping. But we were never satisfied with it, and the more we thought over the matter the greater did our dissatisfaction become.

Every Vermont woodsman knows that:

1. Following an ice storm, when green maple limbs are broken by the load, the broken end of the limb will run sap the first warm day and on the following morning will carry a sap icicle that formed during the colder hours of the night. This sap run from broken limbs will take place whether the ice storm came in December or in February.

2. In sawing down maple trees, sap will wet the saw on any warm day during the whole of winter. The stump of such a tree, cut down during the winter, will run sap following each freeze-up.

3. A young hard-maple tree, say six inches at the butt, cut on a cold winter morning and notched every four feet for conversion into cordwood, will run sap at both bottom and top ends and at every notch if the weather moderates at midday. On one occasion in December, we were thinning out some young hard maple. The poles were cut in the morning and laid together to be sawed that afternoon. The day was bright and the poles lay in full sunshine. When we got back from lunch, icicles were hanging from pole ends and notches. Maximum temperature in the shade was 20 degrees above

zero, but the action of sunlight on the bark of the cut maples raised the temperature inside the bark to the point at which sap flowed. The moment the sap reached the air, however, it froze into icicles. Incidentally, the icicles hung from notches on the side of the poles toward the sun; north-facing notches showed no sap flow.

With these experiences in mind, we began a series of tapping experiments in 1942. We tapped trees in December of that year and in the following January and February. In subsequent years we began tapping trees in October and tapped sample trees in each of the seven months from October to April. Results were quite uniform, year after year:

1. Whenever there was a thaw following a freeze-up, sap ran. This was as true of the autumn and winter months as it was of the spring months.

2. Tapholes, bored in January, or even in December, flowed freely in March and sometimes well on into April, until there was a prolonged warm spell.

3. Trees tapped in October and November were still running sap the following March, but the quantity of sap was less than for spring-tapped trees. In some cases trees tapped in December and January yielded as much sap in early April as trees tapped in February and March.

4. We have gathered sufficient sap to make syrup in every month from November to April. In winters that lasted without a heavy thaw from freeze-up in early December to the breakup in early March, the syrup made during the winter was flavorless, sticky, and dark in color. After a heavy thaw, however, we made good-flavored, good-textured, light syrup.

We wrote to Professor Paul B. Sears, a leading botanist, about the dark, flavorless "winter" syrup. Here is his answer, in part: "I cannot give you any certain explanation of your early flow of dark syrup, but I am inclined to think that the early brief thaw did not permit the full conversion of starch to sugar but did stimulate a partial digestion to intermediate gumlike soluble carbohydrates which under the boiling would perhaps caramelize more easily than the sugar. When the subsequent thaw came, this material, being already in solution, was not further digested before sap containing it was out of the tree. Then perhaps the continuance of the final thaw allowed the final starch to be completely converted to sugar, giving you lighter syrup. If this is the case, the matter was beyond your control."

Our conclusion from these experiences is that it does not pay commercially to tap until spring. The winter periods of sap run are too brief to justify the effort of gathering and boiling. Until a good thaw has followed a hard freeze-up, it is impossible to make acceptable syrup. Once the thaw has occurred, however, excellent syrup can be made at any time sap will flow—witness our having made fancy syrup in December, January, and February.

It pays, however, to tap *before* the first spring sap run. The spouts run equally well if driven before or during the sap run, and if they are in place when the sap run begins, the sugar maker may make from a tenth to a quarter of his entire season's product during those crucial first days. If it were safe to tap only on days when sap would fill the spout, why should the stump of a maple tree, cut in December, run sap the following spring? Surely the air and wind could work their will on such a stump and if drying out were the real factor in checking sap flow, the December stump could not run sap the next spring.

There is a wide variation in the behavior of individual trees. The trees immediately around our sugarhouse were tapped February 19, 1946. By April 2, all but half a dozen of these spouts were dry. One of them continued to run, giving ten quarts of clear sap on April 7 and 8. While all of the neighbor trees had formed scar tissue in their tapholes and stopped running, this tree, backed by a big boulder and with its roots under a small brook, continued to run sap freely. Why this wide differentiation? The tree in question is always a good runner. There are such trees in various parts of every sugar lot. Is it a sport, a genius? Why did its sap not go sour and heal over the taphole? Such variations are met with all through nature and here they are again, cropping up in the maple bush.

There is much talk among sugar makers about retapping, either in the same trees or in fresh trees. Holes that have started to run dry can be reamed. Spouts are pulled and a reamer introduced into the taphole sufficiently large to scrape away the surface of the established hole. We have never tried reaming. As far as we know it is not practiced by sugar makers in our neighborhood. We have tried retapping occasionally. There are wonderful tales about sugar makers who have had their buckets taken down and washed up and who, come a cold spell and a snowstorm, have retapped and made phenomenal amounts of all-but-white syrup. We have never found that extensive retapping late in the season paid.

Early in our sugaring experience we wrote the Vermont Forest Service, asking if it would be beneficial to the trees if we tapped only one section of the bush one year and let the other part rest till the following year. In fact, we had two bushes and could have used them alternately if any benefit to tree or sap yield would have been derived. The reply stated that no experiments on resting of orchards were known to them or recorded in their publications.* They ventured to say that a rest period might tend to increase sugar content but not the flow of sap. In any case, they said, "Chemical studies of maple sugar production indicate that tapping a tree in normal health withdraws a comparatively small proportion of stored carbohydrates. Exceptions to this might be cases of long continued shortages of sunshine and rainfall, defoliation by insects, and very heavily grazed orchards. In other words, tapping such orchards every other year would tend to relieve the tree while recovering from malnutrition."

Our conclusions about tapping might be summed up in

* We found the following in a book by Crèvecoeur: "I owe to nature three to four hundred of these very useful trees, which I have had carefully enclosed and all of whose obtrusive neighbors I have pruned in order to increase the vigor as well as the quantity of their sap. . . . In order not to impoverish them I have divided them into three classes, of which only one is tapped every year." *Voyage dans la haute Pensylvanie et dans l'état de New York*, Paris: Maradan, 1801. Vol. I. P. 280.

these words: Tap when working conditions are right—weather, snow, available labor. Start early enough so that you get the first real run of the spring in your buckets. "As soon as the frost begins to quit its hold of the sugar maple, be prepared to take its luxuriant juice, as the first taken is much the richest." [12] Take your time and do a careful, workmanlike job. One of our neighbors in the valley had a cold, north-facing bush. He always tapped out much later than the rest of us. In fact, in order to save himself unnecessary mental torture as to when, he just set a date, March 20, and come hot or cold weather, did not tap out till that day. And he was as often right as the rest of us who began to get restless around the middle of February.

Gathering the Sap

The buckets have been hung; weather is fine; sap is running. When shall we gather? There are two schools of thought on that. One says: Gather when the buckets are full. The other says: Gather every day.

Most old-timers in our district gather when the buckets are full. "Why bother," they ask, "going to a half-empty bucket? Why not wait till it contains somewhere near fifteen quarts? Suppose a little sap does run over. There is plenty more. We are getting all the sap we can boil, so what more do we want?" An old bachelor, who helps us in sugaring time and who housekeeps for himself, said of our regular and fairly constant gathering, "When I sweep I want it to be worth my while. I wait a week or so for a good accumulation of dirt. That's the way I feel about gathering. I want to find something in the buckets when I go around."

There is another side to the picture. If buckets get more than half full and there comes a hard freeze, there is every likelihood that they will spring and burst, with the resulting loss of both bucket and sap. Later in the season, sap left in the bucket more than one day is likely to ferment and therefore produce inferior syrup. Maple sap is an excellent medium for the nourishment and development of microorganisms.

Hence, with fermentation beginning almost immediately, speed as well as cleanliness in handling is essential. Again, fresh sap makes better-colored and better-flavored syrup. Leander Coburn, in the *First Annual Report of the Vermont State Board of Agriculture,* wrote, "Sap should be gathered and boiled as soon as possible after it has left the trees. This is one of the main points on which good or poor sugar depends, for the longer sap stands after it has left the tree, before it has boiled, the more color there will be in the sugar." [13] One of our oldest neighbors and a careful conservative fellow, who has been making syrup for fifty years, got to the point where he set only one hundred buckets, gathered the sap by hand twice a day, boiled it at once, and made fabulously light syrup and white sugar. Chester Thomas, in 1882, did the same. "If sap runs not more than one-half pint to a tree, gather it up. Do not let it stand in the bucket. . . . I have often had men ask me what I put into my sugar to make it so white, and when I tell them I never put in anything some of them are incredulous, and do not think me honest." [14]

We take a middle position, leaning toward the constant gatherer. We aim to gather whenever there is a reasonable amount of sap in the buckets—anything over two quarts. In any case, we aim to go over our whole bush twice in three days, so that sap does not stand in the buckets more than a day. The following records show the consequent quality of our syrup. From 1937 to 1947 we made a total of 7,334 gallons of syrup from a yearly average of 3,250 buckets. Of this amount 5,533 gallons, or 75 per cent, was fancy grade. In favorable cold sugar seasons such as 1941, 1942, and 1943, we made a total of 2,432 gallons, of which 86 per cent was fancy. In 1942 the percentage of fancy, on a crop of 515 gallons, was 94 per cent.

As authority for this frequent tending of the buckets, we might quote from two government pamphlets, one Washington,[15] and one Canadian.[16] The first says, "In some respects sap is as delicate a product as milk, and the method bringing it from the tree to the storage must be rapid and systematic." The other says, "The sooner the sap is turned into syrup or sugar the better will be the product. Sap deteriorates very quickly after it leaves the tree. For this reason gathering should commence as soon as there is a quart or two in the buckets."

There are times during every sugaring season when sap freezes in the buckets. A mild frost produces loose ice crystals, commonly called anchor ice. Hard frosts convert the sap into a cake of all-but-solid ice, with a thin film of syrup between the ice cake and the sides of the bucket and a small pocket of syrup at the center of the ice cake. Between these two extremes, the buckets will contain a greater or smaller percentage of ice, which is concentrated during the early process of freezing on the sides, top, and bottom of the bucket.

Should sap ice be gathered or thrown away? Most syrup makers throw the ice away—first, because there is no convenient way of gathering it, and second, because the ice contains so small a proportion of sugar. The Vermont Agricultural Experiment Station *Bulletin #103* reports five tests of the sugar content of sap ice. The percentage of sap that was frozen to ice ranged from 33 to 91 per cent. Where there was 33 per cent of ice, 14 per cent of the sugar in the bucket was in the ice. Where there was 91 per cent of ice, 66 per cent of the sugar in the bucket was in the ice. Our own experience in boiling down sap ice leads us to believe that hard sap ice contains by weight about one quarter as much sugar as the sap from which the ice was frozen. We agree with the authors of *Bulletin #103,* however, that "the discarding of sap ice is a wasteful practice." [17] Whether it pays to haul this ice to the sugarhouse is quite another question. The above-quoted bulletin suggests that it would be wise to guard against ice formation in the sap "by keeping up the collection system so that large amounts of sap do not remain in the pails over night when there is a likelihood of a severe freeze." [18]

This is not the whole story, however. We have seen periods of a week or ten days in the middle of the sap season when sap runs a bit between eleven A.M. and three P.M. By sundown, spouts are decked with icicles and the sap is freezing.

In the morning what has dripped is a solid cake. This performance is repeated day after day. The ice cake in the bucket never melts. Each day's sap run adds to its size, until the bucket is full. Then we have seen new sap drip onto the ice cake, freezing as it dropped, until the ice was heaped up above the sides of the bucket.

We meet such a situation by taking a toboggan or a sled, equipped with a rack, and tubs and buckets in it, which we fill with ice cakes, run them down to the sugarhouse, put the cakes in the back pan of the evaporator, and boil them down. Occasionally we have hauled sap ice from more distant parts of the bush, using horse-drawn sled or truck. It is a difficult, cold, mean, unsatisfactory business at best, chiefly because the equipment is so inadequate. However, such situations occur, though rarely, and when they do we handle them that way. On the whole, we agree with the authors of *Bulletin #103:* Keep sap buckets as nearly empty as possible and thereby help to avoid the ice danger.

Much sap is lost in the bush by spilling and slopping. In the 1947 season a twelve-quart pail of sap would make around sixty-five cents worth of marketable syrup. Hence spilling and slopping were expensive practices. We make it a rule to pour carefully from sap buckets into gathering pails, to fill a gathering pail only to within two inches of the top, and to pour slowly into the pipe-line funnels. Occasionally we have lost some sap because of a broken pipe. Sugar makers who haul sap over rough terrain in horse- or tractor-drawn gathering tanks tend to lose considerable sap through slopping.

We have had to learn to be fairly adept at snowshoeing. To struggle afoot without a load through deep soft snow is bad enough, but with a full bucket in either hand it is exhausting and cannot be kept up for long. With the deep snows that fall in our district, snowshoes are a practical necessity and really should be rated among essential sugar tools. We always have half a dozen pairs handy for ourselves and helpers. Once having acquired the knack of their use they are invaluable in carrying heavy loads of sap through deep snow.

Unwieldy and cumbersome as the snowshoes may be,* it would be far worse without them. They make packed paths from tree to tree and from trees to pouring place. On hard frosty mornings we often can follow these paths afoot. There are years, of course, in which the ground is bare for sugaring and we have never touched our snowshoes. In 1943, however, we were on snowshoes in the bush from February 22 to April 23.

Specifically as to gathering on the pipe line, we get best results by having experienced teams of two persons, who know the trees and the lines. On any given morning two men would start out, each with two gathering pails and with a funnel and strainer. They would begin on line 4, for example. The men went to the first standpipe on the line, took the cap off the standpipe, screwed on the funnel, and put the strainer in place. Each then took one side of the pipe line, poured the sap from the sap buckets into the gathering pails, carried the pails to the standpipe and poured them in. After a little experience each man knew exactly which trees should be gathered to each standpipe. Far buckets were gathered first, gradually working in to the center, which lessened the amount of lugging. Few, if any, sap buckets were missed and there was no confusion. When all of the sap around the first standpipe had been gathered, one of the men went on toward the next standpipe, gathering as he went. The other unscrewed the funnel, put the cap back on the standpipe, and carried the whole rig to the next standpipe. By the time he had the funnel on the second standpipe his fellow worker would have his two gathering pails of sap ready to pour down.

The two men would follow line 4 to the end of the line.

---

* "The great difficulty of carrying a load on snow-shoes in the time of a thaw, is one of those kinds of fatigue that it is hard to describe, nor can be conceived but by experience. . . . We had to use nearly our whole strength to extricate the loaded shoe from its hold. It seemed that our hip joints would be drawn from their sockets. . . . So terrible is the toil to travel through deep snow, that no one can have a sense of it till taught by experience." *A Narrative of the Sufferings of Seth Hubbell and Family in his Beginning a Settlement in the Town of Wolcott, in the State of Vermont*, Danville: Eaton, 1826. Pp. 16-18.

Then came down line 3 or line 5, whichever needed gathering. At noontime the chart at the sugarhouse would show lines 4 and 5 gathered. After lunch the men could then start on line 3 or 6. Thus the pipe lines divide the sugar bush into gathering units and allow a very accurate checkup on what has and what has not been gathered and what is next in order.

We have tried gathering with teams of three. Where one person is inexperienced, he is charged with handling the funnel, taking off and putting on the standpipe cap, and pouring sap from nearby sap buckets directly into the funnel. This arrangement has its advantages and disadvantages: a good example of "two is company, three is a crowd."

If conditions underfoot are average, one man can visit fifty to seventy-five buckets an hour, depending on the amount of sap in each bucket. Where there is only a small bit of sap per bucket—a quart or two—the number of buckets visited is greater and the volume of sap gathered per hour smaller. We then have two or even three teams, or single persons, gathering along different lines at the same time.

The speed of gathering with the pipe system astonished us. With buckets averaging six to eight quarts of sap, two experienced men can pour down ten barrels of sap per hour and thus keep a 5-by-16 evaporator more than supplied with sap for boiling. Where trees are close to the sugarhouse the difference between the speed of horse gathering and pipe gathering is not so considerable. The farther the trees are from the sugarhouse the greater the difference in speed, because in both cases the sap must be gathered and poured, and while pipe-conducted sap finds its own way to the sugarhouse, the horse-drawn gathering tank must make a round trip with every load. We estimate that our costs of gathering are only 40 per cent of the costs of gathering the same territory with horses. In addition, we can move our sap more rapidly from the trees to the sugarhouse and thus decrease the likelihood of fermentation.

Let us suppose the teams have taken their assignments and begun gathering. If they are working close to the sugarhouse, within a few minutes the sap begins to pour into the storage tanks. Each tank is equipped with a rough burlap strainer that is washed and dried at the end of each sap day and attached to the pipe, clean and fresh, before gathering begins. (The sap is strained three times: as it is poured into the funnels at the standpipes; as it goes into the storage tanks up in the bush; and third, as it all comes into the main tank back of the sugarhouse. The tanks are washed each time they are emptied. By this means cleanliness is assured and the chances of sap fermentation are reduced. Hiram Cutting says, "Cleanliness is doubtless everywhere next to Godliness, and nowhere is it more apparent than in sugarmaking." [19]) At the beginning of the season it takes about seven barrels of sap to fill our 5-by-16 evaporator. After that, with the evaporator full, the boiler waits till there are five to ten barrels ahead in the storage tank and then he is ready to begin boiling.

Boiling Maple Syrup

With sufficient sap ahead in the storage tanks, with sap coming down fairly constantly through the piping system, and with an inch of sap covering all the evaporator pans, a fire is lighted in the arch. As the evaporator warms, the sides of the pan should be carefully gone over with a wet cloth (a pail of warming water can be set in the pan) in order to clean off the accumulated foam and scum of the last day's boiling. This should be done every day, and during the day when possible. About twenty minutes after starting the fire, if the wood is dry and of proper size, the evaporator is roaring with the steam shot up from the boiling sap.

For several years we ran our evaporator with the front draft open, used dry wood, and boiled with a very hot fire. We took off record batches of syrup in that way. In one ten-hour day of boiling in 1943, we took off sixty-three gallons of fancy syrup. In 1944, in a twelve-hour day we took off sixty-seven gallons, and during that same week in another twelve-hour day we took off seventy and a half gallons of fancy syrup. One of our neighbors, however, who usually boiled with green wood and a much slower fire, made what we considered better-tasting syrup than we did. This may have been the flavor of his bush.* It may, however, have been his rate of boiling. The following quotation from a *Vermont Agricultural Report* might be pertinent. "Rapid boiling is apt to burn it [syrup] a little. When we have a hot fire, and keep it boiling as fast as possible, it burns a little without our knowing it, and my idea is that slow evaporation is better than rapid. Most people believe rapid boiling necessary, and while there is no doubt that it is necessary to convert it into the product as quickly as possible, that is, not to allow it to stand and get sour, still, I would not have the boiling process too fast." [20]

We decided that our boiling temperatures might be too high, that it was no use trying to keep on breaking our own record, and that perhaps we were boiling too fast. We therefore put a movable sheet of metal over the firebox opening, kept the front draft closed more often than not, and built a damper into the base of the smokestack. With this damper we can control the draft, and instead of letting a large percentage of the heat rush up the stack, we keep it concentrated under the firebox. This gives us a steadier fire and we believe it reduces wood consumption by a quarter to a third.

Our 5-by-16 evaporator in action is a two-man job for one man (or woman) on a busy day. Ten hours of boiling will consume from two to three cords of wood (256 to 384 cubic feet). This wood must be taken from the woodshed, moved to the evaporator, and fed into the fire. The evaporator must be fired just enough and not too much or too little. Too hot a fire will scorch the front pans or cause the sap to boil over, and too small a fire will keep the syrup in the pans too long and darken the color and affect the flavor. Firing up should be done regularly and methodically. Never fire up on the taking-off side just before the syrup stage is reached—sap from the adjoining pan will tend to boil over and thin the finished

* Every bush, and possibly every tree, differs radically in flavor. A real connoisseur can taste these fine differences and can even sometimes tell from which bush the syrup came. We have tasted syrup from Ohio that seemed like a different product than our maple syrup.

syrup. Only fire up on one side at a time. The whole pan should be given time to adjust its boiling before firing on the second side. If only one door is open at a time and only one side is filled with cold wood, the evaporator cools less. Keep doors open as little as possible and never open both doors at once for the same reason. A long poker is occasionally handy to stir up the accumulated coals and to shift the wood a bit.

Itinerate visitors to the sugarhouse invariably find the firing process fascinating. There is a lordliness and a sense of power in heaving heavy logs into a blazing furnace and hearing the resulting roar. One fine March day when boiling was proceeding at a great rate, two bowler-hatted long-black-overcoated gentlemen from the city of Boston appeared at the sugarhouse. They were salesmen for the *Encyclopædia Britannica* and had come with hopes for a sale. The lone tender of the rig that day was a mere woman, and admiration and envy loomed high in the men's eyes as they watched her chuck in the logs and tend the huge evaporator. "May we watch?" they asked. And later, timidly, "Could we stoke the fire? We've always wanted to be firemen on a train." Off came the bowler hats and overcoats, and soon they were unrecognizable as white-collar employees of a great and respectable company. While they did not learn the fine art of firing, they proved good workers, and, incidentally good salesmen, as we bought their encyclopædia set!

The evaporator must be carefully watched. Under the best conditions the sap in the pans will be not more than an inch deep and the closer one dares to keep it to half an inch the more quickly the sap turns into syrup. The fresh sap is fed in through an automatic regulator, but as the rate of boiling varies with the heat of the fire, the regulator must be watched lest the evaporator go dry. A galvanized or tin pan that has run dry in any section, with a hot fire raging immediately underneath it, will be smoking with burning syrup the first minute, unsoldered the second, on fire and blazing the third, and burned through, the fourth. Hot syrup burns rapidly, almost to the point of exploding, and if prompt measures are not taken, the sugarhouse will be on fire. It is this fire hazard which makes the insurance rates on sugarhouses so outrageously high—13 per cent per year at the last quotation. The person boiling must therefore know his evaporator, must be eternally vigilant, and must be quick to meet emergencies. As an expert pilot listens to the throbbing of his motor and every creak and snap and hum of his plane, so does an expert boiler know every sound of his evaporator. A lowering in the pitch of the boiling, a drip or a sizzle where there should be none, has him on an immediate tour of inspection to test that all is in order. There are days in our boiling when not one minute can one sit down and take things easy. Fire up, test the depth, check the tank, take off syrup, test depth again, skim off foam, wash cloths or bottles, put up syrup, get wood, fire up, etc. On one's feet all day, round and round like a cart horse one goes, with one job following right on another. One of us wore a pedometer on a busy day. At the end of seven hours it registered 29,090 steps, or an estimated nine miles.

The *American Agriculturist* of March, 1870, in giving directions for the boiling of sap, says, "The most careful and capable hand should take this work,—usually the owner of the sugar-works." "A man that is ready and willing to tend strictly to business is indispensable in the manufacture of the best maple sugar" says another report.[21] It is certainly the most crucial and responsible part of the whole sugaring operation. A Frenchman, writing on cooking, has given the needful qualifications that can be applied to that extremely engrossing and onerous occupation. "If you are extremely clean, if you are very sober, and have above all, a great deal of activity and intelligence, you will succeed one day or other in acquiring that confidence which these qualities always inspire. You have not the power which other artists and mechanics have, of putting off for another day what cannot be done in this; the hour imperiously commands, and the work must be done at the appointed time. Be ever careful then to have all things ready for your work by the time it is required, and proceed without noise or confusion." [22] Thomas

Chester gives his general directions in sprightly form: "When the sap is obtained make lively work of it; put it into sugar or syrup, whichever you want, on the double quick, never letting it cool till you have got it to the consistency you wish." [23]

Maple syrup is 35 per cent water, 62 per cent sucrose, one per cent invert sugar, one per cent malic acid. The making of maple syrup consists primarily of getting rid of the surplus water by evaporation. Daniel Jay Browne words it in this involved fashion: "Maple molasses is made by discontinuing the evaporation before the liquid is of sufficient consistence to consolidate by cooling." [24] The less time the sap is over the fire the better. Quick evaporation is necessary for high-quality production. Consequently, small amounts of sap at constant depth and hot enough to boil, but not to burn, are the constant object of the syrup maker's attention.

The sap is kept flowing from the tank, through the regulator in the backpan, by the perpetual evaporation of water from the sap in the shape of steam. Often, when the fire is roaring and the sap shooting up clouds of steam, the whole sugarhouse is so dense in fog that one can see no farther than a few feet around. Visitors call out on entering, "Is there anybody here?" Startlingly, like a nearby foghorn in a murky harbor, booms an answering voice from a body scarcely discernible, but close by.

From one barrel of sap, consisting of thirty-two gallons, we often must boil away 97 per cent of water, leaving one gallon of finished syrup. Seasons differ, but at all times an enormous proportion of water is drawn off and shot into the air. Some sugar also goes with this ascending steam, as can be witnessed by the sugaring together of one's eyelashes and the general stickiness of one's hair and clothes at the end of a long boiling day.

Another proof that much sugar as well as steam is in the air lies in the fact that most boilers who are in this sweet and sticky atmosphere all day rarely sample the syrup or yearn to lap it up as the occasional visitors or bush help do when they get near the scent and roar of boiling sap. In fact, most

sugar makers during the whole period of boiling become
sated with sweetness in general and eat only sour, vinegared,
pickled, or salted food during sugaring time. It almost seems
as though the sugar might be absorbed through the skin.

With the first boiling of the sap, and while the season is
at its height, a sweet aroma is noticeable at boiling times,
even at quite some distance from the sugarhouse. "A dis-
tinctly agreeable odor marks the process of maple sap evaporation, as every one can attest who has visited the primitive
sugar factories which are operated in the maple-sugar industry." [25]

The sap is now boiling wildly in the evaporator. On the
side of the front pan from which we will take the finished
syrup, the experienced sugar maker can see signs of the
"finishing point." Syrup is usually ready to come off within
forty or fifty minutes after the sap begins to boil—certainly
within an hour. "It requires much practical information, and
the exercise of sound discretion, to determine from the different appearances of the syrup in the time of boiling, the
moment when some material movements or changes ought
to be made." [26] How do we know when the point is reached?
There are several tests. After years of experience one can
judge merely by the look of the boiling liquid, by the color,
and by a certain volcanic or explosive type of bubbling. The
old-timers tested by dripping some from a wooden paddle
and watching how it "aproned." We also watch the boil and
take off "by sight." We have, however, instruments handy to
prove our judgments right.

The thermometer gives us the boiling point at which to
take syrup off. At sea level both water and sap boil at 212
degrees, and syrup at 219 degrees, the sugar in syrup raising
the boiling point by that much. The boiling point is lowered
one degree for each 550 feet of ascent. At the point in elevation at which water boils one should add 7 degrees to get the
syrup temperature. We are almost two thousand feet up, and
we take our syrup off when the mercury stands at 214.

The Baumé hydrometer registers the density of the liquid.
It is a graduated glass tube, weighted at the bottom. It floats

at 31.5 when syrup is at standard weight, or eleven pounds per gallon, the point at which it was found that syrup keeps the best, neither crystallizing from being overheavy nor fermenting from being too thin. We test each batch we take off with the hydrometer.

However, this instrument only gives a hot and a cold test. If syrup is a little less than boiling, or, at the other end of the scale, faintly lukewarm, it will not give a reliable test. A table of correction for the hydrometer, with allowances made for altitude and thermometer variations, has been issued by the Vermont Department of Agriculture, Montpelier.

There is on the market a precision instrument calibrated by expert glass blowers called the hydrotherm, invented and produced by Fairfax Ayres of Arlington, Vermont, which gives the weight and density of the syrup at any temperature. This glass tube has no scale to read or to compute. It simply floats at the level, regardless of temperature, where the syrup will weigh eleven pounds to the gallon. It is an invaluable tool and a money saver to boot, as the syrup can be taken off on the dot of perfect testing. With the Baumé hydrometer, syrup is usually taken off a little on the heavy side to allow for the immediate decrease in temperature of the syrup tested.

Before drawing off a batch of syrup that we have tested to be ready, we take a quick tour around the evaporator. Is all in order? Is there plenty of sap in the tank outside? Is the regulator letting in sufficient sap? Is the back pan deeper than the front? With two or three gallons coming off at a time, the pans might otherwise run dry.

Assuring ourselves that all is in order, we open the syrup gate and let out the ready syrup into a pail set underneath. With the syrup gate open and syrup pouring out, fresh sap, concentrating in density, automatically circulates through the pans to take its place. We test the boiling syrup with the hydrometer as it moves around, and also place the floating hydrotherm in the pail of hot liquid. We watch the point at which the syrup will begin to test below the needed density, and at that point shut the valve, tend to the firing, again take a look all around, at flow of sap, etc., and prepare to take care of the pail or two we have just drawn off.

With our evaporator going full tilt we can take off a twelve-quart pail of syrup every half hour, given normal general conditions. This syrup goes immediately, right off the fire, through flannel and felt strainers to ensure crystal clarity of the syrup. Many folk only strain their syrup once, through a square of flannel, clothes-pinned onto the tops of the taking-off pails. We found that this arrangement impeded the quick flow of syrup from the boiling rig and made it difficult to test the pailful with the hydrometer or hydrotherm, which otherwise could float in the pail. We have made bags of flannel (cotton sugar bags would do) which we insert in the felt bags which hang in our settling tanks. The flannels keep back all foreign matter, allowing the cleansed syrup to go through the felts. In this way the foam and muck of boiling clogs the flannels but not the felts, and at the end of the day they need no washing, only a soaking in boiling sap and a run through the wringer to clean them of syrup for the next day's use.* The felts are tough and unyielding to wash constantly (and costly also); with this system they keep cleaner, and the flannel bags take the wear and tear.

From the settling tanks the syrup can be put up hot or cold, at one's convenience. To bottle hot ensures a sterile pack, and is supposed to keep more flavor and fragrance, ward off crystallization in case it has been overboiled, and enable one to fill to the top of the container. As the syrup cools it leaves a vacuum that allows for possible later expansion in warm weather.

There is one manner of boiling that a few farmers in our district practice. They have a small stove and sugaring-off pan in the sugarhouse, into which they keep putting liquid from the evaporator just before it reaches the syrup point.

---

* Our nearest neighbor, who has farmed in the vicinity for forty years, claims that in his early days here it was the practice to pay the help with the "scum cloths." They could take home at night all the cloths used in straining the syrup, and the sugar they boiled down from them was their wages for the day.

They feel they can finish it off more easily and exactly over a small fire in small batches. We are not in favor of the practice and fail to see its benefits. Continuous boiling in the original pans gives the best results. Reporting a contest for syrup makers in Canada, J. B. Spencer says, "In almost every case the prize-winning syrup was finished in the main evaporator. Reheating is claimed to darken the syrup." [27]

A few more points as to boiling technique. Early in the season the boiling sap throws up a tasteless, pure-white foam that should be skimmed off whenever sufficient quantities rise to the top. This scum rising is a natural cleansing of the sap and, with its coagulation of nitrogenous matter, brings with it any other solid matter that might have got into the sap. Later in the season this foam turns from pure white to a dirty gray or even a brown as dark as cocoa foam. The sap should be kept clear of all such extraneous matter. Samuel Perley says, "Use the skimmer freely while boiling. It is surprising to see the amount of dirt which is thrown up with the foam, even when the sap appears perfectly clean and pure." [28] In a talk on making maple sugar, A. M. Foster says, "If I were going to put in two or three hours I could tell you what was necessary to do to make the best sugar. Entire and absolute cleanliness is necessary—the one thing you cannot disregard. If I were going to have a motto I should say, intelligent enterprise is necessary. Skimming constantly is necessary." [29] Very often this scum is shaken off onto the sugarhouse floor, wherever it happens to land. This makes the floor slippery and dangerous to walk on, and is sloppy to boot. We keep an old sap bucket handy under each side of the evaporator, throw the foam into it, and empty the bucket several times each day. Cleanliness and tidiness are assets to the efficient boiler. In fact, William Chapin rates them highest of the virtues. "Cleanliness is next to Godliness always, and in making the nicest maple sugar it may have to come first with some people." [30]

A "source of great annoyance to many sugar-makers," says Cutting, "is found in the so-called 'sand' or 'niter,' which forms a non-conducting layer on the pans, deteriorates the appearance of the syrup by separating out, on standing, in dirty-looking flecks, and gives an unpleasant grittiness to the sugar." [31] This niter, silica, or sugar sand, as it is variously called, is mainly a malate of lime deposit that no longer remains in solution but precipitates into floating flecks, or cakes the bottoms and sides of the pans. The loose bits are skimmed off with the foam but the surface coating of the pans can only be removed at the end of the syrup season when the pans are emptied, and the hard deposits attacked with a putty knife or some such dull scraping instrument. (If alternate sides of the front pan have been used to take off the finished syrup, the niter would tend to move along and deposit less.)

Other suggested methods to remove niter from pans are to leave the last boiling, at the end of the season, in the pans all summer and winter. This makes a horrendous mess to clean up in the spring, but those who try it say the action of the souring putrescent mass leaves the pans "cleaner'n a whistle." Another way is to scrub the pans with a mild solution of muriatic acid.

This sugar sand, however, is not in its entirety an evil. E. R. Towle considers the malic acid and lime to be "a component part of maple sugar" and the source of "the nice and peculiar maple flavor so much to be desired." [32] Franklin B. Hough quotes a Vermont correspondent as saying that "the best sugar is made in years when there is most niter in the sap." [33] And A. M. Foster says, "Nitre, so called, is more plenty some years than others, and varies in different sugar places; as a rule we find the most in old sugar places and in seasons when we have a large yield of sugar." [34] It might be a fair test of the type of season to expect, to boil some sap very early in the season, and from the relative amount of niter deposit judge the quality and quantity of syrup ahead. This subject could stand more investigation.

One little trick of the syrup maker should be mentioned here. With a hot fire underneath, the inch or two of sap in the pans often rises to the tops of the pans (six to eight inches) in uproarious boiling, and even rolls over onto the floor if the fire is not tempered. One of the ways to control this boundless energy when it gets out of hand is to throw open the arch doors and calm the turmoil by letting a draft of cold air play over the fire under the pans. The dampers in our evaporator flues, when shut completely, will curb the wildest boiling. Another way is to break the surface tension of the foam by tossing a tiny drop of fat (we use a speck of cream or evaporated milk) into the boiling sap. In an instant, as if by magic, the high point of the boiling sap subsides and down it mutters to its accustomed level. If too much is thrown onto the troubled waters the sap takes a long while to get back to a good rolling boil. Only a flick from a pencil point is enough to calm a whole pan in a twinkling. This is a more pleasant adaptation of the old-timer's piece of pork hanging over the kettles which was supposed to keep the sap in automatic order. "If I were obliged to use anything" says W. O. Brigham, "to prevent running over, I would use a few drops of sweet cream; but I very seldom use anything believing that everything that is added has a tendency to make it dark colored."[35] One further method is to rub some type of fat all around the top edge of the evaporator before starting boiling. When the boiling sap reaches the edge it automatically lowers.

One other necessary point in effective boiling is keeping the flues clean. An evaporator, burning two or more cords of wood daily, deposits quantities of soot on the underside of the pan, in the flues, and depths of ashes in the ash pit. The pan bottoms, flues, and ashbox should all be cleaned frequently and a record kept posted so that there is no slip in these essential matters. Soot-covered pans and flues do not transmit heat, and hot ashes, piled against the grates, will warp them out of shape in a surprisingly short time.

If syrup is of proper consistency it will keep from one season to another without deterioration, except that fresh-made syrup possesses a delicate tang and bouquet that old syrup invariably lacks. An 1870 government report cites an interesting if unusual procedure to preserve the syrup and its flavor. "Recipe for the benefit of those who appreciate the saccharine products of the rock maple: To preserve the fine flavor, take the sirup made of the first run of sap, and fill good, sweet, sound jugs, cork tightly with short corks, seal and cover the corks closely with wax; then bury the jugs in the ground three or four feet deep, and in a shady place." [36] Syrup once open to the air may develop a mold on top, just as jelly does. This affects the syrup no more than it does the jelly. It should be put through a sieve, brought to a rolling boil, and put in smaller, sterilized, airtight containers.

Syrup is divided, for commercial purposes, into four different grades of color. Color is one of the chief factors in grading maple syrup. The lighter the syrup, usually the more delicately flavored, and the higher the quality. Government grading stipulates that fancy syrup be maple-sap syrup, free from foreign material, and of a density of 36 degrees Baumé hydrometer reading, weighing not less than eleven pounds to the gallon. (The U.S. gallon has a cubic capacity of 231 inches.) It should be of a color no darker than that designated in the U.S. color standards as light amber. It should possess a characteristic maple flavor, should be clean, free from fermentation, and free from damage caused by scorching, buddiness, any objectionable flavor or odor, or any other means. Grade A syrup must be the same as above except in color. The color is darker than light amber, but no darker than that designated in the U.S. color standards as medium amber. Grade B is the same as above except in color and flavor. The color is darker than medium, but no darker than that designated in the U.S. color standards as dark amber. Grade C syrup should be the same as Grade B except in color. The color is darker than that designated as dark amber in the U.S. color standards. More fancifully expressed, the color of the finest syrup has been compared to a pale ginger ale; Grade A to a Pilsner beer; Grade B to tea; and Grade C to coffee.

Color, clearness, and flavor are important in determining the commercial value of maple syrup but are not essential to the identity of maple syrup as such. Maple sap, and nothing else, as the raw material of its making, is the essential ingredient.

Color and clarity depend upon the weather, the cleanliness of the tools, the regularity of gathering, and the manner of boiling and straining. Flavor depends on imponderable qualities of tree, location, soil, etc. If the sap is kept frequently gathered up, if tools are clean and the evaporator fired with good wood, if sap is boiled shallow, fancy syrup should be made by any careful person in the beginning of an average season. E. A. Fiske gives some rules for making *poor* syrup: "Let the tubs hang upon the trees or lay around the sugar-house for two or three weeks after sugaring is done, and then if you wash them at all, do it with cold water. Do not scald your store tubs during sugaring, or at its close. Let your sap-gatherer stand on the sled in front of the sugar-house through the summer. Never strain your sap, or skim it while it is boiling. Do not wash your pans from the commencement to the close of sugaring. Follow these rules faithfully and the result is guaranteed." [37]

John Lorain, in his book on husbandry, says, "The processes employed in making sugar are so very simple, that care and cleanliness seem to be the principle necessary accomplishments of a sugar boiler." [38] One must be responsible, alert, and on one's toes every minute. Given these not-too-rare qualities and no daydreaming, any person of moderate perspicacity and energy can become an assured sugar maker in one season. However, grim warning is passed on to the prospective sugar maker in the following two quotations. "Do not suffer a hand employed in your sugar camp to ever carry such deadly weapons as guns and rum bottles, nor articles so destructive to success as cards, dice, dominoes, and novels. You must watch and work, and then you need not doubt success. Sugar-making is pleasant, healthy, hard work. A camp is no place for lounging." [39] "Neatness and dispatch is the motto, and must be lived up to in every particular; even the meerschaum, if it must be used, should be taken outside of the sugar house in working hours." [40]

Washing the Buckets

Tapping, gathering, and boiling sap is lively, exciting work. Washing up is less thrilling. The buckets are taken down, spouts are pulled, and covers placed in storage. The buckets are then brought to a central point for washing. The sooner this is done after the sap has ceased running, the better, because the longer sour sap remains in the buckets, the harder they are to clean when the time comes and the more chance the acid has to eat the galvanizing off the buckets.

We usually run a pipe from a small brook to one of our storage tanks, fill the tank with water, let this into the evaporator, keep it hot by means of a slow fire, and scrub and rinse the buckets in galvanized wash tubs. Individual sugar makers have made bucket-washing machines; there are some on the market. We made our first bucket-washing machine during the 1948 season, at a cost of about forty-five dollars. With it, one operator and an assistant easily washed 350 buckets an hour. By hand the best that three washers and two assistants could do was 100 to 125 buckets per hour.

The spouts are boiled in a mild washing-soda solution, cleaned of loose dirt, and packed away in cloth bags—one hundred spouts per bag. We count out the first one hundred clean spouts, weigh them, and then do the balance of the counting with the scales. When we begin tapping out the following spring, instead of counting the buckets we have set out, we simply count our empty spout bags, and keep a record each day of the number of buckets set. By this means we can tell by a glance at our record how much tapping is already done and how much remains to be done.

There is a sigh of relief when the buckets are all washed up, although even that rather tame task achieves a festive air on mild, sunshiny days when tubs are lined up outside on planks across wooden horses, and teams divide up to scrub, rinse, and pile buckets in pyramids to dry in the sun and wind. The long-drawn-out winter is now well over, air and earth are soft and warming, the birds are cheeping, early violets and anemones showing up in the bush, and buds popping on the trees. We shed our heavy woolens, and in shorts and cotton shirts let sun and wind get to the long-beflanneled body.

Underlying the relief of finishing a job is a note of regret that the sugar season is over. Any contest with nature is exciting, and the sap season, coming as it does in the very early spring, carries with it a thrill and a promise that is all but inescapable. How many of our neighbors, getting on into their seventies, have declared their intention, year after year, of making this time the last sugar season. Then, as winter rounds out into the following spring, the fever grips their blood and with the first warm sunshine they are out in the sugar lot scattering buckets, tapping, gathering, and boiling, and telling endless yarns of the wonderful sap seasons in the days of their youth and early manhood.

CHAPTER EIGHT

Making Maple Sugar

"There are in the Valleys of those Forests great store of Maples, from whence may be drawn distill'd Waters. After a long boiling, we made of it a kind of reddish Sugar, much better than that which is drawn from the ordinary Canes in the Isles of America."

Louis Hennepin, A New Discovery of a Vast Country
in America, *1699.*

"I have never tasted any better sugar than what has been made from the maple, when it has been properly refined. It has a peculiarly rich, salubrious, and pleasant taste."

Samuel Williams, A Natural and Civil History of Vermont, *1794.*

"Maple sugar forms a great article of domestic consumption, the material is plenty, the preparation is easy, the taste agreeable, it seldom cloys the stomach, it is an excellent anti-scorbutic, and so innocent that it may be taken in almost any quantity by infants."

Ira Allen, The Natural and Political History of the
State of Vermont, *1798.*

"The first occupation of the spring, or rather the end of the winter, with the Canadian farmer is the making of his sugar. The sap of the

181

maple is possessed of a large quantity of saccharine matter; and when, by long boiling it is reduced into a solid form, yields a sugar by no means unpalatable, even to an European taste. . . . The people of the country are passionately fond of it, and look upon it with the same sort of national feeling as an Englishman does his beer, a Scotchman his scones, or a Mexican his pulqué."

P. La Terriere, A Political and Historical Account of Lower Canada, *1830.*

"This maple prefers cold situations. . . . It is excellent fuel. . . . But the quality for which we could wish to see this tree everywhere more abundant, is its producing maple sugar . . . the most delicious sweet that ever meets the palate."

Samuel Goodrich, Peter Parley's Illustrations of the Vegetable Kingdom, *1840.*

WE HAVE now traversed "the period of the limpid sap" and have come to the preparation of "the granulated condiment," to use the words of Samuel Goodrich.[1] This "tree sugar," or "molasses sugar," as it used to be called, is the solid product resulting from the evaporation of maple sap to syrup and a still further concentration to a higher temperature. The ratio of sap to sugar is thus described by Solon Robinson: "Sap concentrated thirty times makes what we call good sirup, and this concentrated three-eights makes grained sugar, hard enough when taken out of a jar to require a stiff knife, which, as I calculate, is that sap concentrated fifty times in sugar."[2]

From the same author we get the admonition that "although maple sirup is made with very little trouble, it requires much experience and care to make good maple sugar."[3] Here is a pitiable example of Captain Basil Hall who, with no directions and no teacher, gave up in despair. "In April [1826], we tried to make some sugar; but as we had nobody to tell us how to set about it, we did not succeed at all."[4] Says the *American Farmer* of June 17, 1835, "The stirring of maple sugar, to make it good, cannot be learned but by seeing it done, or by a long course of practice." "Nothing but experience," says Moses Mather, "can enable a person to convert syrup into sugar." [5]

Our opinion is that anyone who is moderately expert at making fudge or panocha can learn to make maple sugar. The problems are almost identical and the procedures are practically the same, except that the maple sugar is usually poured into bulk containers or into small molds instead of flat pans. There is a wide range of temperatures for the various sugars, but that is a matter of detail. We would agree with the statement made in 1824 that "maple sugar might be manufactured by the rudest mountaineer as well in the first season after his arrival here, as by the most eminent sugar-refiner in Jamaica." [6] Our first venture into sugar making was at the instigation of an ex-prizefighter turned confectioner in Brattleboro. He demonstrated the method to us and then we went home and tried it on our own stove. We have kept our sugar making a home craft. We do it in a small way, by hand, using no machine mixers. Electric beaters can be used, and even ice-cream freezers, but we beat with a large wooden spoon.

Maple sugar is made by boiling standard syrup until it reaches the necessary temperature, and then stirring or beating it until it reaches the required consistency. Under ordinary conditions a half gallon of maple syrup, in a good-sized kettle, can be converted into sugar within thirty or forty minutes.

The size of the kettle should be about three times the size of the batch. One of the chief difficulties in sugar making is the tendency of the boiling syrup to leave the kettle and even the stove. Over a hot fire, the boiling liquid will erupt like a geyser, rising from an inch in the bottom of the kettle to five or six inches up the side. In a matter of seconds it is dripping from the stove onto the floor. A few more seconds and the spilled syrup on the stovetop has taken fire and is blazing merrily. If the fire gets into the other kettles of boiling syrup the sugar maker will pass an uncomfortable five or ten minutes.

We began our sugar making with large quantities of syrup

in large kettles. When one of these boiled over, as they did occasionally despite our utmost vigilance, a half gallon of boiling syrup would be rolling over the stove before we could turn around. Now we begin boiling with small amounts in large kettles, raise the temperature close to where we want it, then put two kettles together and finish off this larger batch. By this technique we shorten the boiling period, get better color, preserve more of the flavor, and have less trouble with boiling over.

Actually, boiling over can almost always be prevented if the sugar maker puts a wooden spoon or paddle into the boiling syrup and moves it about vigorously when the syrup has risen to within an inch of the top of the kettle. It can also be prevented by putting a little grease—butter, lard, or oil—around the top rim of the kettle. We prefer small amounts of syrup in large kettles, combined with constant supervision.

There is another circumstance in boiling that may precipitate crises. One must have a hot fire to get the syrup to the necessary high temperatures, but the boiling syrup scorches easily on too hot a fire. Therefore, care must be taken to heat the syrup quickly but not too suddenly. An occasional general stirring helps take care of both boiling over and scorching.

These large wooden spoons or paddles rank among the sugar maker's necessary tools. Also necessary are a confectioner's funnel and stick for pouring the molten sugar, small cake tins or tin pans in various shapes, and black rubber molds of varied designs. For the actual boiling we use a large kitchen range, burning dry split hardwood. With this equipment two people can make about seventy-five pounds of sugar in half a day. To do this the top of the stove should be covered with kettles, moving them in rotation to the hottest section and there finishing off at the required temperatures.

As with syrup, the temperature at which to boil sugar varies with the elevation above sea level. The higher the altitude the lower the temperature required; and the harder the sugar is desired, the higher the temperature required.

"Atmospheric conditions affect candy and must always be taken into consideration. In summer one should cook all candies a degree or two higher than in winter. In humid hot weather it is impossible to make good hard candies." [7] This pertains to maple-sugar making as well.

Almost any pure maple syrup can be converted into sugar, except the very earliest "winter syrup," and the late runs, which often are incapable of crystallization. The first-run syrup after a thaw sugars at a lower temperature than that made from late runs. Sometimes, when one is trying to make sugar from late-run syrup, the syrup boils and boils and boils with no perceptible rise in temperature. The best syrup is none too good for making sugar.

Maple sugars range all the way from a soft spread, called maple honey or butter, which has the consistency of slightly granulated, thick honey, through many variants to hard cake sugar that must be broken with a hammer. These various products are turned out at different temperatures and through the employment of different processes. They all, however, comprise merely the boiling down and stirring of the syrup, which in its turn was merely the boiling down of the sap. Nothing is added, but a great deal is taken away, in the shape of water vapor.

When we first ventured into the sugar-making business, maple cream was the rage, so we learned to make maple cream. It is produced by raising the temperature of the syrup to 25 to 27 degrees above the boiling point of water at that elevation, and suddenly cooling the product. (Water boils with us at 205 degrees, so we took off at 232 degrees.) We poured it on a cold marble slab, and without stirring or moving the mass, reduced the temperature as rapidly as possible to 70 degrees. Then we began to turn and beat the sticky mass until tiny white crystals began to appear and the taffy suddenly became a huge lump of finely grained fondant. This cooling and beating tends to produce very small crystals of sugar, which give it a creamy texture.

The fondant was then put in a double boiler, a tiny portion of water was added to help the process of liquification, and then slowly heated until it had the consistency of thin gruel. Whereupon it was poured into a confectioner's funnel and distributed into molds—rubber or tin.

The process was slow and rather tricky, but it produced a semisoft, smooth sugar that all but melted in the mouth. Maple cream is a typical product for an age that savors and relishes cream puffs. No laborious chewing or biting is required. The stuff slides down with one easy gulp.

Maple cream was unstable and would not keep for more than three or four weeks. Then, if the weather was hot and damp, it separated into syrup and crystals. If the weather was cold and dry it hardened and turned an unpleasant mottled plaster color. Stability could be increased by dipping the maple-cream shapes into a supersaturated solution of cane sugar, which is the method used by the big companies who sell vast quantities in the open market.

After some experience with cream making, we wondered why we should join the procession on the sheep run. "If everyone else is making maple cream," we asked ourselves, "why should we not try something different?" So we turned to making old-fashioned grained sugars, such as the Indians made.

Grained sugars are made of crystals that are larger than those in maple cream. The commonest form of grained sugar is a block or cake weighing from an ounce or two to several pounds. Such cakes were formerly made in wooden molds. Now they are generally made in small, sturdy cake or bread tins.

A temperature of 30 to 33 degrees above the boiling point of water is necessary for hard sugar. Higher temperatures are often advised, but would produce a very hard sugar cake— one that must be broken with a hammer after it has dried out for a few weeks. This is quite satisfactory for a housewife who shaves the hard sugar with a sharp knife and serves it on pancakes or waffles, but it is too hard for chewing. So we experimented until we found a temperature that would produce a cake hard enough to hold together, but soft enough to be bitten into readily. We therefore boil syrup to about

237 degrees and let the kettle cool to anywhere from 200 to 210 degrees. The syrup after cooking should be "suffered to remain entirely at rest," says the *Farmer's Dictionary*.[8] "Let no further agitation be had by stirring," warns Solon Robinson.[9] C. T. Alvord stipulates, "If it is desirable to have the sugar of a coarse grain, it should not be stirred while it is crystallizing; but if a finer grain is wanted, by stirring it moderately while cooling, any desired grain can be obtained." [10]

After cooling, we beat the syrup until it begins to grain. If we are using fancy syrup, the graining will begin gradually and then suddenly the entire mass will stiffen. The one who is beating must catch the batch just before this stiffening process takes place, pour it into the confectioner's funnel, and get it quickly into molds. If the batch is poured too soon the forms will be moist around the edges and the center will drop in large cakes. If it is poured too late, the sugar will be rough and uneven on top and so thick that it will barely come out of the funnel.

Sugar cakes were easy to make, rather large in bulk and prosaic in form. We looked around for something a bit out of the ordinary. The answer seemed to lie in fancy shapes and fancy packs. At that time, 1936–1937, maple-sugar shapes of hearts, men, and maple leaves were being sold by the big companies. We decided to utilize the rubber molds for these and other shapes, which were then procurable from a few confectioners' suppliers. This involved the problem of making a sugar for these small fancy shapes (from fifteen to eighty pieces to the pound) that would be attractive in appearance, sturdy enough to stand packing and shipping, and yet not too hard. After experimenting, we decided to use fancy syrup only, to boil it to 240 degrees (or 35 degrees above water boiling), cool it to 220 degrees, beat it as long as possible, and then, with a candy funnel, distribute it quickly into the molds. When the syrup is a fine fancy, the crystallizing process is quite rapid. Often the beating process lasts for only a minute or two. The moment a cloud of small crystals shows in the batch it must be rushed into the funnel and distributed. Even with the greatest speed possible, the batch will sometimes harden before it can be poured. A thermometer can be used to indicate points of boiling and cooling, but, as with fudge, it is a question of judgment on how long to beat the mixture. When a batch is successfully beaten and poured, the sugar is even in texture, with a faint grain, and deliciously appetizing. Poured into rubber molds it is ready to be taken out and stored away as soon as it has cooled to body temperature.

A form of sugar rarely made now is the "stirred," or "granular," sugar. It was made by the Indians and early settlers as it was dry and granular, kept well, and could be used exactly like refined cane sugar. We get a few orders for this "Indian sugar," and make it in the old-fashioned way. Raise the temperature as high as you dare without scorching. The syrup seems to boil almost dry and becomes high in the kettle and almost explosive. A thermometer is of little use as the bottom of the pan must be continuously scraped to prevent scorching. After taken from the fire, as soon as the syrup has subsided in the pan, the batch is beaten briskly for many minutes (ten to fifteen), when it thickens considerably and finally forms in small and separate grains, when it is worked through a sieve for even consistency. Alvord says, "Many families are in the habit of stirring a portion of their sugar, as in this form it retains its flavor better than when it is drained, and is in a more convenient form for use. . . . If it is put into tight boxes or tubs and thus kept, it will retain the fresh maple flavor for some length of time." [11]

One delicious maple-sugar product, never made commercially, is called "sugar on snow," or "maple wax." Hot syrup, just before the hard-sugar stage, is ladled out (unbeaten) on packed pans or banks of new-fallen snow. The thick syrup, when poured out in trailing spoonfuls, is a delicious concoction, fragrant and flavorsome, chewy and ice cold. There is nothing quite like it in the way of sweets. The practice probably originated from the early tests of sugar making. Thomas Fessenden, in 1820, writes, "If you wish to make dry sugar there are various modes of ascertaining when it is boiled sufficiently; perhaps as sure a method is to drop some on snow and let it cool, if it is brittle as rosin it is done." [12] "There are various ways of telling when the sugar is boiled enough. A convenient and good way is, when snow can be obtained, to have a dish of snow, and when some of the hot sugar is put on the snow, if it does not run into the snow, but cools in the form of wax on the surface of the snow, it is done enough to be put into tubs to drain. But when it is to be caked or stirred, it should be boiled until, when it is cooled on the snow, it will break like ice or glass." [13]

Soft sugar is a product that we have made in considerable quantities. Our procedure is: Boil to 227 degrees (20 to 22 degrees above the boiling point of water), cool to 160 degrees, and beat until thoroughly grained and fairly cool. The beating is a tedious process when done with a spoon or paddle. It may take as much as eight or ten minutes for a batch. Soft sugar can vary in degrees of stiffness, and for each degree higher the syrup boils, the sugar becomes that much stiffer.

After the beating has gone on for some time, clouds of whitish crystals begin to form in the batch. There is little danger, as with hard sugars, of sudden stiffening. Cooked to this low temperature and extensively cooled, the process of crystallization is a slow one. After the crystals begin to appear it is often possible to go on beating for three or four minutes. The longer the beating, the whiter the product and the creamier its texture. Also, the cooler the mixture becomes (and the beating helps to cool it) the more chance the sugar will retain the poured surface. If poured too hot, the center of the top often caves in. A way to remedy this is to fill the container only partly full at first, and later, from another kettle, finish to the top.

When crystallization has brought the batch to the consistency of medium-thick cream, it is poured into glass or tin containers. At the end of half an hour the sugar has cooled and is firm in the container, yet can be spooned out or spread on bread like thick honey or peanut butter. If

stored in a cool, dry place, with only a paper cover, this soft
sugar will retain its texture for weeks or months. In warm
damp weather some syrup may separate from the sugar and
form a film on the top of the container. If exposed to the air
in such weather, mold may form on top of the soft sugar as
it does on jams or jellies. As this sugar is fairly moist, and
therefore does not keep easily, we make it up only on order.

Another soft spread can be made that is finer grained than
the soft sugar and is called "maple butter." For this, syrup
is brought to 18 or 20 degrees above the boiling point of
water, then cooled almost to room temperature before it is
stirred. When the sugar is quite cool and crystallization has
commenced, it can be poured into containers.

Another important line of maple products is made by adding flavoring—butter, milk, cream, salt, nuts, or various other
ingredients—to maple syrup and thereby producing maple
fudge and maple panocha. There is always a good market for
such confections, but it is not sugar making. It takes one into
the confectionery field where special taxation and factory
inspection remove it from among the homecrafts.

"Maple sugar is peculiarly an American product," said
John Burroughs,[14] and as such, unadorned and unadulter-
ated, fills a niche of its own. It is a simple, unrefined concoction and can be made by any housewife in any kitchen in
the land. Syrup and sugar can be used in endless ways to add
to the variety of flavors in the menu. It can be used not only
in the proverbial way, on waffles and pancakes, but can serve
to sweeten custards, puddings, pies, baked beans, or pickles.
Both maple sugar and syrup are far superior to white when
used on the morning cereal, with or without fruit. As a sauce,
or sprinkled over ice cream and puddings, it is unexcelled.
It also gives a pleasant flavor when beaten into ice-cold milk.

In the way of suggestion we include in the back of this
volume a few recipes using maple sugar or syrup. There are
various grades and varieties of maple sugar, but the recognized color and flavor are unmistakable. An 1851 traveler
in North America writes, "It is generally preferred of a
brown, and by many of a dark-brown colour, because of the

rich maple flavour it possesses—a flavour which, though novel to a stranger, soon becomes very much relished." [15] Since the improved modern methods of boiling sap have been introduced, the sugar has gained in delicacy of color and also delicacy of flavor. This is not always appreciated by those accustomed to the old-time "tang."

The pages of an early magazine, *Garden and Forest,* were open to a controversy on the qualities of the "tasty" and the "tasteless" sugar. An anonymous writer in the May 3, 1893, issue rants in testy fashion against the new-fangled methods of boiling that cause the sugar to lose all the flavor. "I wish to defend the city people of the imputation of complete ignorance. . . . They do not want the kind of pure maple-sugar that is white. . . . They like the flavor of the maple, and they are perfectly right in objecting to too much refinement of the article. . . . I wonder whether the expert sugar-makers up in Vermont are as well advised about the business as they suppose themselves to be. . . . If the people of our cities want the maple flavor, why should they not have it in proper measure, since it is in the trees? If sugar is wanted that is simply sweet, we can get it much cheaper from cane or beets." Mr. Plumb, in the March 7, 1894, issue, says, "It does seem singular that the market should prefer the sugar on the basis of color rather than quality. . . . Are light-colored, flavorless sugar and syrup preferred because they are fashionable, or is our sense of taste becoming more refined?" That is the point underlined by Mr. Hills on March 28: "The modern palate delights in delicate as distinguished from pronounced flavors. We used to prefer mother's butter, and we are apt to look back to it as the acme of perfection. If it were now placed beside the creamery butter, which we then would have thought flat and which we now admire, it would often be found possessing too strong an aroma."

In the judgment of Mr. Schuyler Matthews, "the sugar made by the old-fashioned, boiling-down method possesses the highest and best flavor; but in the market the super-refined, lighter-colored sugar made by the patent evaporators is of course considered much finer, and brings a higher price." [16] On the presumption that what one wants one is willing to pay more for, shrewd farmers have been known to charge accordingly. The story came our way of the city buyer who approached a Vermont farmer for a gallon of syrup and insisted he get the best. He said, "I don't want any of that light-colored stuff. You can't fool me. I want the good old dark maple syrup." "Well," said the farmer, "I have a little of that left but I keep it for our own use. It's not for sale." "Oh, I'll pay well," replied the city man, "I know the real thing is worth it." "It costs more, you know," said the farmer, wondering how high he could peg the price. "That's all right with me," and off walked the city man happily with a gallon under his arm of Grade B syrup that the farmer kept for his own use—usually for cooking.

As with syrup, so with sugar. "No product of the farm can vary more in quality than sugar as made by different men," says E. A. Fisk. "Like the human race, it is of all shades of color, and I think that this is one of the cases in which prejudice against color is justifiable." [17]

It is all a matter of taste. Duhamel, the eighteenth-century French botanist, came close to a fair description of a good sugar in his treatise on trees. "For the maple sugar to be good, it should be hard, of a brownish color; it should also be somewhat transparent, of a delicate odor, and very sweet on the tongue." [18]

CHAPTER NINE

Marketing Maple Products

"*The manufacturing of maple sugar is an article of great importance to the state. Perhaps two-thirds of the families are engaged in this business in the spring, and they make more sugar than is used among the people. Considerable quantities are carried to the shop-keepers; which always finds a ready sale, and good pay.*"

Samuel Williams, A Natural and Civil History of Vermont, *1794*.

"*Pure maple sugar will always command a market abroad, if we choose to part with the article.*"

Walton's Vermont Register and Farmer's Almanac, *1847*.

"*The sugar product of Vermont is so much sought for by speculators that the price of a good article has been on the increase for the past few years, and I think that our interest and the interest of the next generation requires us to be careful of the sugar maple, for it has been proven that there is no better place than our state to make maple sugar and syrup, and we are going to have the whole world for a market.*"

Lyman Newton, Vermont Agricultural Report, *1886*.

"*We have no reason to fear an overproduction of extra maple syrup and sugar, for the demand for such goods has and always will keep pace with the supply.*"

L. R. Tabor, Vermont Agricultural Report, *1892*.

IF YOU build a better mousetrap, the world will beat a pathway to your door. New England, and particularly Vermont, has a maple mousetrap planted right in the front yard and buyers come from near and far, unurged, to purchase from it.

Maple sugar and syrup are unique products, made in small amounts on a small portion of the globe. They cannot be duplicated elsewhere, any more than bananas can be made to grow in Greenland. Maple syrup and sugar spell New England, and the Vermont label seems to be the closest linked to it in people's minds. The product practically sells itself. The market is all but guaranteed.

Maintenance of quality, of course, is a necessary factor in the matter. As A. M. Foster says in the *14th Vermont Agricultural Report*,[1] "I don't know as I can tell you how to market maple sugar. The first thing I do is to make it just as good as I know how. . . . Have a standard and keep right up to it—that is the way to keep customers." Owing to the weather and to runs of sap, it is all but impossible for the farmer to turn out a grade of syrup uniform in color and flavor, but it is possible to strive for quality under given conditions.

The product not only must be good but must be packaged to the public taste. In olden times the product as well as the package differed considerably from that of today. Says Hiram Cutting in 1886, "The demand of the market changes from year to year. Ten years ago and earlier stirred sugars were in best demand; then tubs and caked sugar; now sugar in tin pails and airtight tin cans. What the next fashion will be no one can tell. It is best to put it up in such a way as to command the quickest sales and fullest prices." [2] Moses Mather, in 1823, says, "About three-fourths of my sugar is stirred off dry and packed into dry casks." [3] In 1884 Hough writes, "Most of the sugar is cast in 2 and 4 pound bricks and packed in boxes. Some of the sirup is shipped in 15 and 20 gallon kegs. The greater portion, however, is put into five-gallon tin cans, cased with wood, and in these packages shipped all over the world." [4] In the same year the *Vermont Agricultural Report* states that Mr. Chester Thomas "puts most of his sugar in 25 pound cans for local demand." [5] That is quite a size for a modern refrigerator. In 1886 Lyman Newton says, "I have learned that small packages generally sell the best," and then proceeds to recommend "those containing from ten to thirty pounds finding the quickest market." [6] Today ten-pound cans of sugar are considered huge and quite unmarketable, and even five-pound cans are looked at askance. Pound cakes are regarded as enormous, and most sales are of quarter and half-pound boxes.

Syrup, which used to sell by the gallon can, is now most popular in quart size, and a large chain grocery store stocks only one-half-pint bottle of maple syrup. People seem to grudge the room to a can of any size. The producer must accommodate himself to the customers' shrunken storage space and smaller families.

Before 1850 sugar was the most marketable maple product, all but a small percentage being sold in wooden tubs. The switch to selling syrup occurred about the time that cane began to undersell maple sugar. Almost a hundred years later, in 1948, the position was completely reversed, around 97 per cent of the total crop being sold as syrup. An important bulletin written by John A. Hitchcock in 1928 [7] states that "practically all of the United States crop entering the wholesale trade leaves the farm as syrup. . . . Establishment on the part of the wholesalers of the practice of furnishing their producers with steel drums in which to ship their syrup has considerably hastened the passing of the sugar tub in Vermont."

Mention of the wholesaler's barrels brings up the question of the proportions sold retail and wholesale. It varies, of course, with the crop. In 1946 and 1947 the bulk buyers got very little as the crop was small, demand keen, and most of the syrup was sold straight from the farms to consumers. A wholesaler of our acquaintance estimates that "in the years previous to 1943 approximately one-half of the maple syrup crop was sold in bulk" and that from 1943 to date (1948) "not over ten percent of that produced in the United States was sold in drums." As the wholesalers have continued to market sugar and syrup, the inference is that Canada now supplies the bulk demands.

On the whole, syrup of the lower grades go to the bulk buyers who in turn blend them for popularly priced syrups, or sell them to tobacco or whisky manufacturers. The better syrup is sold on roadside stands by the producers directly to consumer or by mail to an established list. In the old days, sugar makers kept careful lists of mail customers, and the lists were often sold with the sugar bush when it changed hands. It is still a common practice in Vermont in buying a farm also to acquire the list of regular sugar customers.

There is little sales appeal to the bulky gallon tin, or even to the smaller cans, though brightly colored lithographed models have lately come on the market. In any case it enhances any product for the quality to be seen, so glass is being used more and more widely for maple syrup. Glass is cheaper and comes in an endless variety of shapes and sizes, allowing the ingenuity and artistry of the producer or packer to express itself. A little detail or quirk of packing often makes the difference between a sale and no sale. C. J. Bell, in 1897, even put his distinctive mark on the crate in which he shipped his syrup cans. "Anybody can make a tasty package out of thin lumber, basswood or spruce, for a case for the pails, and then have your pails labeled, and it will all help to sell your goods. I sometimes have customers for two or three gallons, and in such instances I put a handle on their cases. For these handles I use a maple twig and turn the handle up above the case a little. That little maple handle has done a good deal in the way of selling sugar for me." [8]

A gallon of maple syrup weighing eleven pounds produces eight pounds or a little less of sugar. By passing the syrup through this extra process and by packaging the product attractively, one can extend the market and increase returns from the bulk product, which is syrup.

To refer to our own experience, it takes five of us a week, on the average, to make one hundred gallons of syrup. It takes two of us ten half days to turn this hundred gallons into sugar and probably ten full days to pack and ship the sugar. Thus the sugar operation takes somewhat more than half the labor time that the syrup operation requires. In several of its phases it also requires greater judgment and skill. The syrup in the form of sugar, however, sells for about double the sale price of the syrup, thus practically doubling the gross return from the cash crop with no considerable increase in outlay aside from the additional labor power put into the sugar-making process.

Perhaps the reader will pardon us at this point for detailing our own experience in packaging and selling maple syrup and sugar. We had taken the first two steps toward making a cash income from maple. We had learned to convert sap into syrup and syrup into sugar. The syrup and sugar still had to be marketed.

Most of the neighbors put their syrup into steel barrels and sold it at company-fixed prices the first week in May. That practice brought ready cash, but the price level was lower than at any other time of the year, and it was the companies that converted the syrup into sugar that was sold at a gross price double or treble that of the syrup they bought.

Two syrup producers a few miles away from us had decided to break into the sugar-making business. They bought syrup from neighbors, hired some help, and began the manufacture and sale of maple cream in special shapes and fancy packs. The market was expanding rapidly at the time and both of the producers were making a success of their venture. They had stands of their own along two main highways. They also sold their products to other roadstands and to stores and gift shops within a radius of fifty miles.

We discussed the possibility of paralleling their efforts, but decided against it. The moment we went outside to buy syrup we would be compelled to hire help in order to convert it into sugar. Then, having turned out the sugar it would have been necessary to develop a marketing organization. The result would have been a small-scale factory with its distribution problems. We would have been in business up to our eyes and might as well have stayed in the city. If successful, the business would have made money. Successful or unsuccessful, it would have devoured our time and energy and thus would have consumed our leisure and contravened the basic purpose of our enterprise. We decided to keep our maple industry a home craft.

Was there not some middle way between selling syrup wholesale on one hand and setting up a factory on the other? We set out to find it.

We had learned to make syrup and sugar as good as or a little better than that of the average producer. How could we be sure of a market and at the same time a market on a scale small enough to use up our own syrup crop and no more?

We decided that the answer lay in unique packaging. If we could turn out a product a little different from any other, a bit more tasteful, more striking, and more compelling, we were confident that we could market our relatively small amount of syrup and sugar, stop producing for that year, and get back into the market again when the new crop was made. We needed a striking package for syrup and more than a few for sugar.

By chance we picked up a glass bottle shaped like a prim New England matron. We had a large number made up specially for us. These bottles held a little over a pint. We filled them with our best syrup, corked, capped, and labeled them, and took them to roadstands and shops nearby. They sold well, although the price of the container and the type of packaging put it into the expensive gift class. Apparently there was a demand for the item, especially around Christmas, with a red sealing-wax cap on the lady and a red ribbon round her neck holding a sprig of holly or evergreen. We have since had them decorated still further by painting their faces and dresses. We gave them the trade name of *Sweet Old Ladies,* and got double the gallon price for our syrup in this fancy container. The New York market spotted them and for one year we allowed ourselves to be pushed around by a large department store, which swamped us with orders.

Eventually we decided this was not to our liking and *Sweet Old Ladies* are now for sale in small quantities at a few quality shops.

Maple-sugar packaging at that time was rather standardized—in pound cakes and in 4-, 6-, 8-, 12-, and 16-ounce paper boxes. Only a few sugar shapes were used, mostly leaves and hearts, and they were packed in brown-paper candy cups, duplicating the brown of the maple sugar. The boxes were drab brown or white. There was no particular merchandising appeal. People who wanted sugar bought it regardless of the wrapping.

We decided to venture on various innovations. We would pack in candy cups of various colors, and the liveliest colors we could procure. The light brown of the sugar is rather neutral and combines well with most bright colors. The step caught on at once and was gradually adopted by several of the big sugar-making companies.

But it was not enough to have bright colors. We decided to use a wider variety of shapes to attract attention and interest. There were manifold candy forms available on the market, but few we had ever seen used. We ordered a few of each that seemed to offer some possibilities for development, then sat down to play with them. A man, rabbits, daisies, trees, stars—of course, *Little Man in the Woods*. And so he was packed in picture form—rabbits in brown candy cups, daisies in bright orange, trees in green, and stars in blue. The perspective was poor—daisies almost as big as rabbits, little trees and big stars, but the effect was good, and they were fun to make up. *Starry Night* came next, *Woodland Glade,* and *Three Rabbits Out Late*. We put a log-cabin form in red, with red and blue block letters beneath, and had *Little Red Schoolhouse. A Young Man's Fancy* went romantic in pink hearts and blue flowers; *Pigs in Clover* all in kelly green. We saw there were endless possibilities and we kept working out pictures till we had close to two dozen titles. Thus was the idea of *Picture Packs* born.

Our first attempts at packing were all in squarish four-ounce boxes. As we were led further afield in our pattern making and playing with colors, we needed more scope and larger boxes for our *Moonlight and Roses, Country Gentleman, Deep Sea, Hearts Are Trumps,* and *The Three Bears.* We had eight-ounce boxes made up with transparent covers. Many customers said, "They're like samplers. I'm going to hang them on the wall. They're too pretty to eat." The boxes stood out noticeably among the sugar displays on the road-stands; it was not long before we were selling as many as we cared to make and were turning down orders.

Heretofore, the fancy maple shapes had been packed formally—for example, all hearts in a box—or else had been packed in a geometric pattern, with a centerpiece of a maple leaf, around which hearts were grouped. Such packs contained no element of imagination. It was not long before the new possibilities our *Picture Packs* opened up were utilized and copied in modified form by several of the sugar-packing companies. However, their stocks of forms were necessarily large and mostly of one set kind. Their adaptations had to be cumbersome at best, and we were quite willing to keep always a few jumps ahead of them. For instance, at Christmastime, when 40 per cent of the candy supply in the United States is sold, we made up special packs—*Jingle Bells, Silent Night, Jolly Old St. Nick.*

Up to this point we had not packed pound boxes, though there were requests for a large-sized gift box. As long as we were in the gift market we decided to do a superlative job, so we had a wooden pound box made up of California redwood. We would have preferred a Vermont wood, but basswood (about the best for the purpose) would have needed trim, or coloring or finishing, and looked too raw, while the redwood made a soft-hued beautiful container. The box was sturdy as well as attractive, and wrapped in corrugated paper has been sent undamaged through the mails to nearly all parts of the world. With two layers of colored *Picture Packs* inside, this package was an instant success.

Something less ornate was now called for, and something old-fashioned. We would make up the good old-time maple-sugar blocks of darker sugar. We blended various grades of syrup and produced a rich golden-brown cake, wrapped it in cellophane, and called it a *Gold Brick*. We made these in pound and half-pound sizes. Countless numbers of these have been shipped abroad to ease the sugar famine there, and even in the United States, during the wartime sugar shortage, veritable hodsful of *Bricks* were distributed over the country-side. We recommend that *Gold Bricks*, scraped onto waffles or pancakes with a sharp knife, make the baked batter less soggy than when drenched with syrup. The cakes can also be melted down with a little boiling water to make hot syrup. The half-pound brick, with a pint tin of syrup, we packed in a wooden chalkbox with sliding cover and sent out labeled "Maple Messenger." It served as a comprehensive gift and a sturdy, mailable sample.

When we first began making sugar, we found that the usual small unit was a round scalloped patty-cake or a small rectangular block, selling for five or ten cents apiece. We put sticks in some of our larger rubber forms and there were lollipops—of trees, men, bears, pigs, leaves, cabins. No one, so far as we know, had made lollipops before, and no one has made them since we put them on the market. These lollipops were sure sellers to children, so we had to fill a large demand. The largest department store in the world (R. H. Macy & Company, New York City) gave us an order for them so huge that we filed it away as a curiosity. We never dreamed of filling it.

Finally, we developed one package made almost entirely from local materials. "Why," we asked ourselves, "should we go to Boston or New York for all our sugar containers? Why not use something right off the place?" We had seen mention in our researches of the birchbark containers or *Mokuks* that the Indians made for their finished sugar. We decided we would make Indian *Mokuks*. We cut cross sections half an inch thick from a softwood trunk or branch two inches in diameter, stripped thin layers of bark from the white birch, cut 6-by-10-inch rectangles of the best bark, wrapped it round the cross section, fastened it in place with two small tacks, and thus had cylinders of white birchbark about two inches in diameter and five to six inches high. We filled the birch *Mokuk* with assorted small sugar shapes, wrapped the whole in cellophane, and fastened it at the top with bright red florist's cherries. The package is rustic in appearance and tourists like it (some even finding it "an excellent imitation of birchbark"). They call them "little logs" or "loglets" or "firecrackers," but in memory of the Indians we call them *Mokuks.*

One further point, though slight, is the matter of labels. These should harmonize with the package and lend color or distinction as well as contain the necessary data for identifying product and producer.

There are two more maple products made on farms, neither of which we have manufactured. One is maple vinegar. This is made of sap run at the end of the season and was used in many households in the old days. Here is one way it was made: "Boil down three pails of sap into one, adding a little yeast when the liquid is milk-warm. Your barrel when full should set in some sunny place with a piece of glass over the bung-hole: the addition of a gallon of whiskey to the barrel will much improve the strength of the vinegar." [9]

The other maple product is sap beer. "Take one pound of good hops, put them in a clean barrel, and take it to the orchard; fill the barrel with sap and set it away for use; in about two weeks it will be fit for drinking and will remain good till June." [10] A "summer beer" is made by taking "four quarts of Molasses, half a pint of yeast, and a spoonful of race ginger; put these into your vessel, and pour on them two gallons of scalding hot water, shake them well till it ferments; and add thirteen gallons of cold water; before it is quite full put in your yeast to work it; the next day you have agreeable wholesome small beer, that will not fill with wind as that which is brewed from malt or bran, and it will keep good till it is all drank out." [11] Michaux also gives his recipe for making "Maple-Beer": "Upon four gallons of boiling water, pour one quart of Maple Molasses; add a little yeast or leaven to excite the fermentation. and a spoonful of the essence of spruce: a very pleasant and salutary drink is thus obtained." [12]

Personally, we feel with Benjamin Rush, who wrote in 1791, "The sap of the Maple is capable of affording a spirit, but we hope this precious juice will never be prostituted by our citizens to this ignoble purpose." [13] Thomas Jefferson, in a letter to George Washington in the same year, gives "flattering calculations" anent the "sugar-maple tree" and then remarks, thankfully, "that less profit is made by converting the juice into spirit than into sugar." [14] The Reverend Nathan Perkins, on a trip through Vermont in 1789, held up his hands in holy horror at the perversion of sweet syrup into devilish drink. "Brook-water is my chief drink," he maintains. "The maple cyder is horrible stuff." [15]

Given the syrup and sugar, packaged and ready for sale, what was the most economical and efficient way to get it to the market? For a time we took one day each week, during the tourist season, filled our pickup truck with syrup bottles and sugar boxes, and went the rounds of the roadstands. As soon as our products became known we had no difficulty in disposing of all the syrup and sugar that we cared to put up. However, the peddling consumed a lot of time.

The owner of two nearby roadstands was developing a statewide circuit over which he went regularly, delivering maple products. He had noted our packages on the stands and came to see if he could do business with us. We agreed to let him handle our products, and until World War II cut off the gasoline supply in 1941, and tourists stands all but shut up, we made and packed the sugar that he called for and distributed. Other sugar jobbers have handled our products at times, but on the whole we can dispose of our entire output without intermediaries.

Roadstand dealers buy from the producers at a third off. For an item selling at one dollar they pay sixty-five cents. The jobber-distributor takes ten to fifteen cents on a dollar package. That leaves the producer fifty or fifty-five cents on a dollar item.

We often talked over the possibility of direct advertising

and a mail-order business, but our volume of production was such that we were afraid that we would outsell ourselves. One advertising manager of a nationally known home magazine that sent us rates, and to whom we replied as above, wrote and said, "I want to thank you for your letter of April 9th in which you very frankly said that you felt *House and Garden* would bring you too many returns. This is the first time we have ever had a letter of this sort." At about this time, with the war sugar shortage, the demand for maple products rose so steeply that we could sell our output almost as fast as we could make it, and any thought of markets was how to keep them within bounds, and not how to increase them. We supplied three or four shops in different parts of the country, sold syrup and sugar to mail-order customers, and sold a fair amount to travelers who happened along the back road on which we live. We also took our wares to the local fairs each year and sold our goods there personally.

Other things being equal, direct marketing is far and away the most advantageous. The income, of course, is larger. But principally, the personal contact, whether by correspondence or in person, is pleasant; we have many friends throughout the country made through our marketing of maple sweets. We have a card list of several hundred past customers. Once a year, in April or May, we send them a simple announcement of the new syrup crop, including a list of sugar packs and prices. That announcement sells as much syrup as we desire to part with, as well as some sugar.

Thus far our household production-unit project has worked out satisfactorily. We have sold enough to provide a minimum cash income, have done the necessary work in less than half of our time, and thus have enjoyed a wide margin of leisure, on top of the thorough enjoyment that always comes from doing a workmanlike job.

Marketing the product that we ourselves gathered and converted proved to be of almost as much interest as the rest of the process. It completed the stages of sap to syrup to sugar to consumer, and rounded out the whole procedure.

"In conclusion, we remark that the production of maple

sugar and sirup is among the agricultural industries admitting of large development within the districts favored by nature with the conditions requisite for success. The maple grove that is planted by a young man may be enjoyed by him through more than half of an ordinary lifetime. With proper care it will perpetuate itself through a long course of years, and for aught we know (if the young growth is protected) forever. It will occupy broken grounds that could not otherwise be cultivated, and the timber, when taken out at greatest maturity, has a value which is gaining every year, aside from the annual revenue to be derived from the sap. The maple adorns and beautifies perhaps more than any other of our native forest trees. The demand for pure, cleanly and carefully made maple sugar and sirup is increasing every year, as the articles become better known, and there is scarcely a possibility of overstocking the markets. The sugar season comes at a time when farm labor is least employed, and the occupation presents amenities beyond those which any other form of farm labor can afford." [16]

PART III

A Living from Maple

CHAPTER TEN

Pioneers, O Pioneers!

"It is one of the noblest employments to assist nature in her bountiful productions. Instead of being ashamed of their employment, our laborious farmers shall, as a great writer says 'toss about their dung with an air of majesty.'"

Samuel Deane, The New-England Farmer, *1790.*

"Agriculture is confessedly the most useful of all the Arts. Bodily health and activity of mind are eminently promoted by the Exertions it requires. It is better calculated than other Occupations for preserving the simplicity of manners, and purity of morals, which constitute the surest Basis of a prosperous Tranquillity in States."

J. P. Bardley, Essays and Notes on Husbandry, *1801.*

"I write more particularly for those who have not been brought up as farmers—for that numerous body of patient toilers in city, town, and

209

village, who, like myself, have struggled on from year to year, anxious to break away from the bondage of the desk, the counter, or the workshop, to realize in the country even a moderate income, so that it be a sure one. Many such are constantly looking round in this direction for something which, with less mental toil and anxiety, will provide a maintenance for a growing family, and afford a refuge for advancing age —some safe and quiet harbor, sheltered from the constantly recurring monetary and political convulsions which in this country so suddenly reduce men to poverty. But these inquirers find no experienced pioneers to lead the way, and they turn back upon themselves, too fearful to go forward alone."

> *Anonymous,* Ten Acres Enough: A Practical Experience, Showing How a Very Small Farm May be Made to Keep a Very Large Family with Extensive and Profitable Experience, *1864.*

THE proposition we are advancing in this book is based on experience in our locality and in one industry. But its application is as far-reaching as the oft-repeated conversion of villages into cities, of farm operators into factory hands and tenement dwellers—with the inevitable reaction of urbanites toward a freer life in the countryside.

"A place in the country" has beckoned city folk ever since there were cities. Nature lovers wanted it for fresh air, sunshine, gardening, hiking. Home lovers wanted it to bring up children away from dust, smoke, noise. Lovers of solitude wanted it to "get away from it all." Many and many a one repeats the proverb, "Man made the town, but God made the country."

Several different ways were found to answer this urge for country living. The rich had their country houses as well as their town houses; their country clubs as well as their city clubs. Schoolteachers and other professionals with regular periods of leisure built summer homes in the mountains, on the plains and deserts, along rivers, lake shores, and seacoasts. Nature lovers hiked to the country on holidays and week ends. Surburbanites commuted from small communities around railroad stations, or along good roads. Old folks with pensions or a property income tucked themselves away on the outskirts of some village. A few hardy souls, still young, vigorous, and enthusiastic, thumbed their noses at the city and all its works, took their courage in their hands, moved out bag and baggage and went to live year round in the country.

Up our way, in southern Vermont, would-be country dwellers drift by in shoals during the open summer season. Latterly, they are coming also for winter sports. "This is the life!" they exclaim, sniffing the tangy mountain air and running their eyes enviously over the ranging hills. "You have this all year—just for the taking. How we wish we could live like this."

Time flies. Around September when the best weather of the year sets in, when the nights are snappy and the days golden and warm, when the mapled hills are a riot of burnished color, when flies and mosquitoes are a thing of past memory, the "summer people" are on the afternoon train or moving in traffic lines along auto-littered highways toward their cliff dwellings amid the turmoil, noise, and stench of the city. They have relished the full blaze of strident summer suns. They miss, however, the rich glory that autumn alone possesses. Nor do they ever feel that gripping of the heart that accompanies the first winter storm, swept down from arctic cold by a searing north wind. The cityite dabbling now and then in comfortable country living is a dilletante. He comes while the coming is easy, and slips away before ice and snow make the going hard. He samples daintily the dessert of country living, but misses the robust meal of the three seasons that precede and follow the lush summer. Each year he comes back for his pastry and sweets—eating them on a surfeited city stomach. If he would savor the true riches of country living he must follow the rugged path past autumn, across winter, and through spring. Then only does he know summer, not merely for itself, but for the contrast it makes with its fellow seasons.

Cityites go where their bread is buttered, where their jobs are, to the white-lighted regions where they make more and spend more. But do they keep more?

Country bread is also buttered. Both bread and butter may
be homemade, and much of their savor lies in joy that always
links effort and reward. Probably half of the folk who reluc-
tantly go back in the autumn to stuffy offices or sterile counting houses could stay in the country and live as well, minus
the frills and the thrills, as they do in cities. It takes initia-
tive; it takes gumption; it takes a certain amount of daring
to leave the rut and cut out a new path. In the old pioneering
days it took pluck to turn backs on Europe and come to
America, to say farewell to the East and to go on West. Once
in the city with its creature comforts and allurements it takes
backbone and fortitude to forsake all that the city has to offer
and chance it in new, untried rural surroundings.

The country-to-city and city-to-country movements seem to
go in cycles. At certain periods the flow from city to country
is stronger. Sometimes the country streams to the city. The
general movement from countryside to city has been going
on in Europe and America for many generations. Some observers feel that it reached its greatest momentum fifty years
ago. Since then business depressions and obliteration bomb-
ing have combined with good roads, speedy transportation,
and increased leisure to enhance the lure of the countryside.
Lewis Mumford tells about this movement in his *Culture of
Cities*.[1] It may be observed in the old world of Europe and
the new world of North America. It is only a few years since
New Englanders were mostly farmers and villagers, with only
a few towns and cities in their midst. Advertising, higher
education, jobs, the lure of city lights pulled young ambitious
country folk cityward. As lately as 1890, two people out of
three in the United States were still "rural," but in 1900 it
had dropped to three out of five, and in 1920 to one out of
two. New England, settled early, had moved much further
cityward. The census of 1940 showed one Vermonter in three
an urban dweller. In Connecticut, however, two out of three,
and in Massachusetts and Rhode Island, nine out of ten (89.4
per cent and 91.6 per cent) were urban.

Along with this growth of cities went the abandonment of
the countryside. Take our township of Jamaica, Vermont, as

an example. Back in 1840 Jamaica township had a population of 1,586. Fifty years later, in 1890, it was 1,074. In 1940,
there were only 567 people in Jamaica, or just over a third
of the 1840 population. The neighboring town of Stratton,
where Daniel Webster spoke to a gathering of 20,000 in 1840,
had a population of 302 in 1880. In 1930 the town listed 55
inhabitants. These figures can be duplicated in one rural area
after another, all over northeastern United States.

Take a walk across the countryside in our neighborhood.
You will see huge piles of rotting sawdust, slashed timber,
brush-covered mowings, run-down orchards, old cellar holes,
pastures grown up to merchantable timber. Nearly two centuries ago these lands were cleared by pioneers. Today the
forest has re-established itself.

This is not the place to urge the importance of the earth in
comparison with the pavement. The facts are plain enough.
Abandoned farms and deserted villages are danger signals.
From the land come food, the fibers for clothing, lumber, and
other building materials. Men still must live off the land even
though they spend their days perched high in office and apartment buildings. Where does the city dweller get his milk for
baby, his bananas for breakfast, his steak for dinner, his
woodpulp for comics, his leather for belts and shoes, his
mahogany for desks, and his sugar for coffee? These materials
are not produced in the city. They are processed and consumed there. The raw materials are all country produced.
Without the country the city would be nowhere. Without the
city the countryfolk could plod along as they did for millen-
niums before the cities came into being.

Is there any way out? Can the pavement pounder get his
feet on the land and keep them there? Sentiment and delight
in lovely scenery are admirable; it is all very well to cry "back
to the land," but can anyone make a living there? If the land
is so attractive and so secure, why have so many people left
it in recent years? And why do so many stay in the cities,
when once they get there?

Technically, the answer is simple. New lands in the Amer-
icas and Australasia, opened up by railroads and hard roads

and farmed by power machinery, have provided mankind with such a large and temporary increase in the supply of cereals, cotton, and timber that the food supply of a community can be provided by one able-bodied person out of five working the land and leaving the other four free to move cityward, perhaps even compelling them to go cityward.

How strong is that compulsion? As strong as the stimulated itch for things—more things, bigger things, grander and gaudier things. Once the commodity market is set up, it is the business of advertisers and salesmen to make the gadgets attractive. Buyers, to satisfy their acquisitive urge, need only one thing: money. Money is to be had in factory, office, and store, in exchange for labor power. The would-be buyer takes a job, rents an apartment or room, dons the badge of serfdom—the business suit—and enters the city treadmill. He has exchanged his contacts with Mother Earth, with sunshine, starlight, cloud-decked sky, wind, driving mist and pelting storm, the light-drenched days and the gorgeous, silent, limitless nights for the floors, ceilings, walls, elevators, subways, one-way streets, teeming intersections, and traffic lights of man-made metropoli.

Friday night brings the pay envelope or pay check. The landlord takes his share; a larger portion goes to the grocery store and the delicatessen. Street cars and telephones demand a cut, not to mention house-furnishing establishments, clothing stores, doctors, dentists, and undertakers. Besides that there are the incessant demands for hard and soft drinks, smokes, and an endless variety of shows to fritter away the off-hours. Come Monday or Tuesday, the money is all but gone, and the wage slave puts in another forty hours of time and energy on a routine, pointless, dead-end job that at best will yield him a bank account and two weeks of vacation freedom to match his fifty weeks of job serfdom, and at worst will force him to die in a flophouse, and leave his body in a potter's field. So the years pass over frustrating labor, specious pleasures, drugged boredom, and futile, purposeless old age. Once the city is entered, once its pattern of labor and spend are accepted, the average urbanite is like any ant in any anthill—a helpless creature of circumstances set up by landlord, merchant, factory owner, and banker, to snare the unwary, reduce them to dependence, and force them into a life of servitude in the impersonal mechanism of an acquisitive society.

Can the cityite escape? Even if he longs for dawn across the mountains and the smell of fresh air, has this victim of cave dwelling and pavement pounding half a chance to make a living back on the land? Has he the knowledge, the strength, the stamina to make the break and to survive such an ordeal? Or will he be hurled back, broken and defeated by the relentless nature forces that preside over life in the countryside?

Others have done it. Others are doing it all the time. Milton Wend has written a book on *How to Live in the Country Without Farming*,[2] giving a detailed description of various methods other than soil cultivation, of making a country living. Among many methods, Wend recommends the production of maple syrup and maple sugar. We have been trying out that method for more than a dozen years. This book is a report on possibilities and a record of progress. It is also a guide, designed for anyone who would like to do likewise.

Wend is not alone. Since Bolton Hall, almost half a century ago, published his *Three Acres and Liberty*,[3] the back-to-the-land movement has been gaining momentum in peacetime and losing it in wartime. Ralph Borsodi's *Flight from the City*,[4] Arthur E. Morgan's *The Small Community*,[5] Thomas Hewes's *Decentralize for Liberty*,[6] and Willis D. Nutting's *Reclamation of Independence*[7] are examples of a rapidly growing literature devoted to distributism or decentralism. There are many books by private individuals and pamphlets issued by the United States Department of Agriculture and the state agricultural colleges and experiment stations giving careful directions for various types of farming, gardening, building construction, craft work, and related subjects.

More specifically, there are many books and pamphlets now on the market telling in detail how individuals have succeeded in moving from city to country, with noteworthy advantage to themselves and their families. There is, for example, *The Have-More Plan* by C. and E. Robinson,[8] a detailed account of a city couple's successful tackling of country living in Noroton, Connecticut. W. M. Teller's book, *The Farm Primer*,[9] Teller's and Larson's *What is Farming?*,[10] *Success on the Small Farm* by Haydn S. Pearson,[11] *Pleasant Valley* by Louis Bromfield,[12] *This Country Life* by Samuel R. Ogden,[13] J. I. Rodale's book *Pay Dirt*,[14] F. H. Faulkner's *Plowman's Folly*[15]—all these record tried-and-tested experiments in living on the land and making a living off the land.

City dwellers who contemplate a plunge into country living should note several important differences between the two patterns. The city man must make money enough to pay rent, buy food and clothes, pay carfare, and meet the ceaseless demands of movie houses, soda fountains, restaurants, theaters, tobacco shops, and the like, to spend, spend, spend. The country dweller has to provide shelter, food, clothing, fuel, and implements for himself and his family. Most or all of these he can have in exchange for his own labor on his own land. He needs a small cash income out of which to pay taxes and to buy the products that he cannot easily produce at home, but the bulk of his real income will be the direct result of labor performed within the household. Roof repairs, a new woodshed, a sandbox and swing for the youngsters, stovewood and fireplace chunks from the woodlot, greens and winter roots from the garden, wild and cultivated berries and fruit, early and late flowers, a Christmas tree and cones from the sprucewoods—all these can be had for the making and the taking. The good earth with its fertility, its resources, and its eager response to cultivation and conservation holds out to all comers its horn of plenty—in exchange for forethought, planning, and well-directed labor.

The United States is a country occupied by a few ugly, dirty, noisy cities, but it still consists mostly of immense reaches of plains, valleys, and mountains. The choicest countryland is relatively high in price. But up our way hill land from which lumbermen have cut the timber can still be bought for a song, even in these days of inflated prices. What do we mean by a song? Two young folks from a distant part of the country journeyed to Vermont in 1943, liked our valley, picked out a piece of cut-over land off a town road, found an abandoned housesite and well on the land, bought seventy-five acres "more or less" for three hundred dollars, and settled down to build themselves a stone house. Where to live meanwhile? They got some rough lumber, built a tar-paper shack, fitted it up, and used it as shelter for themselves and their baby while they worked on the stone house. In the wintertime they cut some cordwood to sell in the village and in sugaring the man worked with a neighbor. This supplied their cash income. In the summer they kept a good garden, storing their root crops for winter use. A couple of goats supplied them with milk. Their clothes cost them little or nothing as they wore overalls and their own cast-offs. From well-to-do homes, college bred, this couple made a way for themselves in the wilderness.

Do we hear a chorus of commiserating "ohs" and "ahs" from city softies in their steam-heated apartments and air-conditioned offices, restaurants, and theaters? Well, think a moment. Are these young people, hewing out a home in the wilds, any better or worse off than our great-grandfathers and grandmothers in northeastern U.S.A.? We know what pioneer life contributed to the stamina of those folks in the early days. Does anyone question what steam heat, air conditioning, and food processing are doing to their descendants? Maybe these young people have found the only rational alternative to the devastating environment provided by the "biggest" and "richest" urban ant heaps.

Dare we pioneer? Dare we break away from a social pattern that all the best people endorse as the last word in human achievement? Dare we fly in the face of parental wishes, run the gantlet of neighborhood gossip, abandon the irresponsibility, boredom, ennui, and personal stagnation of life in an urban strait jacket for the responsibility, elbow room, and victory over environmental obstacles offered by the countryside?

Certainly in North America the answer lies almost wholly with ourselves. While most of the free land is gone, there is still plenty of cheap land in out-of-the-way places—farms with buildings on them that cost no more than low-priced or middle-priced pleasure cars; farms that, after a dozen years of well-directed labor, can be converted into admirable establishments for both children and adults, and that, during those dozen years, will give the entire family a more thoroughgoing education than the average higher educational institution can offer. Many who have pioneered during recent years can vouch for this.

Man has been pioneering ever since he began to use sticks and stones, build fires, weave fibers, shape clay, and smelt metals. In each generation there will be adventurous, determined, imaginative young people (and some not so young) who will count it their choicest privilege to leave the beaten path and blaze out new trails. It is of such stuff that old pasts become new futures.

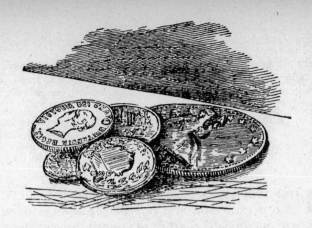

CHAPTER ELEVEN

The Money in Maple

"From the value of these trees, and the many uses to which their sap has been applied, the new settlers have learned to preserve them with as much care, as if they were apple, or other fruit trees. From the facility with which they may be cultivated, and the profit which can be had from them, it is plain, that a farmer could raise nothing on his farm with less labour, and nothing from which he could derive more emolument, than the sugar maple tree."

Agricola, American Museum, *October 1788.*

"It must appear obvious to every unprejudiced person that the sugar-maple is of undeniable value to the American agriculturalist. . . . The inhabitants of any other country upon earth, with equal opportunities and facilities, would make double, if not treble the quantity of sugar which those of America content themselves with manufacturing."

E. A. Talbot, Five Years Residence in the Canadas, *1824.*

"Probably there is no article of production or manufacture connected with farming less likely to be affected by stringency in the money market than good maple sugar. It contributes alike to the luxuries of the rich and the necessities of the poor. It adds very materially to the productive industry of the state, and may be made a constantly increasing source of wealth."

A. M. Foster, Report of Vermont Board of Agriculture, *1874.*

"Except the labor of the ordinary forces on the farm, at the most impracticable season for other farm-work, the outgoes are so small, that at least ninety percent is net income, earned, as it were, incidentally, while waiting for the frost to come out of the ground."

J. R. Dodge, Report of Commissioner of Agriculture for 1876.

MAPLE provides syrup and sugar for the household. It is also a cash crop and one of the sources of money income upon which thousands of country folk in the northeastern part of the United States rely. "The production of maple products has an important place in the future development of Vermont's agricultural program, especially on marginal farms where the land is ill suited to ordinary crop production. The sugar bush is usually located on land not adapted to cultivation, hence the better areas on such marginal farms can be otherwise employed and the total farm income becomes augmented. There are many such farms in Vermont which would hardly be worth cultivating were it not for the sugar money."[1] The income from maple varies slightly from year to year, with weather and economic cycles, but by and large, maple is money any time. Which reminds us of the story of the energetic though deluded Englishman who, finding sugaring so lucrative, stated that he, for one, was going to sugar the year round.

Thus far we have written about past and present ways of turning maple sap into syrup and sugar and of marketing these products. In this final section we want to broaden the discussion by relating maple production to the livelihood problems of a technical, mechanized age.

Modern social practices have done four things to the household. First, by converting the village into a city, they have replaced the personalized village neighborhood by an agglomeration of human beings, most of whose relations are as impersonal as those between passers-by on a busy street or fellow passengers in a bus or subway car. Second, they have stripped the household of many of its old-time tasks: the barnyard, the woodpile, food preservation, cooking, the work-shop, construction, the making of implements and utensils, the making of cloth and clothing, laundering, and transferred these and other activities to factories and stores. Third, they have taken adults out of the household into factories, stores, and offices and children into schools and playgrounds. Fourth, through organizing an extensive amusement industry, they have induced both adult and juvenile members of the house-hold to spend a great deal of their spare time away from home. Such changes have gone a long way toward destroying the villages of households and have done much to break up the family.

Those of us who regard the family as the building unit out of which the present-day community is constructed are deeply concerned, because we do not believe that a stable society can be established so long as the family-household units are themselves crumbling. Such an effort might be likened to the work of brickmasons, laying up a wall with bricks that crumble as they are laid in place.

Feeling a concern for social stability, we are impelled to seek out ways in which existing instabilities may be remedied. It is our conviction that this remedial social process must begin with the social building unit—the family in the house-hold. Beyond a rebuilt household lies the rebuilt neighbor-hood and the rebuilt community. For the moment we shall confine our attention to the household.

It is not enough to have the members of a family and a household feeling and thinking together. They should also act together. To achieve this result the household should be so related to its livelihood that all of its adult and semi-adult members can make a contribution to the common family needs and household tasks. Such possibilities exist outside the denser centers of population and in those productive activi-ties that offer a variety of occupations suited to the strength and experience of different age groups.

Our experience has convinced us that maple production is one of the means of family and household rehabilitation. It offers occupational variety and a modest source of cash income. Having written at some length about the methods of maple production and marketing, we now wish to call attention to its cash-income possibilities.

Maple production has had a curious history, which began, like so many farm practices, on the level of a use economy, but, unlike such agricultural operations as grain- and fruit-raising and the production of cane sugar, it has not fallen into the hands of big business. It still remains essentially a household industry.

American Indians produced maple syrup and sugar largely for use, though on occasion sugar cakes were employed by them as a medium of exchange. Early settlers, following this lead, tapped their hard maples, boiled the sap down to sugar, packed it in containers, and stored it away as their year's sugar supply. Surpluses, however, went to the store or trading post in exchange for hardware and other essentials, and maple sugar eventually became an object of trade in itself. "The farmers, after laying aside a sufficient store for their own consumption, sell the residue to the shop-keepers in the small towns of the neighborhood, at 8 cents a pound, by whom it is retailed at 11 cents." [2] As a news note in *The American Farmer* of November 18, 1828, it was mentioned that "Upwards of 300 barrels of Maple Sugar have been received in New York by the Canal, which has been sold at five cents a pound." The *American Agriculturalist* for October, 1844, quoted the *New York Sun* as stating that ten thousand hogsheads of maple sugar were sold annually in the city. It is therefore evident that by the middle of the century maple sugar was an article of commerce as well as an important element of food in a use economy.

The wide distribution of maple production is indicated by the census of 1850. In that year cane sugar was produced in nine states—Tennessee, Kentucky, South Carolina, Georgia, Florida, Alabama, Mississippi, Louisiana, and Texas. The total quantity produced was 247,577,000 pounds. At the same time, maple sugar was made in twenty-seven states, including all of the New England states, all of the Middle Atlantic states except Delaware, all of the southern states except Florida, Mississippi, and Texas, and all of the states as far west as Minnesota, Iowa, and Missouri. The total quantity of sugar produced, as reported by this census, was 34,253,436 pounds and of syrup, 12,700,534 gallons. These figures show that, with the exception of a few states where the hard maple does not thrive, farmers were making maple sugar all over the United States.

Small wonder that with (1) the all but universal demand for sugar, (2) the countrywide distribution of sugar maples and maple-sugar production, and (3) fortunes being made at that time in the cane-sugar industry, big business made repeated attempts to invade the maple-sugar field and monopolize it as it had already monopolized the cane-sugar industry. There were four possible points at which big business might have achieved its objective: (1) in making maple syrup; (2) in marketing maple syrup; (3) in converting maple syrup into sugar and marketing the product; and (4) in manufacturing the machinery needed in the maple industry. In practice the business interests succeeded only in controlling the manufacture and distribution of maple sugar and the manufacture of sugar and sugar tools and machinery.

At the point of initial production—that is, in the sugar bushes and sugarhouses—the maple industry has always been carried on in household units. With minor exceptions, it has never been conducted on a large scale, and it cannot be conducted as a large-scale industry so long as there are several tens of thousands of households continuing to operate it along its present lines.

Here is a typical case in our neighborhood. The household is made up of a man, his wife, and five children, the oldest a boy of fifteen. Sugartime comes in late February or early March. The snow is so deep in the woods that logging and wood cutting (the usual winter occupations) are difficult or impossible. In the homestead there is little to do beside the regular chores. The family has a sugar bush, a sugarhouse, 1,500 buckets, covers, and spouts, an evaporator, a gathering tank, a team of horses standing idle in the barn, a supply of sugar wood. Not a single cash outlay is involved in the entire sugar operation. School allows the children a three-week "sugaring vacation." The man and his family tap out. All gather. He boils and she puts up the syrup. In the course of five or six weeks, if weather is favorable, the household can produce 350 to 400 gallons of maple syrup. If the syrup is put into steel drums, provided by one of the companies that buy syrup, there is not a nickel of necessary cash outlay, unless there are replacement parts for worn-out equipment.

If this operation were put on a business basis, not only would insurance, depreciation, wages of management, and other overhead and operating costs be charged as part of the costs of operation, but the team and man would cost $10 a day at going rates, at least one helper would get $7 or $8 a day, and the wood for boiling would cost at least $10 per cord. For forty days of operation, including tapping out and washing up, the cash outlay would be: men and team $700, 20 cords of wood $200, plus operating and overhead costs. In short, a business concern, operating at a high level of efficiency, would be compelled to spend from $1,200 to $1,500 to produce the 350 or 400 gallons of syrup.

The household that we have described works for no wages, gets all the syrup for its own use that it wants, sells the balance, and has cash in pocket. Their only outlay is the time and energy of family and horses, otherwise more or less idle at this time of year. As Benjamin Rush wrote to Thomas Jefferson in his letter of August 19, 1791,[3] sugaring comes "in a season of the year in which nature provides no sustenance to man or beast. . . . The time required for the labour, if it deserves that name, is at a season when it is impossible for the farmer to employ himself in any species of agriculture." A writer in *The New England Farmer* for April 26, 1823, also decries the outlay and work involved for a farmer in sugaring. "The trees would yield 200 pounds of sugar an acre, deducting only a trifle, not so much for labor as for a short attention in the leisure month of February."

In our valley in the 1947 season, five of the eleven sugar bushes were operated. The average number of buckets hung was around 1,800. Two of the five bushes hired wage labor.

One of the two hired one man for part time. There are perhaps seven thousand operating sugar bushes in the state of Vermont, the great majority run on the household basis, with little or no hired labor.

We know that there are sugar outfits that hang from five to ten thousand buckets and make it pay. One near us, which taps three large bushes, is operated by a trained engineer, who acts as manager of the enterprise. If he charged for his services at the going wages of management, he would be in the red. Another large enterprise, which operates a mill, hangs seven thousand buckets and, when sap is running, transfers personnel from mill to sugar bush for the duration of the run. Such instances are highly exceptional, however.

If big business could not enter the maple-sugar industry profitably at the point of production, it could buy the syrup directly and immediately from the farmers who produced it. The business was well organized, with half a dozen companies doing most of the buying. A sale price was fixed and drums distributed to the farmers at the beginning of the season. The farmers filled the drums and hauled them to designated assembly points. There a company agent graded and weighed the syrup and handed the farmer a check.

There is a fourth way in which business might participate in the sugar industry—by the manufacture and sale of the needed tools and equipment. With the exception of evaporators and storage tanks, there is little high-cost equipment used in sugaring. The sugar tool manufacturers buy sap buckets ready-made from bucket factories. Sugar tools have a relatively long life and replacements are infrequent. In general, the manufacture and sale of sugar equipment are still conducted on a small scale.

Organized business has been unable to take over the maple industry. The co-operative movement has been equally unsuccessful, except in some parts of Canada. A wide organization for maple producers has been proposed, such as those formed by the large orange, apple, raisin, and nut growers on the West Coast.[4] This would be a central clearinghouse to which small growers would belong and where buying, selling, packaging, and advertising would be centralized and expedited. This would leave small producers and families still in the field but would co-ordinate and consolidate their powers. Whether sugar makers would take to such an organization is a matter of question. F. L. Allen, in the 22nd *Annual Report of the Vermont Maple Sugar Makers' Association,* says, "By our unorganized, haphazard, every-man-for-himself methods, the pure maple products on the general market are as varied as the methods of the different producers, coupled with changing weather conditions, can make them. . . . I believe the time has come for a cooperative organization for the production, standardizing, grading and marketing our maple products." [5] The Vermont Maple Sugar Makers' Association, organized in 1893, has a considerable membership among maple producers and busies itself with pricing, marketing, and state legislation involving the production and sale of maple sugar and syrup. A similar association in New Hampshire also promotes the maple industry. Such associations would be eminently useful for producers and could be educational for consumers.

We went to Vermont strongly predisposed toward co-operation, and we are trying to operate our own plant co-operatively. It is the hard way. Hill dwellers are rugged individualists, mistrustful, cautious, and shrewd. Some day we hope to have our enterprise on a full co-operative basis. Today it is only partly so. Benjamin Rush hoped for co-operative sugaring plants as long ago as 1792, when he wrote, "It has been a subject of inquiry whether the maple sugar might not be improved in its quality and increased in its quantity by the establishment of boiling houses in the sugar maple country to be conducted by *associated* labour. From the scattered situation of the trees, the difficulty of carrying the sap to a great distance, and from the many expenses which must accrue from supporting labourers and horses in the woods in a season of the year in which nature affords no sustenance to man or beast, I am disposed to believe that the most productive medium both in quantity and profit of obtaining this sugar will be by the labour of private families." [6]

A stand of hard maple, even if located in the backwoods of northeastern United States, will yield the owner-operator a living. This has been the case for at least 150 years. It is still true today. Maple alone among the trees can be used as firewood, as logs, and as sweetener.

Hard-maple logs are always salable. There have been times in recent years when soft maple and beech logs could find no market. To our knowledge this has never been true of hard maple. Whether made into flooring, furniture, or some more specialized product, hard maple usually tops the list of logs that millmen buy. With white oak, yellow birch, and white ash, hard maple usually commands higher prices per log foot than any of our other northern hardwoods. Consequently, the owner of a hard-maple stand, who is planning to establish a sugar bush, can count on selling any marketable logs that may result from his thinning or culling operations.

The same holds true for cordwood. In terms of available heat units, hard maple ranks close to yellow birch, white oak, and beech. Every cordwood market welcomes hard maple. In these days of diminishing forests and widespread building of fireplaces, hard maple is a much sought-after fuel. Thinnings and cullings from a hard-maple forest, that will not make logs, will make firewood. And unless the wood is rotten, limbs down to three inches in diameter are as acceptable as trunkwood. Since hard-maple trees, under favorable circumstances, quite commonly attain a height of seventy to eighty feet and a total limb spread up to fifty feet, a good-sized tree will frequently yield more than a cord of marketable wood, in addition to the logs it contains.

We have no way of estimating the annual value of hard-maple logs and cordwood marketed in the United States, but it totals up to a tidy sum. In the field of maple-syrup and sugar production, however, the facts are more readily available. Census Bureau officials, the Federal Department of Agriculture, and state agricultural departments have been tabulating and publishing information on the production and sale of syrup and sugar for almost a century. The last reports of cash receipts of United States farmers on their total syrup and sugar crop were between eight and ten million dollars.

UNITED STATES MAPLE PRODUCTION

	Maple Sugar (thousand pounds)	Maple Syrup (thousand gallons)	Index of Total Production
1860	40,120	1,597	100
1870	28,444	921	68
1880	36,576	1,796	96
1890	32,953	2,258	96
1900	11,929	2,057	54
1910	14,060	4,106	89
1920	9,692	3,508	71
1930	2,134	3,712	62
1940	434	2,597	40
1948	253	1,399	22
1949	341	1,611	31

Both maple-syrup and sugar production have diminished with the years. Instead of increasing with the population of the country, which is almost five times as large as it was in 1860, maple-sugar production has fallen off sharply since 1890, and has neared the vanishing point in the 1940's. This decline is due in part to the increase in the proportion of maple sap made into syrup and sold in that form. But this is only one part of the explanation. Syrup production in 1940 was just about what it was in 1890. Figures from the U.S. Tariff Commission reports on maple sugar and syrup give the total production, in pounds of sugar, as 52.9 millions in 1859, 51 millions in 1889, 46.9 millions in 1909, 34.8 millions in 1926, and 11.4 millions in 1948.

There are several reasons for the decline in maple production. First, the maple industry, being conducted chiefly on a household basis, of necessity is carried on in the country. A United States Census survey of April, 1947, showed that 83 per cent of American households are now located in urban areas, where maple production is, of course, impossible. Second, even the rural households now buy much of their food, including sugar, from the food processors and packers. It is easier and quicker to eat out of boxes or cans than to prepare the ground, sow, weed, harvest, preserve, and store food. This invasion of the countryside by commodity foods has played havoc with the rural households' use economy. Third, with modern transportation the adults in a rural household travel miles to and from work each day, exchange their labor power for wages and spend their money for commodity foods, clothing, fuel, and shelter. It is no longer true that February and March are "leisure months" when able-bodied adults are idle and might just as well tap out their maples. Many of them have regular jobs, which they cannot afford to give up for a few weeks of more or less uncertain sugaring. Maple production, like every other phase of use economy, has suffered severely in the trend away from use and toward commodity economy. Finally, wage costs have increased considerably and the price of syrup has risen correspondingly. Maple is undersold by cane and beet sugars and is no longer considered a staple. Less than one per cent of the sugar consumed in the United States is from maple. It cannot compete with cane and has become a luxury except in the localities and in the households where it is made.

Maple production, essentially a household operation and an aspect of a use economy, cannot compete financially with commodity economy and wage labor. The winters of 1945 to 1948 found men earning from $6 to $15 a day in industry, transport, and trade, and in the woods. If maple producers valued their labor at such a figure, their syrup would sell at somewhere around $10 a gallon—a price far above the customary market rate of $2 to $3 a gallon in the 1922–1942 period.

Nevertheless, maple is a cash crop and can be used to keep farm operators in the black. "Those who have made the industry of the manufacture of maple-sugar a study, estimate a net profit of 10% on the capital invested. If this is the case there is no good reason why it should not be profitable, for, unless it be the Walnut, or possible the Chestnut, there is no tree worth growing for its timber that will yield yearly so large an income." [7] There was a brief period in 1930–1932 when there was some difficulty in marketing maple syrup.

This was due to the large carry over of syrup produced at 1929 price levels and frozen by the price collapse of the following years. With that exception, in our experience, the market for maple syrup and sugar has always absorbed the entire product. Unlike perishable agricultural products, which must be marketed quickly or lost entirely, maple syrup may be kept in storage for years without serious deterioration in either color or flavor.

The price of maple syrup and sugar varies considerably. During early years, maple sugar and cane sugar sold on a parity—at around ten cents per pound. "In 1874 the price rose from 10 to 22 cents. In Canada, at the beginning of 1878, new maple sugar was selling at 10 to 11 cents, about the price of the best cane sugar; and in April, 1882, the new season's sugar was quoted at 22 cents." [8] Beginning in the 1870's the price of cane sugar, and later of beet sugar, was cut by the introduction of new processes and machinery. By 1875 cane sugar began to undersell maple. Since 1885 maple sugar has gradually come to be considered a confection or a luxury article.

Maple syrup, up until 1915, sold for about a dollar a gallon, rarely over. In 1895 it was reported as low as sixty-three cents average price. World War I, with its restrictions on ocean freight shipments, cut cane sugar imports into the United States, and pushed up the price of both maple syrup and sugar. Coupled with the price inflation that accompanied the war, maple-syrup prices rose to $3 a gallon.

In the early 1930's, prices dropped again to $1 per gallon (wholesale) for fancy syrup. During our early experience with syrup production (1933–1935) syrup sold at retail for $1.50. By the end of the 1930's however, the price had risen to $2.50 or $3. World War II, with its sugar rationing, brought a government-regulated top price of $3.39 per gallon for syrup sold direct by the producer to the consumer. When the ceiling price was removed in 1946, the price of syrup shot up sharply. The 1945 and 1946 crops had been subnormal, with little or no carry over. When warm weather in early 1947 threatened a third bad maple harvest, buyers paid fantastic prices for early-run syrup. During that spring Vermont fancy syrup sold at retail anywhere from $4.50 to $8 a gallon. The average price was $6 to $7, with maple sugar selling from $1 to $2 a pound.

Present prices of both syrup and sugar are unstable and unpredictable. The upward-moving price spiral will tend to raise them. Labor shortage on the farms and the considerable advance in wages will have a like effect. On the other hand, consumers long accustomed to paying around $2.50 for a gallon of maple syrup hesitate a long time before paying $6 or $7. A series of heavy crops during the next few years would certainly result in a price reduction.

If the old adage is accepted—a gallon of syrup is worth one day's labor—maple-syrup prices are not seriously out of line. In the 1890's when men worked for a dollar a day, syrup sold at a dollar. In the 1930's with wages at $2 to $3, syrup brought about that amount. In the late 1940's, with wages at $7 to $10 a day, syrup is selling at a little less than those figures. Other things being equal, the price of a gallon of maple syrup will tend to hold at about the level of going day wages.

There is no guaranteed price of maple products. Some unforeseeable technical improvement in syrup production might cut costs drastically. C. J. Bell envisaged such in 1897. "In this age, when we have so many new improvements, so much machinery, I am expecting it will be only a few years when I can start out from my home in the morning and sit on the back end of my sled and, by some electric device, gather the sap from the trees, and at the close of the day carry home the product and hardly know that I have been at work at all." [9] A period of general impoverishment would make a sharp cut in the demand for a semiluxury article like maple syrup. A new war would push maple prices upward until price control stopped the rise. Rising prices would bring unused or little-used sugar bushes back into full production.

What are the probabilities of enlarged syrup production? The trend in recent years points to less rather than more tapping of sugar maples. Not only have many long-established sugar orchards been sold to lumbermen at fancy on-the-stump prices, but numbers of farms in New England and neighboring states have been bought up by summer people who do little farming and no sugaring. Then again, there is the matter of help. Children leave the farms early and either go away to school or get jobs in towns and cities, thus stripping the farms of the semi-adult workers who play such an important part in sugaring operations conducted on a household basis.

It seems probable that those producers who continue to produce maple syrup and sugar will find an increasing rather than a diminishing market. We travel about North America on occasion. In the course of our journeyings outside the maple-producing area we meet many people who say, "When can I get a taste of real maple syrup?" The blended syrups and the chemical flavorings with which chain stores have been supplying them do not meet the demands of those who have once enjoyed the true maple flavor.

Taking all of these matters into consideration, there seems every likelihood that a family or a co-operating group entering the maple industry has a reasonable assurance that their products will be salable at prices approximating one gallon per day for the work done in the sugar bush and sugarhouse.

The decentralist movement, which is being urged by theorists and is being pushed by the course of events, will find an ideal abiding place in the maple industry. The maple bush, because of its configuration, must be relatively small. The initial investment is moderate. Households or small co-operating units are the logical production units. The market is all but assured. The crop is sold for cash. The syrup market welcomes small containers. A mail-order business is easily built up. When syrup is converted into sugar and packed in fancy boxes, its market is greatly extended. Autos and improved roads have brought tourists who take packages of syrup and sugar back to town as souvenirs. Roadstands on the main highways handle the output of those who live on back roads.

Sugar-country economy is, and apparently will remain, decentralized. Supplemented by a measure of co-operation and coupled with community integration and co-operation, it seems a logical area in which decentralists may test out their theories. Those who are looking to decentralism as a means of rehabilitating households and stabilizing community life have at least part of an economic basis for their efforts in the areas where maple production is commercially practicable. Unlike many other household craft activities, maple production offers opportunities to people of different ages, strengths, and experience to make a contribution to the sum total of household livelihood.

From our point of view, maple production has another immense advantage in its discontinuity. The work is seasonal and only seasonally grinding. Animal husbandry yields a cash income in exchange for seven days a week and fifty-two weeks a year of constant care. A dairy or a chicken farmer must be on the spot, day in, day out. A maple farmer need be on hand during March and April to gather and boil sap, and must, during any unspecified time of the year, cut his wood. Otherwise he is not tied to the place. If the syrup is made into sugar, another two months would be added for labor, making in all perhaps five months work out of the twelve. If the five months of maple production are wisely handled, they will provide a cash income adequate to meet the minimum cash demands of the entire year. "It has always seemed to the writer that the effort and expense in making, say $1,000, from a well operated sugar bush, is considerably less than the effort and expense required to make a similar amount from a herd of cows." [10]

Lest readers get a false impression, let us repeat that maple, like any other household craft, will not enable its practitioners to spend at the level of subordinate corporation executives. On the contrary, it provides the cash necessary to support only a modest subsistence economy. It has no relation to city living, and cannot be compared in terms of cash income, with city salaries or even city wages. "What a farmer earns he gets," says an anonymous author in 1864.[11] "He loses none of his gains, if he attends to his business. They may be smaller, on paper, than those realized by dashing operators in the city, but they are infinitely more tangible."

Maple farming has many points in its favor. It helps to make life in the country financially practicable; it helps to integrate and unify the household; it is an interesting and even an exciting occupation with never ending variations, problems, and demands on ingenuity and endurance, and it provides a generous margin of leisure. Maple trees sometimes die or are broken by storms, but they never stray. Sugaring equipment requires little or no attention except in preparation for the sap season and during actual operations. Most of the work connected with the industry is done under the open sky, in the early days of spring, one of nature's most unmissable periods. "We do hope that those who have it in their power, will in future exert themselves to increase and improve the manufacture of both sugar and molasses. We know by experience that sugaring is extremely laborious, but it is most certainly a sweet employment, and in a good season it is also very profitable." [12]

CHAPTER TWELVE

A Life as Well as a Living

"Agriculture was one of the first employments of mankind; it is one of the most innocent, and, at the same time, the most pleasing and beneficial of any. By its variety, it keeps the mind amused and in spirits; by its exercise and regularity, it conduces to give vigour and health to the body; and in the end, it is productive of every other necessary and convenience of life."

Thomas Heyward, American Museum, *January 1789.*

*"It may very truly be said
  That his is a noble vocation,
Whose industry leads him to spread
  About him a little Creation.
He lives independent of all
  Except th' Omnipotent Donor:
Has always enough at his call—
  And more is a plague to its owner.*

*"He works with his hands, it is true,
  But happiness dwells with employment,
And he who has nothing to do
  Has nothing by way of enjoyment.
His labors are mere exercise,
  Which saves him from pains and physicians;
Then, Farmers, you truly may prize
  Your own as the best of conditions."*

Thomas Green Fessenden, The Independent Farmer, *1806.*

"Listen, Young Farmer, to the moral muse, and catch the useful lessons of her song. Be frugal and be blest; frugality will give thee competence;

thy gains are small, too small to bear profusion's wasteful hand. Make temperence thy companion; so shall health sit on thy brow, and brace thy vigorous frame to every useful work. And if to these thou happily shalt join one virtue more, the love of Industry, the glowing joy felt from each new improvement, then fair peace with modest neatness in her decent garb shall walk around thy dwelling; while the great, tired with the vast fatigue of doing nought, filled with the ills which luxury await, impatient curse the dilatory day, and look with envy on thy happier state."

Daniel Adams, The Agricultural Reader, *1824*

> *"Here, brothers, secure from all turmoil and danger,*
> *We reap what we sow, for the soil is our own;*
> *We spread hospitality's board for the stranger,*
> *And care not a fig for the king on his throne;*
> *We never know want, for we live by our labor,*
> *And in it contentment and happiness find."*

John L. Blake, Farmers' Every-Day Book, *1850*.

THROUGH this book we have drawn upon libraries, laboratories, and personal experience, and have presented certain conclusions regarding the making and marketing of maple products. In the previous chapter we tried to show that the maple industry was so unique that big business had never been able to take it over, and that it still provided at least a partial basis for a household economy. In this chapter we propose to deal with some of the thinking that led us toward semisubsistence agriculture in general and maple production in particular, and to relate this thinking and practice to that larger sphere of human experience that is sometimes called the art of living.

Originally, we had no intention of going into maple production. On the contrary, we were unaware that maple offered us an opportunity to try out the life pattern we had in mind. Broadly, the purposes we had in mind when we turned our backs on the city and our faces toward the country might be summed up in this manner:

First, we wanted to control our own source of livelihood. The community had left us no choice in the matter by deny-

ing the chief wage earner of our family group the opportunity to practice his profession—which is teaching. While we
were not anxious to own land, we were compelled to face
the fact that under existing conditions in North America, the
renter, share-tenant, or worker was at the mercy of the
landlord or job owner. The weakness of the teacher's position, for example, lay in the fact that the businessmen who
made up the boards of education and the boards of college
trustees could deprive a teacher of his job and blacklist him
in his profession, not on the basis of academic efficiency, but
because of differences in political and social viewpoints.
What was true of teaching was more or less true of any field
in which one man owned or controlled the job on which
another depended for his livelihood. Under these circumstances we were looking for a source of livelihood that was
beyond the reach of the privateers who were operating big
business.

Second, we wanted to get away from the cities, which
seemed to us more and more hectic, disorganized, and dis-
orderly. We had lived in cities all over the world, and with
minor exceptions, the story was the same everywhere. The
city was artificial from top to bottom, imposing upon its
victims a life pattern based upon superficialities and upon
an endless grind of routine that had as its chief purpose the
fleecing of the poor and weak for the profit of the rich and
powerful. Furthermore, we found cities in general squalid
and corrupt; ruthless, policemanized concentration camps in
which men and women were persuaded or compelled to
spend their lives and in which children were forced to grow
up unaware of any alternative to the wealth-power pattern.

Third, we wanted to get our feet on the earth and to get
our hands into it—to make and keep that incomparably
important contact with nature which balances life at the
same time that it cleanses it, rejuvenates it, and keeps it sane.
We also wanted to find a place near a large body of water—
preferably the ocean. This wish we did not realize, in part
because the capital outlay involved in such choice spots was
so heavy that the place could hardly be self-supporting, and

in part because waterside areas were being rapidly converted into stately and select summer colonies or into miniature Coney Islands.

Fourth, we wanted to live simply, doing as much good as possible to our fellow humans and fellow beings, and at the same time doing them as little harm as possible. The negative part of this aim could be fulfilled anywhere on earth. The positive part made it impossible for us to withdraw to the inaccessible mountains of Guatemala or India or to the remote Pacific Islands, to which, indeed, we were inclined to go. The place had to be so located as to enable us to reach other people and to enable people who so desired to reach us.

Fifth, we wanted to live solvently. That is, we did not want to beg or borrow or steal, and we did want to produce our living with our hands and in the closest possible contact with the earth. That meant an annual budget that would cover a simple but adequate livelihood and show a surplus rather than a deficit.

Sixth, we wanted, in one sense most important of all, to make a living in about half of our working time—say four or five hours a day—so that we would be freed from the livelihood problem and enabled to devote the other half of our time to study, teaching, writing, music, travel. We had frequently read and heard theoretical advocacies of such a daily time schedule: four hours for bread labor, four hours for one's vocation, and four hours for social intercourse, but we had seldom seen it practiced in our acquisitive society.* We have succeeded, better than we dared to hope, in putting such a formula into practice, but subject to minor modifications. There are times during the year, such as the syrup-making

---

* In a letter to General Koscuisko in February 26, 1810, Thomas Jefferson wrote, "I am retired to Monticello where . . . I enjoy a repose to which I have been long a stranger. My mornings are devoted to correspondence. From breakfast to dinner, I am in my shops, my garden, or on horseback among my farms; from dinner to dark, I give to society and recreation with my neighbors and my friends; and from candle light to early bed-time, I read." *The Writings of Thomas Jefferson*. Washington: Memorial Association, 1907. Vol. XII. P. 369.

weeks, when we work eight or ten or twelve hours a day. These we balance with at least an equal number of weeks when we do no bread labor whatever. During the balance of the year, we succeed moderately well in carrying out the daily 4–4–4 formula.

Last, we wanted to demonstrate a pattern that might be followed by those who felt with us that self-respect could properly be maintained only at arms' length from the centers of exploitation and only under conditions where the able-bodied individual was doing his share of the necessary social labor at the same time that he was satisfying his own creative urges in his chosen fields of the sciences, the arts, and social intercourse.

That sounds like a big order. It was and is. We spent years in the search for a locale, finally picking on an area in southern Vermont that seemed to come as near as any we had seen to meeting the varied requirements for a place to try out our ideas. The district we selected is in a high valley in the chain of Green Mountains that stretches from the Canadian border southward. "But why not the summerlands of Florida or southern California?" might be asked. We have a theory, which we are not able to defend to our complete satisfaction, that soft climates probably produce soft people and certainly produce parasitic people. Life, like a magnetic field, cannot operate without its positive and its negative poles. A year of all summer is as deadening as a year of all winter would be. A sequence of varied seasons maintains interest by providing the basic ingredient of climatic change. We look forward to winter with as much or perhaps more anticipation than to any other season. But more than that, we enjoy the procession of the seasons across the hills and through the varied activities of our daily lives.

We are located on a side hill of a valley directly facing Stratton Mountain, the highest peak in southern Vermont. The first place we bought required an outlay of $300 cash, and the assumption of an $800 mortgage. It had a farmhouse in poor repair, a good barn, and sixty-five acres of land well stripped of timber, but with plenty of firewood in the wood-lot. That was in 1932. We soon added a much larger piece of land, lumbered over between 1916 and 1919, which we were able to buy for $3 an acre. As things then stood, we decided that by foresting this area, beginning with the cutting of cordwood and going on with logging as the timber matured, we could make our cash income and set up a solvent economy. We began our venture with some minor house repairs, built a stone cabin off in the woods, dug a swimming pool beside it in a brook, established a garden, and got out our firewood.

We had no sooner stabilized our thinking in terms of forestry as a source of cash income than we discovered that we were in the heart of the Vermont maple country. The valley where we had settled contained thousands of sugar maples at all stages of growth from tiny seedlings to mighty trees twelve feet in girth. There were maples on our place. We accepted our destiny, tapped half a dozen trees near the house and made a few gallons of maple syrup on the kitchen stove. We hired out, free of charge, to neighboring farmers, watched their system (or lack of system, as the case might be), and learned while we helped them.

Within a year we were so fortunate as to be able to buy the place next door. It had a fairly good stand of timber and included an old but excellent sugar bush, several buildings in bad repair, and a decrepit sugarhouse. When we bought the place, it was being sugared on shares by a neighboring family. We continued the share arrangement and worked under the guidance of these competent sugar makers for five years.

At the outset we accepted the local pattern in sugar making and followed it implicitly, as though we had been hired hands. We were told what to do—in the typical indirect manner of mountain folk—and to the best of our ability we did it. Our neighbors were patient and we learned as quickly as we were able.

While we took orders, we kept looking for ways to improve

the plant and the techniques.* As recounted in the pages of this book, we invested a little money and a deal of labor in good tools and housing, improved the bush, and "learned maple" until it now affords a comfortable living, country style, with a minimum of gadgets and a maximum of leisure time to do other work, to study, and to travel.

We have said perhaps enough to show how, in a few years, novices in maple production can turn their energy and ingenuity into a craft that offers scope for imagination and new ideas, and pays sufficient financial returns to provide a simple but adequate living.

We were now turning about half of our annual syrup crop into sugar. Roughly, a gallon of syrup, which sells for three or four dollars, converted into cake sugar will sell for about double, and made into fancy shapes and packs will sell for nearly triple. Our gross sugar sales therefore greatly exceeded our syrup sales and gave us a considerable margin, a part of which was used for capital improvements.

Much of the equipment used by our sugar-making neighbors was primitive and inadequate. We made various improvements and innovations and, by doing much of the work in our spare time, we cut money costs and paid the expenses out of our syrup income.

For instance, our first sugarhouse was completed for $242 cash outlay. At the then retail price of syrup ($1.50 a gallon) this made the building cost about 160 gallons of syrup, or something more than a third of our share of the year's syrup crop. With a little attention the building should last anywhere up to thirty or forty years, and was as completely fireproof as such a building could be. The concrete stack

* "On the turn of middle age and whilst gradually quitting public employments, the author sat down on a farm in Maryland, and became enthusiastically fond of husbandry. Farmers in the neighborhood informed him of their modes of practice; but they taught him nothing of the principles of the art. Whilst they knew how to practice in the manner common to the country, he knew neither principles nor practice; but began however with observing their practices, which he continued to imitate; until gaining information from a number of instructive experiments, he was encouraged to deviate from some of them." John Beales Bordley, *Essays and Notes on Husbandry and Rural Affairs*. Philadelphia: Dobson, 1801. P. iv.

that we later attached to the building cost us $66, making the total cost of the sugarhouse not much more than $300.

The woodshed was erected in 1944 at high-price levels for both labor and materials, and cost $167 in cash, or the equivalent of 50 gallons of syrup at the price of syrup that year.

Our second sugarhouse, including its concrete stack and the attached woodshed, cost $457. Compared with the cost of the sugarhouse built in 1935, it seemed excessive. But at 1935 price levels the first sugarhouse, with its stack, cost us 205 gallons of syrup, whereas on the 1946–1947 price levels the new sugarhouse, with stack and woodshed, cost us only 65 gallons of syrup.

Our first evaporator, bought in 1935, cost about $450, which at that time represented the value of 300 gallons of fancy syrup. Our second evaporator, bought in the autumn of 1946, cost around $650, which in terms of 1947 syrup prices (the first season in which the evaporator was used) cost less than 100 gallons of syrup. If we had had a good run of sap in 1947 the new evaporator would have made 100 gallons of syrup in two days. Actually the season was disappointing. However, like all farmers, we look ahead with the slogan, "Things will be better next year."

Furthermore, with the two sugarhouse units and added boiling capacity, we were in a position to take two more people into our enterprise and virtually assure them a minimum cash income in exchange for about three months work per year.

We have gone into this detail concerning our capital improvements because we want to urge the desirability of: (1) improving a capital plant, instead of letting it deteriorate; (2) using modern methods of accounting, setting aside depreciation and similar funds; and (3) using these funds to replace and, where possible, to improve capital equipment as it wears out.

We like to be connected with a solvent enterprise. Still more do we like to have it a bit better equipped at the end of each year than it was at the beginning. We like to look ahead, make plans, try them out, modify them where they prove inadequate, better them, and finally see them embodied in workmanlike, useful, and pleasing forms that are fulfilling their share of a general program. Such developments are particularly satisfying to one who has helped carry the stone, gravel, and sand, mix the concrete, cut the trees, peel and hew the timbers, prepare them, put them in place, lay the roof, put in windows and doors, and install the tools and implements. Those who have not felt the joy of seeing an enterprise pay its way, and improve itself as it goes along, would do well to test out the experience and find out how profoundly satisfying it is to man's urge for growth and betterment. We are convinced that a city family, spending ten thousand dollars on amusement, diversion, and entertainment during a social season, will not get a tithe of the solid satisfaction that we get from an experience that pays us while we have the joy of participating in a productive, creative, going enterprise.

Improvements in capital equipment provide the economic foundations for broadening social equipment. We enjoy seeing our capital plant improving from year to year. We would not be satisfied unless parallel improvements were being made in our social equipment. This is not the place for a detailed description of the changes we have made in our social setup, but we might mention some of them in order to show that our project yields a fuller life as well as a living.

For seven years we stayed on in the rather unsatisfactory wooden farmhouse that we bought when we first went to Vermont. We then selected a site about a quarter of a mile distant for a combination dwelling and work unit, built a stone lumbershed as the first structure in the project, filled it with green lumber straight from the mill, and let it season for a year. Next, we laid out and constructed a road to the new house site. The dwelling, in three units, we constructed over several years. We needed a place to make, pack, and store sugar and house the necessary supplies of boxes and other packing materials essential to such a business. We incorporated such a unit into our plans and made the work place a part of our living place. Four years after we began work on the new house we left the old farmhouse and moved in.

The whole project we built of stone and concrete, using a modified Flagg system of double movable forms. We believe we have demonstrated what Flagg claimed: that people of moderate intelligence, with no particular training, can build satisfactory stone houses easily and cheaply if they take their time, dispense with architects and contractors, and do much of their own work. Suffice it to say that we have a combined stone and concrete dwelling and workshop, equipped with stone floors, hewed timbers, fireplaces, and wood-paneled walls, cool in summer and warm in winter, good to look upon and pleasant to live in. We paid for it as we went, by making and selling syrup and sugar, and going only as fast as we had cash to buy materials. Throughout the entire operation we paid no interest on loans and no fees to architects or contractors.

This is literally a home that sugar built. With the exception of logs, cordwood, maple syrup, and maple sugar, upon which we relied for our cash income, we did not sell anything. Whenever there was a surplus in the garden or on the place we shared it with neighbors or visitors. When the guesthouse was empty, the next comer was welcome to use it. Whoever set foot on the place at mealtime was invited to share what there was on the table. We were trying to combine the techniques of efficient, simple living with the essential social principle: each for all and all for each.

We have our social theories and we expound them whenever we get a chance. We also have our pattern of living. In this book we have by-passed the theories almost entirely and have concentrated our attention on practical economic and social detail dealing with syrup and sugar production. We have done this deliberately because we believe that a solvent, sane life pattern can be set up even under conditions of comparative difficulty and adversity. Furthermore, we believe that this can be done by foresight, determination, and hard work, quite irrespective of the social theories held by the pioneer in these directions.

We have been trying to demonstrate four livelihood propositions in the fifteen years of experimentation and construction that we have put into the Vermont enterprise.

1. A modest subsistence may be secured and all but guaranteed in exchange for approximately half time, devoted to planned, well-organized, co-ordinated labor.

2. The other half of the time (taken off in daily hours or in larger units) is leisure, which may be spent in active outside, or sedentary inside, pursuits.

3. The capital tools of a household economic unit are neither complicated nor unduly expensive, provided they are acquired gradually in exchange for labor and are not based on borrowing, mortgaging, and interest payments.

4. Facilities for the effective use of leisure time and for building up and maintaining satisfactory, co-operative, creative relations with neighbors, friends, and acquaintances may be enlarged at the same time that the productive enterprise is set going.

In short, what we have been developing is a source of livelihood from the earth—from maple, as it happens, for any one of many household crafts would have served the same purpose. It is hardly possible to overemphasize the importance of this relationship with the earth, its rhythms, seasons, and cycles.

It is semi-independent in that a family or small group is able to make its plans, lay out its programs, put them into action, and see them come to fruition, day by day, season by season, year by year, with little or no necessary help or contact with the outside world.

It is social because we have the time and means to share our livelihood and our lives with people outside of our immediate circle. Thus we play our part in setting up a good town, state, nation, and world. We are not isolated in any but a very limited sense of that word.

Life is interesting, full, rewarding. The day is never long enough to finish all of the things that seem worth doing.

Each dawn renews the promise of a multitude of opportunities for planning, building, planting, harvesting, improving, sharing, learning. There are difficulties, obstacles, mistakes, setbacks, but never a dull moment.

We think we are rediscovering the secrets that some of our forebears in the Green Mountains knew so well: the secrets of simplicity, adequacy, decency, neighborliness, self-respect, and a never ending attachment to the marvels of the life of nature and of society that we contact on every side and of which we are integral parts.

We have earned from maple and found a means of livelihood. We have also learned from maple. The occupation of sugaring has been a thorough-going education and broadened our contacts with life in its many aspects. The young Thoreau in his Journal wrote, "Had a dispute with father about the *use* of my making this sugar. . . . He said it took me from my studies. I said I made it my study and felt as if I had been to a university." [1] A complete syrup and sugar maker comprises in himself a woodcutter, a forester, a botanist, an ecologist, a meteorologist, an agronomist, a chemist, a cook, an economist, and a merchant. Sugaring is an art, an education, and a maintenance. "May it long be the mission of the maple thus to sweeten the cup of life."

MAPLE RECIPES

"*Economy now calls your attention to your maple trees. Make all the sugar you can, for you know not what may happen to prevent its importation. Besides, there is a great satisfaction derived from living as much as possible upon the produce of one's own farm; where no poor slave has toiled in sorrow and pain; where no scoundrel has lorded over your fields; but where honest industry walks peaceful amidst the smiling fruits of his labour.*"

Robert B. Thomas, The Farmers' Almanac, *March 1807*

"*Hurrah for the Sugar-Orchard! Let the sunny South boast her sugar-cane, and the West her beet or corn-stalk sugar; but we Green Mountain Boys will stand by the rock-maple—no unfit emblem for our hardy mountaineers and the sweetest mountain nymphs to be found the whole world over. Stick to the maple; and so long as the maple forests stand, suffer not your cup to be sweetened by the blood of slaves.*"

Walton's Vermont Register and Farmers' Almanac, *1844.*

"*The sugar maple is the glory of the Vermont forests. . . . The form of the maple and the intenseness of its foliage, the first to bud and leave out in the spring, and the first to fade in autumn, renders it a pleasing object of contemplation in itself. But the increasing use made of it for sugar and molasses, must greatly enhance its value and comeliness in the eyes of the Vermonters, on whose soil it stands pre-eminent and most frequent.*"

Hosea Beckley, The History of Vermont, *1846.*

"*The true Vermonter never loses his taste for the sweet of the maple. Although in after years his home may be in the great city, or on the prairies of the West; or he may search for wealth in the mines of the Pacific slope, or sojourn in a foreign land; yet, year by year, when he knows that it must be early spring in the old homestead, his thoughts go back to former days, and he forgets the weariness and toil, the bitter part of his early life, and remembers the sweet alone. . . . May it long be the mission of the maple thus to sweeten the cup of life.*"

E. A. Fisk, Report of Vermont Board of Agriculture, *1874.*

CANDIED SWEET POTATOES

Cook sweet potatoes until tender but not soft. Peel and slice lengthwise. Arrange in buttered baking dish and cover with maple sugar or syrup and dot with butter. Add a little water. Bake until potatoes are glazed. Carrots may be prepared in the same way.

BAKED APPLES

Wash and core some good tart apples. Set in baking dish and fill center of apples with maple sugar or syrup. Pour a half inch of hot water to cover bottom of dish. Bake in a moderate oven until soft, basting occasionally with maple syrup.

MAPLE APPLE SAUCE

One cup maple sugar or syrup, with half a cup of water, should be brought to a rolling boil in a deep pan. Then fill pan with unpeeled sections of apples. Stir up until all pieces are coated with syrup. Cook only long enough to tenderize apples. The slices remain unbroken and glazed.

MAPLE NUT COOKIES

Mix altogether in a large bowl 1½ cups maple sugar, 1 cup butter, 3 eggs, 3 cups flour, 1 teaspoon baking powder, 1 teaspoon soda dissolved in half a cup of hot water, 1 cup walnut meats, and 1½ cups dates cut in pieces. Drop from a teaspoon on baking sheet and bake in a moderate oven. Store in a tin can; they improve with age.

MAPLE NUGGETS

Boil one cup maple syrup (or one cup maple sugar with a few tablespoons of water) until 235°. Remove from fire, add 2 tablespoons butter and beat until it begins to thicken. Add 3 cups puffed rice or wheat which have been crisped over

heat. Mix thoroughly. Drop on waxed paper. Needs no cooking.

MAPLE ICING

Bring 1 cup maple syrup to a brisk boil. Beat the white
of 1 egg until stiff. Add the syrup gradually while continuing
to beat. When it holds its shape, cool and spread on cake.

MAPLE MOUSSE

Make a usual custard, using 1 cup maple syrup, ⅔ cup
milk, and the yolks of 4 eggs. Whip 1 pint of cream and
thoroughly mix with the custard. Place in refrigerator until
proper consistency.

MAPLE NUT CANDY

Use maple sugar with sufficient water to dissolve it, one
tablespoonful of vinegar to 2 pounds of sugar, and butter
the size of a walnut. Boil until 260° or hard-ball stage. Pour
immediately into buttered pan in which chopped nuts have
been placed. Mark in strips before cold.

MAPLE DIVINITY FUDGE

Boil 2 cups maple syrup to 235°. Add a pinch of salt and
pour slowly over 2 egg whites that have been beaten stiff.
Beat the whole mixture until it holds its shape. Add a third
of a cup of chopped nut meats and pour into pan lined with
waxed paper. Needs no cooking.

MAPLE PUFFS

Cook 1½ cups maple syrup, 2 pounds maple sugar, 1 cup
of water, and a pinch of salt to 260°. Remove from the fire
and let stand for 3 or 4 minutes. Then slowly pour in the
well-beaten whites of 4 eggs. When thick, stir in 2 cupfuls
of walnut meats and drop, in spoonfuls, on heavily waxed
paper. Work quickly so that all can be finished before the
batch hardens. Needs no cooking.

MAPLE HERMITS

Beat to a cream one-half cup of butter. Gradually beat in ¾ of a cup of maple sugar, ¼ teaspoonful cloves, 1 teaspoonful cinnamon. Dissolve ½ teaspoonful soda in 1 tablespoonful milk, and beat this into the sugar and butter. Add 1 well-beaten egg. Then add 2½ cups flour, ½ teaspoon soda, and ½ cupful currants. Roll out an inch thick and cut in squares. Bake in a hot oven 12 minutes.

MAPLE CUSTARD PIE

Line pie plate with fluted-edge pastry. Fill with the following custard: 1 packed cup maple sugar, 2 tablespoons butter, 1½ cups scalded milk. Stir over fire till sugar dissolves and mixture bubbles. Dissolve 1 tablespoonful cornstarch in ½ cup cold milk, 3 slightly beaten eggs, and ½ teaspoonful salt. Add to sugar mixture and pour into pie plate. Sprinkle nutmeg lightly over top of custard. Bake 10 minutes in a hot oven, then reduce heat and finish baking in moderate oven for about 25 minutes, or until knife inserted comes out clean.

MAPLE GINGERBREAD

Mix 1 cup maple syrup with 3 tablespoons shortening and 1 teaspoon ginger. Sift and stir in sufficient flour to make the mixture stiff as can be. Then add 1 cup boiling water to which has been added 1 teaspoon soda. Beat well and bake in a quick oven.

MAPLE SUGAR CINNAMON TOAST

To 1 cup grated or granulated maple sugar add ¾ of a teaspoon cinnamon. Blend thoroughly. Melt ¼ cup butter or margarine in saucepan. Remove from fire. Add the sugar and cinnamon. Mix in ½ cup chopped walnut or pecan meats. Spread on toast and place under moderate broiler. Heat for a few minutes until mixture bubbles. Watch carefully. Cut in strips or triangles and serve immediately.

NOTES

Chapter One

1. "The chief pleasure and pastime which commeth by wild woods is . . . that it is pleasant to the sight: for by its diversity of greenenesse it marvellously delighteth, and with great contentment recreateth the sight." John Liebault, *The Countrey Farme*. London: Adam Flip, 1616. P. 657.

2. Edmond Bordeaux Székely, *Medicine Tomorrow*. London: The C. W. Daniel Company, Ltd., 1938. Pp. 49-50.

3. R. H. Francé, *Germs of Mind in Plants*. Chicago: Charles H. Kerr & Company, 1914. P. 144.

4. John Evelyn, *Sylva*. London: Martyn, 1670. P. 245.

5. F. Schuyler Mathews, *Familiar Trees and Their Leaves*. New York: D. Appleton-Century Company, Inc., 1896. P. xiii.

6. Henry David Thoreau, *Winter*. Boston: Houghton Mifflin Company, 1888. P. 200.

7. Henry David Thoreau, *Maine Woods*. Boston: Houghton Mifflin Company, 1893. P. 165.

8. Walt Whitman, *Specimen Days in America*. Philadelphia: Rees Walsh, 1882. P. 89.

9. John M. Coulter, *Plant Relations*. New York: D. Appleton-Century Company, Inc., 1905. P. 2.

10. Francé, *op. cit.*, p. 118.

11. Virgil, Fourth Eclogue. "*Dura quercus sudabunt roscida mella.*"

12. W. W. Skeats, *The Past at Our Doors*. London: The Macmillan Company, 1912. P. 45.

13. G. Imlay, *A Topographical Description of the Western Territory of North America*. London: Debrett, 1792. P. 113.

14. Benjamin Mosely, *A Treatise on Sugar*. London: Nichols, 1800. P. 76.

15. Joseph B. Felt, *The Customs of New England*. Boston: Marvin, 1853. P. 67.

16. W. G. Freeman and S. E. Chandler, *The World's Commercial Products*. Boston: Ginn & Company, 1908. Pp. 76-78.

17. H. V. Knaggs, *The Romance of Sugar*. London: The C. W. Daniel Company, Ltd., 1931. Pp. 11-12.

18. E. N. Transeau, *Textbook of Botany*. New York: Harper & Brothers, 1940. P. 108.

19. Jagadis Chander Bose, *Plant Autographs*. New York: The Macmillan Company, 1927. P. 165.

20. François André Michaux, *Histoire des Arbres Forestiers de l'Amérique Septentrionale*. Paris: Haussmann, 1810. Vol. II, pp. 218-219.

21. U. S. Department of Agriculture Bulletin No. 134, 1910. P. 10.

22. John Gerade, *The Herball or Generall Historie of Plantes*. London: Norton, 1597. P. 1300.

23. Barnabe Googe, *The Whole Art and Trade of Husbandry*. London: More, 1614. P. 104.

24. Charles Sprague Sargent, *The Silva of North America*. Boston: Houghton Mifflin Company, 1892. P. 101.

25. Samuel Strickland, *Twenty-seven Years in Canada West*. London: Bentley, 1853. Vol. II, p. 304.

26. Richard Parkinson, *A Tour in America*. London: Harding, 1805. Vol. II, p. 640.

27. E. Jones, *The Acer Saccharinum*. London: Colyer, 1832. P. xv.

28. Joseph Bouchette, *The British Dominions in North America*. London: Longmans, Green & Company, 1832. Vol. I, p. 371.

29. Alexander Reed, in *The New England Farmer*, May 22, 1824. P. 341.

30. Francis A. Evans, *The Emigrant's Directory and Guide*. Dublin: Curry, 1833. P. 109.

31. Samuel F. Perley, in *Maine Agricultural Report*, 1862. P. 48.

32. Andrew J. Blackbird, *History of the Ottawa and Chippewa Indians of Michigan*. Ypsilanti: Ypsilantian Job Printing House, 1887. P. 72.

33. François Alexandre Frédéric de la Rochefoucauld-Liancourt, *Voyage dans les Etats Unis de l'Amérique*. Paris: Du Pont, 1799. P. 217.

34. Benjamin Rush, *An Account of the Sugar Maple-Tree of the United States*. Philadelphia: Aitken, 1792. P. 72.

35. William Chapin, in *Vermont Agricultural Report*, 1887-1888. P. 325.

36. Anonymous, *The Book of Trees*. London: Parker, 1852. P. 43.

37. J. P. Brissot de Warville, *Nouveau voyage dans les Etats-Unis*. Paris: Buisson, 1791. Vol. II, p. 60.

38. Henri Nouvel, *Jesuit Relations and Allied Documents*. Cleveland: Burrows, 1899. Vol. LVI, p. 101.

39. Thomas Fessenden, *Original Poems*. Philadelphia: Bronson, 1806. P. 183.

40. John Lincklaen, *Journals of John Lincklaen*. New York: G. P. Putnam's Sons, 1897. P. 11.

41. Coxe Tench, *A View of the United States of America*. Philadelphia: Hall, 1794. P. 77.

42. Robert B. Thomas, *The Farmer's Almanack*, 1803.

43. *Ibid.*, 1805.

44. *Walton's Vermont Register and Farmer's Almanac*, 1840.

45. William Drown, *Compendium of Agriculture*. Providence: Field & Maxcy, 1824. P. 255.

46. Zadock Thompson, *History of Vermont*. Burlington: Goodrich, 1842. P. 210.

47. Benjamin Rush, *op. cit.*, p. 76.

48. M. Bonnet, *Les Etats-Unis de l'Amérique à la fin du 18ième Siècle*. Paris: Maradan, 1802. Vol. II, p. 285.

49. M. Bonnet, *Tableau des Etats-Unis de l'Amérique*. Paris: Testu, 1816. P. 43.

50. E. Jones, *op. cit.*, p. xvii.
51. *Ibid.*, p. v.
52. *Ibid.*, p. xix.
53. *Ibid.*, p. xix.
54. M. Bonnet, *op. cit.* 1802, p. 283.

Chapter Two

1. William H. Keating, *An Expedition to the Source of St. Peter's River*. London: Whittaker, 1825. Vol. I, p. 114.
2. Sebastien Rasles, *Lettres édifiantes et curieuses*. Paris: Le Clerc, 1726. P. 252.
3. Robert Beverley, *History and Present State of Virginia*. London: Parker, 1705. Part II, p. 21.
4. Joseph François Lafitau, *Mœurs des Sauvages Amériquains*. Paris: Saugrains, 1724. Vol. II, p. 155.
5. Nicolas Bossu, *Nouveaux Voyages aux Indes Occidentales*. Paris: Le Jay, 1768. Vol. I, p. 216.
6. P. F. X. de Charlevoix, *Journal d'un Voyage dans l'Amérique Septentrionnale*. Paris: Giffart, 1744. Vol. I, p. 192.
7. H. W. Henshaw, in *American Anthropologist*, October, 1890. Vol. III, p. 342.
8. J. D. Hunter, *Manners and Customs of Several Indian Tribes*. Philadelphia: Maxwell, 1823. P. 313.
9. Erminnie A. Smith, "Myths of the Iroquois," *Second Annual Report of the Bureau of Ethnology*, Washington, 1883. P. 115.
10. Henry P. Schoolcraft, *History, Condition and Prospects of the Indian Tribes of the United States*. Philadelphia: J. B. Lippincott Company, 1852. Vol. II, pp. 55-56.
11. Henry P. Schoolcraft, *Indian Tribes of the United States*. Philadelphia: J. B. Lippincott Company, 1884. Vol. I, p. 199.
12. R. L. Allen, *The American Farm Book*. New York: Saxton, 1849. P. 220.
13. C. P. Traill, *The Canadian Settlers' Guide*. London: Edward Stanford, Ltd., 1860. P. 66.
14. W. L. Smith, *The Pioneers of Old Ontario*. Toronto: Morang, 1923. P. 264.
15. Henry P. Schoolcraft, *op. cit.* 1884, p. 199.
16. W. J. Hoffman, "The Menomini Indians," *14th Annual Report of the Bureau of Ethnology*. Washington, 1896. Part I, p. 288.
17. J. D. Hunter, *op. cit.*, p. 298.
18. *Ibid.*, pp. 296-297.
19. P. F. X. de Charlevoix, *op. cit.*, Vol. VI, p. 47.
20. Alvar Nunez Cabeca de Vaca, *La relación y comentarios dos jornados qui hizo a las Indias*. Valladolid, 1555.
21. George Catlin, *Letters and Notes on the Manners, Customs and Conditions of the North American Indians*. Philadelphia: Hazard, 1857. Vol. I, p. 98.
22. Harmon Morse, in *Vermont Agricultural Report*, 1890. P. 85.

23. James Smith, *An Account of Remarkable Occurences during Captivity with the Indians, 1755-59*. Philadelphia: Grigg, 1831. P. 75.

24. W. J. Hoffman, *op. cit.*, p. 288.

25. Alexander Henry, *Travels and Adventures in Canada and the Indian Territories between the Years 1760 and 1776*. New York: Riley, 1809. P. 69.

26. Joseph François Lafitau, *op. cit.*, p. 154.

27. Samuel Hopkins, *Historical Memoirs Relating to the Housatonic Indians*. Boston: Kneeland, 1753. P. 38.

28. *Ibid.*

29. James Smith, *op. cit.*, pp. 44-45.

30. Frances Densmore, "The Uses of Plants by the Chippewa Indians," *44th Annual Report of the Bureau of Ethnology*. Washington, 1928. P. 312.

31. Henri Joutel, *Journal historique du dernier Voyage que feu M. de la Sale fit dans la Golfe de Mexique pour trouver l'embouchure et de cours de la Riviere de Missicipi*. Paris: Robinot, 1713. P. 352.

32. Joseph François Lafitau, *op. cit.*, p. 157.

33. Sebastien Rasles, *op. cit.*, p. 295.

34. James Smith, *op. cit.*, p. 44.

35. *Ibid.*, pp. 52-53.

36. *Ibid.*, pp. 50-51.

37. Pehr Kalm, *Huru Socker göres uti Norra America af åtskilliga slags trän*. Stockholm: Kungliga Svenska Vetenskaps Academiens Handlingar, 1751. P. 155.

38. *Ibid.*, p. 157.

39. Alexander Henry, *op. cit.*, p. 70.

40. *Ibid.*, p. 218.

41. Jonathan Carver, *Travels through the Interior Parts of North-America*. London: Walter, 1778. P. 262.

42. Benjamin Rush, *op. cit.*, p. 74.

43. John Heckewelder, *History, Manners and Customs of Indian Nations*. Philadelphia: Small, 1819. P. 185.

44. Samuel Goodrich, *Manners, Customs and Antiquities of the Indians of North and South America*. New York: Allen, 1844. P. 204.

45. Benjamin Perley Poore, *History of the Agriculture of the U. S.* Report of Commissioner of Agriculture, Washington, 1866. P. 500.

46. W. J. Hoffman, *op. cit.*, pp. 139-140.

47. *Ibid.*, p. 286.

48. Johann Georg Kohl, *Kitchi-Gami*. Bremen: Schunemann, 1859. P. 133.

49. George Catlin, *op. cit.*, p. 204.

50. Johann Georg Kohl, *op. cit.*, pp. 139-140.

51. Frances Densmore, *op. cit.*, p. 312.

52. *Ibid.*

53. William D. Ely, "The Sap and Sugar of the Maple-Tree," *Garden and Forest*, May 6, 1891.

Chapter Three

1. Hector St. John de Crèvecoeur, *Sketches of 18th Century America*. New Haven: Yale University Press, 1925. P. 98.

2. A. M. Hemenway, *The Vermont Historical Gazeteer*. Burlington: Hemenway, 1867. Vol. I, p. 313.

3. William Grimshaw, *History of the United States*. Philadelphia: Grigg & Elliott, 1840. P. 194.

4. Robert B. Thomas, *The Farmer's Almanack*, March, 1798.

5. W. O. Brigham, in *Vermont Agricultural Report*, 1878. P. 105.

6. Francis A. Evans, *The Emigrant's Directory and Guide*. Dublin: Curry, 1833. P. 105.

7. Anonymous, "Advice to American Farmers about to Settle in New Countries," *American Museum*, March, 1789. Pp. 226-227.

8. Jeremiah Wilson, *Report of the Commissioner of Patents*, 1844. P. 297.

9. C. P. Traill, *The Canadian Settlers' Guide*. London: Edward Stanford, Ltd., 1860. Pp. 62-64

10. C. T. Alvord, *Report of Commissioner of Agriculture for Year 1862*. Washington, 1863. P. 397.

11. François André Michaux, *Histoire des Arbres Forestiers de l'Amérique Septentrionale*. Paris: Haussman, 1810. Vol. II, p. 227.

12. Solon Robinson, *Facts for Farmers*. New York: Johnson, 1866. Vol. II, p. 837.

13. G. Imlay, *A Topographical Description of the Western Territory of North America*. London: Debrett, 1797. P. 472.

14. C. T. Alvord, *op. cit.*, p. 401.

15. Solon Robinson, *op. cit.*, p. 836.

16. Samuel Strickland, *Twenty-Seven Years in Canada West*. London: Bentley, 1853. Vol. II, p. 300.

17. L. R. Tabor, in *Vermont Agricultural Report*, 1894. P. 142.

18. J. J. Thomas, *The Illustrated Annual Register of Rural Affairs*. Albany: Tucker, 1863. P. 246.

19. W. T. Chamberlain, in *American Agriculturalist*, February, 1870. P. 58.

20. *Country Gentleman*, February 20, 1862.

21. Amos Fish, in *Country Gentleman*, March 13, 1862.

22. Samuel F. Perley, in *Report of the Maine Board of Agriculture*, 1862. P. 51.

23. F. L. Rice, in *Maine Agricultural Report*, 1858. P. 203.

24. Solon Robinson, *op. cit.*, p. 837.

25. *Ibid.*

26. L. R. Tabor, *op. cit.*, p. 141.

27. Benjamin Rush, *An Account of the Sugar Maple-Tree of the United States*. Philadelphia: Aitken, 1792. P. 7.

28. Solon Robinson, *op. cit.*, p. 838.

29. Harmon Morse, in *Vermont Agricultural Report*, 1889-1890. P. 84.

30. John Lorain, *Husbandry*. Philadelphia: Carey, 1825. P. 299.

31. Zadock Thompson, *History of Vermont*. Burlington: Goodrich, 1842. Part III, p. 58.

32. O. M. Spencer, *Indian Captivity*. New York: Waugh & Mason, 1835. P. 115.

33. *Remarks on the Manufacturing of Maple Sugar*. Philadelphia: Society of Gentlemen, 1790. P. 7.

34. E. A. Talbot, *Five Years Residence in the Canadas*. London: Longmans, Green & Company, 1824. Vol. I, p. 276.

35. C. P. Traill, *op. cit.,* p. 65.

36. Timothy Wheeler, in *Garden and Forest,* March 15, 1893. P. 120.

37. John Burroughs, *Signs and Seasons.* Boston: Houghton Mifflin Company, 1914. P. 242.

38. W. T. Chamberlain, in *American Agriculturalist,* March, 1870. P. 98.

39. Nicolas Denys, *Histoire Naturelle.* Paris: Barbin, 1672. Vol. II, p. xx.

40. Louis de la Hontan, *Nouveaux voyages dans l'Amérique Septentrionale.* Hague: L'Honoré, 1703. Vol. II, p. 59.

41. Society of Gentlemen, *op. cit.,* pp. 5-6.

42. *American Museum,* June, 1790. P. 304.

43. *Frank Leslie's Illustrated Newspaper,* April 12, 1873. P. 80.

44. Thomas Ashe, *Travels in America.* London: Phillips, 1808. Vol. II, pp. 237-238.

45. Leander Coburn, in *Vermont Agricultural Report,* 1872. P. 214.

46. E. A. Fisk, *Vermont Agricultural Report,* 1873-1874. P. 717.

47. Anonymous, in *American Agriculturalist,* March, 1844. P. 89.

48. Roswell Field, in *New England Farmer,* June 17, 1835. P. 385.

49. John Woolidge, *Systema Agriculturae,* 1687. P. 95.

50. *New England Farmer,* April 17, 1824. Pp. 298-299.

51. Mackenzie, *Five Thousand Receipts in All the Useful and Domestic Arts.* Philadelphia: Kay, 1831. P. 417.

52. C. P. Traill, *op. cit.,* pp. 62-64.

53. C. T. Alvord, *op. cit.,* p. 297.

54. *Ibid.,* p. 398.

55. G. H. Loskiel, *Geschichte der Mission der Evangelischen Brüder unter den Indianern in Nord Amerika.* Leipzig: Jummer, 1789. P. 93.

56. Timothy Wheeler, in *Garden and Forest,* March 15, 1893. P. 120.

57. Anonymous, in *American Museum,* August, 1789. P. 100.

58. Society of Gentlemen, *op. cit.,* p. 10.

59. Samuel F. Perley, *op. cit.,* p. 53.

60. *Ibid.*

61. *Agricultural Report for 1862.* Washington, 1863. P. 54.

62. Harmon Morse, *Vermont Agricultural Report,* 1890. P. 84.

63. Solon Robinson, *op. cit.,* pp. 839-840.

64. A. M. Foster, in *Vermont Agricultural Report,* 1874. P. 729.

65. Hiram A. Cutting, in *Vermont Agricultural Report,* 1886. P. 301.

66. W. J. Chamberlain, in *American Agriculturalist,* February, 1871. P. 49.

67. H. Allen Soule, in *Vermont Agricultural Report,* 1872. Pp. 220-221.

68. W. O. Brigham, in *Vermont Agricultural Report,* 1878. P. 105.

69. A. M. Foster, in *Vermont Agricultural Report,* 1893-1894. P. 132.

70. Samuel F. Perley, in *Maine Agricultural Report,* 1862. P. 55.

71. Jeremy Belknap, *History of New-Hampshire.* Dover: Crosby & Varney, 1812. Vol. III, p. 86.

72. Samuel F. Perley, *op. cit.,* p. 55.

73. Franklin B. Hough, *Report on Forestry.* Washington: U.S. Department of Agriculture, 1884. Vol. IV, p. 404.

74. C. T. Alvord, *op. cit.,* p. 54.

75. Isaac Weld, *Travels through the States of North America and the Provinces of Lower Canada.* London: Stockdale, 1799. P. 220.

76. Patrick Campbell, *Travels in the Interior Inhabited Parts of North America*. Edinburgh: Guthrie, 1793. Pp. 82-83.

77. Johann David Schopf, *Reise durch einige mittlern und südlichen Vereinigten Nordamerikanischen Staaten*. Erlangen: Palm, 1798. Vol. I, p. 417.

78. R. L. Allen, *The American Farm Book*. New York: Saxton, 1849. P. 221.

79. John L. Blake, *Farmer's Every-Day Book*. Auburn, N.Y.: Derby Miller, 1850. P. 435.

80. Hector St. John de Crèvecoeur, *More Letters from an American Farmer*. New Haven: Yale University Press, 1925. P. 99.

81. C. T. Alvord, *op. cit.*, p. 398.

82. Frances Densmore, in *44th Annual Report of the Bureau of Ethnology*. Washington, 1928. P. 311.

83. C. P. Traill, *op. cit.*, p. 64.

84. L. R. Tabor, *op. cit.*, p. 142.

85. Pehr Kalm, *Huru Socker göres uti Norra America af åtskilliga slags trän*. Stockholm: Kungliga Svenska Vetenskaps Academiens Handlingar, 1751. P. 156.

86. François André Michaux, *op. cit.*, p. 229.

87. J. G. Palfrey, *History of New England*. Boston: Houghton Mifflin Company, 1883. Vol. IV, p. 303.

88. Robert Holditch, *The Emigrant's Guide to the U.S. of America*. London: Hone, 1818. P. 6.

89. C. P. Traill, *op. cit.*, p. 62.

90. J. L. Hills, in *Vermont Agricultural Report*, 1893. P. 106.

91. *Ibid.*, p. 108.

92. Coxe Tench, *A View of the United States of America*. Philadelphia: Hall, 1794. P. 81.

Chapter Four

1. Samuel F. Perley, in *Maine Agricultural Report*, 1862. P. 49.

2. Moses Mather, in *American Farmer*, February 28, 1823. P. 397.

3. John Lorain, *Husbandry*. Philadelphia: Carey, 1825. P. 393.

4. Hiram A. Cutting, in *Vermont Agricultural Report*, 1885-1886. P. 275.

5. Hiram A. Cutting, in *Vermont Agricultural Report*, 1881-1882. Pp. 64-65.

6. Hector St. John de Crèvecoeur, *More Letters from an American Farmer*. New Haven: Yale University Press, 1925. P. 99.

7. Isaac Weld, *Travels through the States of North America and the Provinces of Lower Canada*. London: Stockdale, 1799. P. 222.

8. Charles T. Jackson, *Report on the Geology of the State of Maine*, 1839. P. 168.

9. Josiah T. Marshall, *The Farmers and Emigrants Complete Guide*. Cincinnati, 1854. P. 308.

10. Joseph C. G. Kennedy, in *United States Census of 1860*. P. clxx.

11. Julia Ellen Rogers, *The Tree Book*. New York: Doubleday, Doran & Company, Inc., 1935. P. 374.

12. E. N. Transeau, *Textbook of Botany*. New York: Harper & Brothers, 1940. P. 325.

13. Timothy Dwight, *Travels in New-England and New-York*. New Haven: T. Dwight Jr., 1821. Vol. I, p. 40.

14. John Burroughs, *Winter Sunshine*. Boston: Houghton Mifflin Company, 1881. P. 108.

15. *Ibid.*, p. 109.

16. John Evelyn, *Sylva, or a Discourse of Forest-Trees*. London: Martyn, 1664. P. 108.

17. Horace Greeley, *Recollections of a Busy Life*. New York: Ford, 1868. Pp. 298-299.

18. Franklin B. Hough, *Report on Forestry*. Washington: U.S. Department of Agriculture, 1884. Vol. IV, p. 406.

19. *Garden and Forest*, September 4, 1889. P. 423.

20. G. Imlay, *A Topographical Description of the Western Territory of North America*. London: Debrett, 1792. P. 473.

Chapter Five

1. Leander Coburn, in *Vermont Agricultural Report*, 1872. P. 215.

2. Solon Robinson, *Facts for Farmers*. New York: Johnson, 1866. Vol. II, p. 837.

3. Paul D. Evans, *The Holland Land Company*. Buffalo: Buffalo Historical Society, 1924. Pp. 63-65.

4. C. T. Alvord, in *Vermont Agricultural Report*, 1862. P. 401.

5. J. B. Spencer, in *Maple Sugar Industry in Canada*. Ottawa, 1913. Pp. 36-37.

6. *Ibid.*

7. Samuel F. Perley, in *Maine Agricultural Report*, 1862. P. 52.

8. A. M. Foster, in *Vermont Agricultural Report*, 1894. P. 133.

9. *Ibid.*, p. 143.

Chapter Six

1. E. F. Benson, *The Book of Months*. New York: Harper & Brothers, 1903. P. 39.

2. E. A. Strasburger, *A Text-book of Botany*. London: The Macmillan Company, 1903. P. 177.

3. *Ibid.*, p. 178.

4. Nicolai A. Maximov, *Plant Physiology*. New York: McGraw-Hill Book Company, Inc., 1938. P. 279.

5. John M. Coulter, *Plant Structures*. New York: D. Appleton-Century Company, Inc., 1904. P. 301.

6. Bulletin No. 103, Vermont Agricultural Experiment Station, 1903. P. 47.

7. Timothy Wheeler, in *Vermont Agricultural Report*, 1856. P. 276.

8. Albert P. Sy, "The History, Manufacture and Analysis of Maple Products," *Journal of Franklin Institute*, July, 1908. Vol. 166, p. 263.

9. C. H. Jones, *22nd Annual Report of Vermont Maple Sugar Makers' Association*, 1915. P. 18.

10. Bulletin No. 228, Canadian Department of Internal Revenue, 1911 P. 8.

11. John Burroughs, *Winter Sunshine*. Boston: Houghton Mifflin Company, 1881. P. 107.

12. Joseph François Lafitau, *Mœurs des Sauvages Amériquains*. Paris: Saugrains, 1724. P. 154.

13. Walter H. Crockett, Bulletin No. 21, *Vermont Agricultural Report*, 1915. P. 31.

14. Bulletin No. 39, U.S. Department of Agriculture, Bureau of Forestry. P. 35.

15. Franklin B. Hough, *Report on Forestry*. Washington: U.S. Department of Agriculture, 1884. Vol. IV, p. 400.

16. Jagadis Chander Bose, *Physiology of the Ascent of Sap*. New York: Longmans, Green & Company, 1923. P. 151.

17. Samuel Deane, *The New England Farmer*. Worcester: Isaias Thomas, 1790. P. 242.

18. Nicolai A. Maximov, *op. cit.*, p. 322.

19. Walter H. Crockett, *op. cit.*, p. 30.

20. Bulletin No. 103, Vermont Agricultural Experiment Station, 1903. Pp. 61-62.

21. *Ibid.*, p. 54.

22. C. H. Jones, *op. cit.*, pp. 18-20.

23. Timothy Wheeler, in *New England Farmer*, October 9, 1869.

24. Bulletin No. 103, Vermont Agricultural Experiment Station, 1903. Pp. 57-60.

25. Bulletin No. 59, U.S. Department of Agriculture, Bureau of Forestry. P. 35.

26. Anonymous, *The Book of Trees*. London: Parker, 1852. P. 46.

27. Timothy Dwight, *Travels in New-England and New-York*. New Haven: Converse, 1821. Vol. I, p. 59.

28. P. F. X. de Charlevoix, *Journal d'un Voyage dans l'Amérique Septentrionnale*. Paris: Giffart, 1744. Vol. V, p. 179.

29. J. P. Brissot de Warville, *Nouveau voyage dans les Etats-Unis*. Paris: Buisson, 1791. Vol. II, p. 65.

30. *The Philosophical Magazine*, July, 1799. P. 218.

31. Edmund O. von Lippmann, *Geschichte des Zuckers*. Berlin: Springer, 1929. Pp. 667-670.

32. Ira Allen, *Natural and Political History of the State of Vermont*. London: Myers, 1798. P. 9.

33. François André Michaux, *Histoire des Arbres Forestiers de l'Amérique Septentrionale*. Paris: Hausmann, 1810. Vol. II, p. 227.

34. John Burroughs, *op. cit.*, p. 105.

35. H. L. Duhamel du Monceau, *Traité des Arbres et Arbustes*. Paris: Michel, 1809. Vol. IV, p. 27.

36. James Johnston, *Notes on North America*. Boston: Little, Brown & Company, 1851. Vol. II, p. 50.

37. Frances Wright, *Views of Society and Manners in America*. London: Longman, Green & Company, 1821. P. 333.

38. John Burroughs, *op. cit.*, p. 107.

39. C. T. Alvord, *Report of Commissioner of Agriculture for Year 1862.* Washington, 1863. P. 402.

40. Hiram A. Cutting, in *Vermont Agricultural Report*, 1885-1886. P. 287.

41. Samuel Williams, *Natural and Civil History of Vermont.* Walpole, N. H.: Thomas & Carlisle, 1794. P. 75.

42. G. B. Emerson, *Report on Trees and Shrubs.* Boston: Little, Brown & Company, 1850. P. 493.

43. Lawrence Southwick, in *New England Homestead*, February 25, 1939.

44. Alexander Reed, in *American Farmer*, May 7, 1824.

45. Alexander Reed, in *New England Farmer*, May 22, 1824.

46. Solon Robinson, *Facts for Farmers.* New York: Johnson, 1866. Vol. II, p. 843.

47. François André Michaux, *op. cit.*, p. 230.

48. Timothy Wheeler, in *Garden and Forest*, April 19, 1893.

49. Anonymous, "The Green Mountains in Sugar-time," *Harper's*, April, 1881. P. 646.

50. E. A. Talbot, *Five Years Residence in the Canadas.* London: Longmans, Green & Company, 1824. Vol. I, p. 276.

51. Franklin B. Hough, *op. cit.*, p. 398.

52. A. H. Bryan and W. F. Hubbard, in Bulletin No. 56, Department of Agriculture, 1912. P. 20.

53. *Vermont Agricultural Report*, 1893-1894. P. 147.

54. Charles W. Janson, *Stranger in America.* London: Cundee, 1807. P. 57.

55. C. H. Wilson, *The Wanderer in America.* Northallerton: Langdale, 1820. P. 105.

Chapter Seven

1. Timothy Wheeler, in *Garden and Forest*, April 19, 1893.

2. Hiram A. Cutting, in *Vermont Agricultural Report*, 1883-1884. P. 75; also 1885-1886, pp. 277-279.

3. Franklin B. Hough, *Report on Forestry.* Washington: U.S. Department of Agriculture, 1884. Vol. IV, p. 400.

4. Solon Robinson, *Facts for Farmers.* New York: Johnson, 1866. Vol. II, p. 840.

5. François André Michaux, *Histoire des Arbres Forestiers de l'Amerique Septentrionale.* Paris: Haussmann, 1810. Vol. II, p. 235.

6. Hiram A. Cutting, in *Vermont Agricultural Report*, 1885-1886. P. 91.

7. H. L. Duhamel du Monceau, *Traité des Arbres et Arbustes.* Paris: Michel, 1809. P. 37.

8. Dr. Reid, *Rochefoucault's Travels in America.* Berwick: Lochhead, 1795. P. 91.

9. *The American Farmer*, June 19, 1829.

10. Dorothy A. Bennett, *The Golden Almanac.* New York: Simon & Schuster, Inc., 1947. P. 30.

11. "Eminent Literary Men," *Eighty Years of Progress of the United States.* Hartford, Conn.: Stebbins, 1868. P. 126.

12. Robert B. Thomas, *The Farmer's Almanac*, 1800.

13. Leander Coburn, in *First Annual Report of the Vermont State Board of Agriculture*, 1872. P. 216.

14. Chester Thomas, in *Vermont Agricultural Report*, 1882. P. 61.

15. Bulletin No. 59, Bureau of Forestry. P. 39.

16. J. B. Spencer, *Maple Sugar Industry in Canada*. Ottawa, 1913. P. 34.

17. Bulletin No. 103, Vermont Agricultural Experiment Station, 1903. P. 140.

18. *Ibid.*

19. Hiram A. Cutting, in *Vermont Agricultural Report*, 1885-1886. P. 274.

20. A. P. Paine, in *Vermont Agricultural Report*, 1893. P. 127.

21. C. M. Fisher, in *Vermont Agricultural Report*, 1878. P. 109.

22. Louis E. Ude, *The French Cook*. Philadelphia: Carey, Lea & Carey, 1828. P. xx.

23. Thomas Chester, in *Vermont Agricultural Report*, 1882. P. 61.

24. Daniel Jay Browne, *The Sylva Americana*. Boston: Hyde, 1832. P. 111.

25. H. W. Wiley, "Foods and Food Adulterants," Bulletin No. 13, U.S. Department of Agriculture, Chemical Division. P. 675.

26. Leonard E. Lathrop, *The Farmer's Library*. Windsor, Vt.: Spooner, 1826. P. 273.

27. J. B. Spencer, *op. cit.*, p. 61.

28. Samuel F. Perley, in *Maine Board of Agriculture Report*, 1862. P. 54.

29. A. M. Foster, in *Vermont Agricultural Report*, 1894. P. 135.

30. William Chapin, in *Vermont Agricultural Report*, 1887-1888. P. 326.

31. Hiram A. Cutting, in *Vermont Agricultural Report*, 1886. P. 302.

32. E. R. Towle, in *Vermont Agricultural Report*, 1881-1882. P. 410.

33. Franklin B. Hough, *op. cit.*, p. 405.

34. A. M. Foster, in *Vermont Agricultural Report*, 1874. P. 833.

35. W. O. Brigham, in *Vermont Agricultural Report*, 1878. P. 106.

36. *Agricultural Report*. Washington, 1870. P. 420.

37. E. A. Fisk, in *Vermont Agricultural Report*, 1874. P. 716.

38. John Lorain, *Husbandry*. Philadelphia: Carey, 1825. P. 399.

39. Solon Robinson, *op. cit.*, p. 840.

40. *Vermont Agricultural Report*, 1878. P. 109.

Chapter Eight

1. Samuel Goodrich, *Recollections of a Lifetime*. New York: Miller, Orton & Mulligan, 1856. Vol. I, p. 68.

2. Solon Robinson, *Facts for Farmers*. New York: Johnson, 1866. P. 843.

3. *Ibid.*, p. 835.

4. Basil Hall, *Travels in North America*, Edinburgh: Cadell, 1829. Vol. I, p. 315.

5. Moses Mather, in *The American Farmer*, March 7, 1823.

6. E. A. Talbot, *Five Years Residence in Canada*. London: Longmans, Green & Company, 1824. P. 276.

7. Mary Elizabeth, *My Candy Secrets*. Philadelphia: Frederick A. Stokes Company, 1919. P. xxiii.

8. D. P. Gardner, *Farmer's Dictionary*. New York: Harper & Brothers, 1846. P. 482.

9. Solon Robinson, *op. cit.*, p. 841.

10. C. T. Alvord, in *Agricultural Report*, 1863. P. 404.

11. *Ibid.*

12. Thomas Fessenden, *The Husbandman and Housewife.* Bellows Falls, Vt., 1820. P. 80.

13. C. T. Alvord, *op. cit.*, p. 403.

14. John Burroughs, *Winter Sunshine.* Boston: Houghton Mifflin Company, 1881. P. 110.

15. James F. W. Johnston, *Notes on North America.* Boston: Little, Brown & Company, 1851. Vol. I, p. 303.

16. F. Schuyler Mathews, *Familiar Trees and Their Leaves.* New York: D. Appleton-Century Company, Inc., 1896. P. 201.

17. E. A. Fisk, in *Vermont Agricultural Report*, 1874. P. 716.

18. H. L. Duhamel du Monceau, *Traité des Arbres et Arbustes.* Paris: Michel, 1809. P. 38.

Chapter Nine

1. A. M. Foster, in *14th Annual Vermont Agricultural Report*, 1894. P. 138.

2. Hiram A. Cutting, in *Vermont Agricultural Report*, 1886. P. 302.

3. Moses Mather, in *American Farmer*, March 7, 1823.

4. Franklin B. Hough, *Report on Production of Maple Sugar in U.S. and Canada.* Washington, 1884. P. 410.

5. *Vermont Agricultural Report*, 1884. P. 75.

6. Lyman Newton, *Vermont Agricultural Report*, 1886. P. 119.

7. John A. Hitchcock, Bulletin No. 285, Vermont Agricultural Experiment Station, 1928. P. 17.

8. C. J. Bell, in *Vermont Agricultural Report*, 1897. P. 43.

9. Samuel Strickland, *Twenty-seven Years in Canada West.* London: Bentley, 1853. Vol. II, p. 311.

10. *Walton's Vermont Register and Farmer's Almanac*, 1859.

11. *New England Farmer's Almanac*, 1816.

12. François André Michaux, *Histoire des Arbres Forestiers de l'Amérique Septentrionale.* Paris: Haussmann, 1810. P. 230.

13. Benjamin Rush, *An Account of the Sugar Maple-Tree of the United States.* Philadelphia: Aitken, 1792. P. 74.

14. *The Writings of Thomas Jefferson* Washington, 1907. Vol. VIII, p. 190.

15. Nathan Perkins, *A Narrative of a Tour through the State of Vermont.* Woodstock, Vt.: Elm Tree Press, 1920. P. 23.

16. Franklin B. Hough, *Report on Forestry.* Washington: U.S. Department of Agriculture, 1884. Vol. IV, p. 414.

Chapter Ten

1. Lewis Mumford, *Culture of Cities.* New York: Harcourt, Brace & Company, Inc., 1938.

2. Milton Wend, *How to Live in the Country without Farming.* Garden City: Doubleday, Doran & Company, Inc., 1944.

3. Bolton Hall, *Three Acres and Liberty*. New York: The Macmillan Company, 1908.

4. Ralph Borsodi, *Flight from the City*. New York: Harper & Brothers, 1933.

5. Arthur E. Morgan, *The Small Community*. New York: Harper & Brothers, 1942.

6. Thomas Hewes, *Decentralize for Liberty*. New York: Smith, 1945.

7. Willis D. Nutting, *Reclamation of Independence*. Nevada City, Calif.: Berliner & Lanigan, 1947.

8. C. and E. Robinson, *The Have-More Plan*. New York: The Macmillan Company, 1947.

9. W. M. Teller, *The Farm Primer*. Philadelphia: David McKay Company, 1942.

10. W. M. Teller and G. F. Larson, *What Is Farming?* New York: D. Van Nostrand Company, Inc., 1945.

11. Haydn S. Pearson, *Success on the Small Farm*. New York: McGraw-Hill Book Company, Inc., 1946.

12. Louis Bromfield, *Pleasant Valley*. New York: Harper & Brothers, 1943.

13. Samuel R. Ogden, *This Country Life*. New York: A. S. Barnes & Co., 1946.

14. J. I. Rodale, *Pay Dirt*. New York: Devin-Adair, 1945.

15. F. H. Faulkner, *Plowman's Folly*. Norman: University of Oklahoma, 1943.

Chapter Eleven

1. Vermont Commission on Country Life, *Rural Vermont*. Burlington, 1931. P. 91.

2. François André Michaux, *Histoire des Arbres Forestiers de l'Amérique Septentrionale*. Paris: Haussmann, 1810. P. 233.

3. Benjamin Rush, *An Account of the Sugar Maple-Tree of the United States*. Philadelphia: Aitken, 1792. P. 71.

4. Pierre Dansereau, *Les Conditions de l'Acericulture*. Bulletin No. 1 du Service de Bioleographie. Montreal, 1945. P. 44.

5. F. L. Allen, in *22nd Annual Report of the Vermont Maple Sugar Makers' Association*, 1915. Pp. 38-41.

6. Benjamin Rush, *op. cit.*, p. 8.

7. Floyd Wright, in *Garden and Forest*, August 10, 1892.

8. C. G. Lock, *Sugar: A Handbook*. London: Spon, 1888. P. 412.

9. C. J. Bell, in *Vermont Agricultural Report*, 1897. P. 45.

10. Editorial in *Rutland Herald*, March 1, 1945.

11. *American Museum*, August, 1789.

12. Anonymous, in *The New England Farmer*, March 13, 1829.

Chapter Twelve

1. Henry David Thoreau, *Early Spring in Massachusetts*. Boston: Houghton Mifflin Company, 1893. P. 200.

BIBLIOGRAPHY

Abel, Mary Hinman. "Sugar as Food," Farmer's Bulletin No. 93, U.S. Department of Agriculture, 1899.

Alvord, C. T., "The Manufacture of Maple Sugar," *Report of Commissioner of Agriculture for Year 1862-1863*. Washington, 1863.

Barbeau, Marius, "Maple Sugar: Its Native Origin," Transactions of the Royal Society of Canada, 1946. Third Series, Vol. XL, Sec. II, pp. 75-86.

Bartlett, James M., "Maple Syrup," Bulletin No. 143, Maine Agricultural Experiment Station, 1933.

Beverly, Robert, *The History and Present State of Virginia*. London: Parker, 1705. Part II, Chap. IV.

Blake, John L., *The Farmer at Home*. New York: Saxton, 1852.

Boehringer, K., *Über Zuckererzeugung aus dem Safte der in den Oesterreichischen Staaten wild wachsenden Ahornbäume*. Vienna, 1810.

Bose, Sir Jagadis Chander, *Motor Mechanism of Plants*. London: Longmans, Green & Company, Inc., 1928.

——, *Physiology of the Ascent of Sap*. New York: Longmans, Green & Company, Inc., 1923.

——, *Plant Autographs*. New York: The Macmillan Company, 1927.

Brown, Nelson Courtlandt, *Forest Products*. New York: John Wiley & Sons, Inc., 1919.

Browne, Daniel Jay, *The Trees of America*. New York: Harper & Brothers, 1846.

Bryan, A. Hugh, "Maple-Sap Sirup: Its Manufacture, Composition and Effect of Environment thereon," Bulletin No. 134, U.S. Department of Agriculture, 1910.

——, William F. Hubbard, and Sidney F. Sherwood, "Production of Maple Sirup and Sugar," Farmer's Bulletin No. 1366, U.S. Department of Agriculture, 1937.

Carr, Lucien, "The Food of Certain American Indians and their Methods of Preparing It," Proceedings American Antiquarian Society, 1896. New Series, Vol. X, pp. 155-190.

Chamberlain, A. F., "The Maple Amongst the Algonkian Tribes," *American Anthropologist*, 1891. Vol. IV, pp. 39-44.

——, "Maple Sugar and the Indians," *American Anthropologist*, 1891. Vol. IV, pp. 381-383.

Collingwood, G. H., and J. A. Cope, "Maple Sugar and Syrup," Bulletin No. 297, New York State Experiment Station, 1938.

Cook, A. J., *Maple Sugar and the Sugar Bush*. Medina, Ohio: Root, 1887.

Cooke, W. W., and J. L. Hills, "Maple Sugar," Bulletin No. 26, Vermont Agricultural Experiment Station, 1891.

Coxe, Tench, *A View of the United States of America*. Philadelphia: Hall, 1794. Chap. V.

Crockett, Walter H., "How Vermont Maple Sugar Is Made," Bulletin No. 21, Vermont Agricultural Experiment Station, 1915.

Cutting, Hiram A., "The Maple Sugar Industry," *Vermont Agricultural Report*, 1886. Pp. 272-303.

Dana, Dorathea, *Sugar Bush*. New York: Thomas Nelson, 1947.

Dansereau, Pierre, "Les Conditions de l'Acericulture," Bulletin du Service de Biogeographie No. 1. Montreal, 1945.

Dudley, Paul, "An Account of the Method of Making Sugar," Transactions Royal Society of London. Philadelphia, 1720.

Duhamel du Monceau, H. L., *The Elements of Agriculture*. London: Vaillant, 1764. Vol. I, Chap. VI.

——, *Traité des Arbres et Arbustes*. Paris: Michel, 1809. Vol. IV.

Edson, H. A., "Micro-organisms of Maple Sap" Bulletin No. 167, Vermont Agricultural Experiment Station, 1912.

Fechner, Gustav Theodor, *Nanna, oder Über das Seelenleben der Pflanzen*. Hamburg: Voss, 1908.

Fernald, Merritt Lyndon, and Alfred Charles Kinsey, *Edible Wild Plants of Eastern North America*. Cornwall-on-Hudson, N. Y.: Idlewild Press, 1943.

Finlay, Margaret Curtin, *Our American Maples*. New York: Georgian, 1935.

Follett, Muriel, *A Drop in the Bucket*. Brattleboro, Vt.: Stephen Daye, 1941.

Fox, William, and W. F. Hubbard, "The Maple Sugar Industry," Bulletin No. 59, U.S. Department of Agriculture, 1905.

Hayward, F. W., "Factors in the Preparation of Maple Cream," Bulletin No. 720, New York State Agricultural Experiment Station, 1946.

——, "The Storage of Maple Sirup," Bulletin No. 719, New York State Agricultural Experiment Station, 1946.

—— and C. S. Pederson, "Some Factors Causing Dark-colored Maple Sirup," Bulletin No. 718, New York State Agricultural Experiment Station, 1946.

Henry, Alexander, *Travels and Adventures in Canada and the Indian Territories*. New York: Riley, 1809.

Henshaw, H. W., "The Indian Origin of Maple Sugar," *American Anthropologist*, 1890. Vol. III, pp. 341-351.

Herr, C. S., "Maple Syrup and Sugar Production in New Hampshire," Bulletin No. 52, University of New Hampshire Extension Service, 1938.

Hills, J. L., "The Maple Sap Flow," Bulletin No. 104, Vermont Agricultural Experiment Station, 1904.

Hitchcock, John A., "Cost and Profit in the Sugar Orchard," Bulletin No. 292, Vermont Agricultural Experiment Station, 1904.

——, "Economics of the Farm Manufacture of Maple Syrup and Sugar," Bulletins No. 285, 1928; No. 286, 1929, Vermont Agricultural Experiment Station.

——, "The Grazing of Maple Sugar Orchards," Bulletin No. 414, Vermont Agricultural Experiment Station, 1937.

Hough, Franklin B., "Report on the Production of Maple Sugar in the U.S. and Canada," *Report on Forestry*. U.S. Department of Agriculture, 1884. Vol. IV, pp. 394-414.

Hubbard, William F., "Maple Sugar and Syrup," Farmer's Bulletin No. 252, U.S. Department of Agriculture, 1906.

Johnson, Cuthbert W., *The Farmer's Cyclopedia and Dictionary of Rural Affairs*. Philadelphia: Carey and Hart, 1848.

Jones, C. H., "The Exclusion of Lead from Maple Sap," Bulletin No. 439, Vermont Agricultural Experiment Station, 1903.

—— and J. L. Bradlee, "The Carbohydrate Contents of the Maple Tree," Bulletin No. 358, Vermont Agricultural Experiment Station, 1933.

——, A. W. Edson, and W. J. Morse, "The Maple Sap Flow," Bulletin No. 103, Vermont Agricultural Experiment Station, 1903.

Jones, E., *The Acer Saccharinum*. London: E. Colyer, 1832.

Lafitau, Joseph François, *Mœurs des Sauvages Amériquains*. Paris: Hocherau, 1724. Two vols.

Lippman, Edmund O. von, *Geschichte des Zuckers*. Berlin: Springer, 1929.

Lorain, John, *Nature and Reason harmonized in the Practice of Husbandry*. Philadelphia: Carey, 1825.

McIntyre, A. C., "Maple Industry in Pennsylvania," Pennsylvania State Bulletin No. 280, 1932.

McKay, A. W., "Marketing Vermont Maple-Sap Products," Bulletin No. 227, Vermont Agricultural Experiment Station, 1922.

McNair, James B., "Sugar and Sugar-Making," Leaflet No. 13, Field Museum of Natural History. Chicago, 1927.

Mathews, F. Schuyler, *Familiar Trees and Their Leaves*. New York: D. Appleton-Century Company, Inc., 1908.

Maximov, Nicolai A., *Plant Physiology*. New York: McGraw-Hill Book Company, Inc., 1938.

Meyer, Bernard S., and D. B. Anderson, *Plant Physiology*. New York: D. Van Nostrand Company, Inc., 1939.

Michaux, François André, *The North American Sylva*. Philadelphia: Dobson, 1817. Two vols.

Morse, F. W., and A. H. Wood, "The Composition of Maple Sap" Bulletin No. 25, New Hampshire Agricultural Experiment Station, 1895.

Perley, Samuel F., "Maple Sugar," *Maine Board of Agriculture Report*, 1862. Pp. 47-56.

Pfeffer, Wilhelm, *Pflanzenphysiologie*. Leipzig: Engelmann, 1904. Two vols.

Phythian, J. Ernest, *Trees in Nature, Myth and Art*. Philadelphia: Jacobs, 1907.

Pitkin, Royce S., *Maple Sugar Time*. Brattleboro, Vt.: Stephen Daye Press, Inc., 1934.

Robinson, Solon, *Facts for Farmers*. New York: Johnson, 1866. Two vols.

Rush, Benjamin, *An Account of the Sugar Maple-Tree of the United States*. Philadelphia: Aitken, 1792.

Schuette, H. A. and Sybil C., "Maple Sugar: A Bibliography of Early Records," Transactions of Wisconsin Academy of Science. Madison, Wisconsin, 1935. Vol. 29, pp. 209-236.

Seely, H. M., "Profits of Sugar Making," *Vermont Agricultural Report*, 1878. Pp. 111-114.

Smithsonian Scientific Series, *Old and New Plant Lore*, 1931. Vol. II.

Society of Gentlemen, *Remarks on the Manufacturing of Maple Sugar*. Philadelphia, 1790.

Spencer, J. B., "The Maple Sugar Industry in Canada," Bulletins No. 2B, 1913; No. 30, 1923. Canadian Department of Agriculture.

Sy, Albert P., "History, Manufacture and Analysis of Maple Products," *Journal of Franklin Institute*, July, 1908. Vol. 166, pp. 249-280, 321-352, 433-445.

Traill, C. P., *The Canadian Settler's Guide*. London: Stanford, 1860.

Transeau, E. N., H. C. Sampson, and L. H. Tiffany, *Textbook of Botany*. New York: Harper & Brothers, 1940.

Tressler, C. J., and W. I. Zimmerman, "Three Year's Operation of an Experimental Sugar Bush" Bulletin No. 699, New York State Agricultural Experiment Station, 1942.

United States Tariff Commission, *Maple Sugar and Maple Syrup*. Washington, 1930.

Vaillancourt, C., "Erablières," Agriculture Bulletin No. 134, Quebec, 1934.

Wiley, H. W., "The Northern Sugar Industry," Bulletin No. 3, U.S. Department of Agriculture, Chemical Division, 1884. Pp. 190-215.

Weir, J. G., "Care of the Sugar Bush," Bulletin No. 71, Vermont Agricultural Extension Service, 1932.

——, "Suggestion for Making High Quality Maple Syrup," Bulletin No. 73, Vermont Agricultural Extension Service, 1933.

AFTERWORD

WE LOOK back almost forty years to our first tapping out, sap gathering, boiling, taking off of syrup, and converting syrup into maple sugar. We believe that during those four decades sugaring stands out as the most enthralling, satisfying, and rewarding of our many activities.

Since we left Vermont and settled in Maine on a saltwater farm devoid of maple trees, we have nostalgically followed all available news of mapling. There have been a few changes in the business—which we do not necessarily consider improvements. Many sugar makers now boil sap with gas or oil; use plastic bags (which we found flavored the sap unpleasantly) instead of buckets; and use plastic pipe. We are conservative innovators and favor some of the old ways, particularly boiling with wood.

There are far fewer sugar bushes now in operation throughout the country. One of the reasons that the industry has shrunk instead of gaining adherents is that sugaring is not a big moneymaker. There is much more money and far less labor in selling the big trees for lumber and then making large profits on the stripped land. Real estate values have skyrocketed in Vermont, with sugar bushes being sliced up into small building lots. (Our own beautiful sugar bush, which cost us about $25 an acre, is being sold off at $8000 an acre to ski fanciers, who are building flimsy vacation chalets.)

Sugaring remains a family craft, and how many families stay together and work together nowadays? Sugaring is hard work, and how many people want to do hand labor for long hours? People are satisfied with substitute living.

They buy imitation maple syrup in the supermarkets. They watch television in comfort instead of getting out of doors. They stand in line for ski lifts or roar about in snowmobiles instead of snowshoeing through the woods or skiing cross-country.

We deplore these modern tendencies and recommend sugaring as a hearty, exciting occupation that brings returns in many ways. It provides absorbing interest, health, vitality, and recreation, as well as food and a modest income.

HELEN AND SCOTT NEARING

Forest Farm
Harborside, Maine
October 1970

INDEX